THE

BOUNDARIES

OF ETHNICITY

MCGILL-QUEEN'S STUDIES IN ETHNIC HISTORY (ISSN 0846-8869)

Series Two: John Zucchi, Editor

THE
BOUNDARIES
OF ETHNICITY

German Immigration and the
Language of Belonging in Ontario

Benjamin Bryce

MCGILL-QUEEN'S UNIVERSITY PRESS

Montreal & Kingston | London | Chicago

© McGill-Queen's University Press 2022

ISBN 978-0-2280-1394-5 (cloth)
ISBN 978-0-2280-1395-2 (paper)
ISBN 978-0-2280-1488-1 (ePDF)
ISBN 978-0-2280-1489-8 (ePUB)

Legal deposit fourth quarter 2022
Bibliothèque nationale du Québec

Printed in Canada on acid-free paper that is 100% ancient forest free
(100% post-consumer recycled), processed chlorine free

This book has been published with the help of a grant from the
Federation for the Humanities and Social Sciences, through the Awards to
Scholarly Publications Program, using funds provided by the Social Sciences
and Humanities Research Council of Canada.

Funded by the Government of Canada   Financé par le gouvernement du Canada   Canada

Canada Council for the Arts   Conseil des arts du Canada

We acknowledge the support of the Canada Council for the Arts.
Nous remercions le Conseil des arts du Canada de son soutien.

LIBRARY AND ARCHIVES CANADA CATALOGUING IN PUBLICATION

Title: The boundaries of ethnicity : German immigration and the language of
    belonging in Ontario / Benjamin Bryce.
Names: Bryce, Benjamin, author.
Series: McGill-Queen's studies in ethnic history. Series two ; 54.
Description: Series statement: McGill-Queen's studies in ethnic history.
    Series two ; 54 | Includes bibliographical references and index.
Identifiers: Canadiana (print) 20220260559 | Canadiana (ebook) 20220260621 |
    ISBN 9780228013945 (cloth) | ISBN 9780228013952 (paper) | ISBN
    9780228014881 (ePDF) | ISBN 9780228014898 (ePUB)
Subjects: LCSH: Germans—Ontario—Ethnic identity—History—19th century. |
    LCSH: Germans—Ontario—Ethnic identity—History—20th century. |
    LCSH: German language—Social aspects—Ontario—History—19th century. |
    LCSH: German language—Social aspects—Ontario—History—20th century. |
    LCSH: German language—Ontario—Religious aspects—History—19th
    century. | LCSH: German language—Ontario—Religious aspects—History—
    20th century.
Classification: LCC FC3100.G3 B79 2022 | DDC 971.3/00431—dc23

To my father, Gregory,

a lapsed Ontarian who gave me a passion for history

CONTENTS

Figures and Tables

Figures

Tables

Acknowledgments

Many people have assisted me with this project, and I would like to thank them for a great number of things. Michel Ducharme, Tristan Grunow, and Roberto Perin generously read the entire manuscript and got me to rethink several themes at crucial stages of the revision process. Two external reviewers provided excellent advice about how to broaden the focus of this book and hone its contribution. For all of your comments and suggestions on drafts of this manuscript, many thanks! Kyla Madden at McGill-Queen's was everything I could have asked for in an editor, and she helped this book take on its final form in ways that I wouldn't have expected when I first sent her a proposal. Scott Howard did an excellent job editing the manuscript and sifting through endnotes. Kathleen Fraser and Filomena Falocco, along with others who worked behind the scenes at the press, were extremely helpful and professional throughout the production process.

This book grows out of a dissertation that compared German-language education and religion in Canada and Argentina. My co-supervisors Roberto Perin and Gillian McGillivray, committee member Marcel Martel, external examiner José Moya, and other examiners Paul Axelrod, Anne Rubenstein, and Willie Jenkins helped me think through a lot of concepts that remain in this book. I am grateful to all of you for your generous and insightful feedback.

A number of people took the time to read different chapters, and the final product is considerably better because of it. Brittany Luby and Andrew Watson were encouraging and inquisitive writing group partners, and this book has been much improved because of their questions and suggestions. Anna Casas Aguilar, Jason Ellis, Eagle Glassheim, Joanne

Markle, Marcel Martel, Daniel Ross, Gabriele Scardellato, David Sheinin, and Jamie Trepanier commented on different chapters, and I deeply appreciate their advice, disagreement, and requests for clarity. The members of the York University Immigration History Research Group kindly took the time to comment on my work, and our meetings were a wonderful forum in which to present my research. My colleagues Tamara Myers, Ted Binnema, and Bob Brain all gave me great advice about revisions and academic publishing.

My family in both Canada and Spain has given me important intellectual and emotional support, and I am sure they all see or would have seen their influence on this study about religion, language, and children. Anna Casas Aguilar has given feedback and opinions on ideas as they developed on street corners, in airplanes, and around the house, and she has offered deep insights on various versions of my written work. She has also been a wonderful companion since the start of my academic career. I have greatly benefitted from our many conversations, her questions, her support, and her love.

Our son Gabriel has been a wonderful distraction from research and writing ever since he showed up, and he has ensured that life played the dominant role in work-life balance. I first started writing about children's autonomy and their bilingualism several years before Gabriel made it very clear that little people have power, shape adults' behaviour, and are crucial in the linguistic make-up of families and communities. He strikes me as a pretty clear reminder of why we should pay attention to children in the history of language and ethnicity in Canada. This book is unfortunately not about dinosaurs or even salmon, but I hope the next one will be!

In Ontario, the staff at several institutions took their time to help me find my way. Pasang Thackchhoe generously guided me through the impressive collection of the Multicultural History Society of Ontario. The staff at the Archives of Ontario, the University of Toronto Libraries, York University Libraries, the Archives of Wilfrid Laurier University, the Archives and Rare Books Collection at the University of Waterloo, and the Kitchener Public Library helped me find a wealth of documentation. Susan Mavor at the University of Waterloo deserves special thanks. The

Congregation of the Resurrection at St Jerome's University and the public and Catholic school boards of the Waterloo Region showed a warm interest in my project. Mary Bertulli at the University of Northern British Columbia library helped me track down all sorts of rare documents through interlibrary loans. Librarians at both UNBC and the University of British Columbia also helped track down dozens of other primary and secondary sources. In addition, several private institutions in Ontario granted me access to their collections. In Kitchener, the directors of St Matthews and St Paul's Lutheran churches, the Grand River Hospital, St Mary's Hospital, and Kitchener-Waterloo Collegiate Institute all kindly allowed me access to their private collections. The directors of St John's Lutheran Church in Waterloo as well as the leaders of First Lutheran Church and the Redemptorist congregation in Toronto expressed interest in my research and shared their archives with me.

Two student research assistants at UNBC, Cassandra McKenney and Emilio Caputo, helped me add more archival material to this book, and their work was much appreciated. They were funded by the Undergraduate Research Experience program and a seed grant from the UNBC Office of Research.

I am extremely thankful for the Ontario Graduate Scholarship Program and the Sir John A. Macdonald Graduate Fellowship. The Social Sciences and Humanities Research Council, the Spletzer Family Foundation and the Chair in German-Canadian Studies, the German Academic Exchange Service (DAAD), the Avie Bennett Historica-Dominion Institute, York University, and the Canadian Centre for German and European Studies at York have all generously funded my research, as did the UNBC Office of Research. This financial support has made this book possible.

An earlier version of chapter 1 appeared as "Linguistic Ideology and State Power: German and English Education in Ontario, 1880–1912," *Canadian Historical Review* 94, no. 2 (2013): 207–33. An earlier version of chapter 4 appeared as "Entangled Communities: Religion and Ethnicity in Ontario and North America, 1880–1930," *Journal of the Canadian Historical Association* 23, no. 1 (2012): 189–226. I thank the editors of these journals for permission to include and expand on those articles here.

A Note on the Cover Image

The artist of the image on the cover, Woldemar Neufeld, was a German-speaking Mennonite born in the Russian Empire in 1909. He immigrated with his family to Waterloo, Ontario in 1924, and he enrolled in Waterloo Lutheran College soon after arriving. He moved to Toronto in the early 1930s, but he spent much of his professional life in the United States. That he moved in and out of Waterloo County, that he attended a Lutheran college, and that he moved between Ontario and the United States makes him particularly representative of some themes that appear regularly in this book. He worked within some and crossed many other boundaries of ethnicity. The image is courtesy of the Robert Langen Art Gallery, Wilfrid Laurier University. "Bay Street, Toronto" by Woldemar Neufeld, 1933, Courtesy of Wilfrid Laurier University Permanent Art Collection, http://images.ourontario.ca/Laurier/3307884/data?n=36.

THE

BOUNDARIES

OF ETHNICITY

THE BOUNDARIES OF ETHNICITY

In the half century between 1880 and 1930, the boundaries of ethnicity faded, sharpened, shrank, grew, and morphed into new spaces in Ontario. School reformers increasingly pushed for a monolingual society, which in turn cut into the previous boundaries drawn around three speech communities in Ontario – English, French, and German – between the 1850s and 1880s. Lutheran and Catholic churches, however, maintained linguistic boundaries around various local communities, making German-language spaces across the province. Over time, however, the boundaries of denomination and language themselves became porous, and most congregations became bilingual spaces. In these cases, generational difference more than ethnic heritage marked certain boundaries. Both the Lutheran and Catholic Churches operated in Ontario and in a broader North American space. Local communities shared ideas, worked together to publish periodicals, and met at annual meetings and youth events; their pastors took up new positions around the province and across the Canada-US border. In these cases, the boundaries of ethnicity extended into a much larger network.

Outsiders drew other boundaries around groups of people – of various backgrounds – and created their own topographies of ethnic difference. According to a francophone school promoter in Ottawa or a bureaucrat in Toronto, there were German schools all over the western portion of the province. Census takers labelled Germans and dozens of other groups according to their visions of "national" and "racial" origin, even if the people in question were born in Canada and were of mixed heritage. During the First World War, other boundaries were drawn, which by 1918 lumped together recent immigrants and naturalized immigrants from Germany, Austria-Hungary, and Russia, and ultimately German speakers born in Canada and the United States.

Using German speakers as an illustrative case study, this book shows how people defined and contested the meaning of cultural and linguistic belonging in a region transformed by mass migration. It argues that children, parents, teachers, and religious communities shaped the meaning of German ethnicity in Ontario society. This negotiation, in turn, gave form to the nature of cultural pluralism in the province and became the foundation upon which later multiculturalism, and government attempts to manage that diversity, emerged in Canada. Alongside state power and economic forces, German speakers, hundreds of thousands of other immigrants, and other Canadians of different ethnic backgrounds created a framework between 1880 and 1930 that defined the relationships between the public sphere, communities, family, language, and religion in Canada that would persist throughout the twentieth century.

Questioning ethnic categories, this book asks what it meant to be "German" in Ontario, what factors produced competing meanings of ethnicity, and how that changed over time. The Germans who make up the core of this study did not have a uniform, homogeneous groupness, and the distinction between insiders and outsiders was often unclear. Boundaries were crossed as often as they were respected. The meaning of being German varied based on age, religious denomination, educational experience, country of birth, personal and family decisions, and social structures. Having personal or recent family ties to Germany or to the territory that became the German Empire in 1871, to regions of the Austro-Hungarian Empire (such as Galicia, Bohemia, or Austria), to regions of the Russian Empire (around the Volga River, the Black Sea, or elsewhere), or to German-speaking communities in the United States also conditioned people's understanding of themselves and others. Yet local factors, children's choices, the Ontario school system, and religious organizations influenced the evolving boundaries of ethnicity more than did geographic origins.

Ethnic categories are situational, overlapping, and contradictory, and ethnicity is something constructed in a dialogue with the surrounding ethno-social context.[1] A person speaking about their own or other people's ethnicity could try to define it by focusing on important markers of cultural difference such as language or religion. In the case of using language as a marker of ethnicity, it is worth stressing that language can be defined by any combination of linguistic ability, linguistic behaviour, and linguistic identity, which can be contradictory forms of measure. Ethnicity could also be defined by group identification, categories of citizenship, or feelings of belonging. As Tobias Brinkmann cautions in a study of German-speaking Jews in Chicago in the mid-nineteenth century, linguistic, denominational, national (German), or civic (American) labels and identifications all mattered and, in the eyes of these German-speaking Jews, "were closely related."[2]

The term "German speakers" appears often in the pages that follow, not uncritically but as part of the central analytical focus. German speakers were immigrants and the children or grandchildren of immigrants. All had some proficiency in German, but it was bilingualism that permeated their lives. Many adults worked or had relationships in English while they concurrently socialized, read, or worshipped in German. Many children spoke German at home, attended German-language Sunday school, and learned German grammar for three hours per week at a state-controlled public or Catholic separate school. Yet they otherwise had a range of social interactions in English.

The term "bilingualism" can describe an imperfect balance between languages, and that imbalance evolves throughout one's formative years. A three-year-old might speak German as a dominant language, but by the time she is eleven and attends public school, she has a more complex relationship with language. She may be a German speaker, but a native speaker of English might also assess the same child as an anglophone. This eleven-year-old may master the pronunciation of German phonemes and have an advanced proficiency in the language when talking about food or family. Yet many of the children of German speakers in North America, even those who attended bilingual schools, were more comfortable talking about sports, novels, politics, or finances in English. This is what linguists call the *complementarity principle*: different languages are used in different contexts, with different people, and for different reasons.[3]

In addition to language, religion – or denominational identity – was also fundamental in many people's understanding of German ethnicity. Combined, language and religion comprised an important way that people thought about and created ethnic boundaries. The competing Canada Synod and the Canada District of the Missouri Synod were the two largest German-language institutions in the country from 1880 to 1930, and together with Catholic religious congregations and orders they created German-language spaces that played an essential role in educating children and fostering social relationships along ethno-linguistic lines. Religious communities left behind vast amounts of documentary evidence – in German and often in private repositories in Ontario – that show how language and denomination intersected. Organized religion also played an important role in family life, thereby linking children and communities together. As Steven Mintz notes, "childhood plays a crucial role in the intergenerational transmission and development of collective identities."[4] As I show, transmitting language and fostering a specific denomination was an important motivator for many people. Those most adamant about reproducing German ethnicity over time often stressed the interconnectedness of language, denomination, and children.

Most German speakers in this period were Lutherans or Catholics, yet both groups remain largely absent in the study of German speakers in Canada. In contrast, an important body of literature on Mennonites exists.[5] Fewer than one in ten people recorded as "German" in both Ontario and Canada in the 1911 census were Mennonite.[6] In fact, there were five times as many Lutherans in Ontario as there were Mennonites.[7] Lutherans were the makers of the largest German-language religious bodies in Canada between 1880 and 1930. A study of Lutherans and Catholics illustrates the role of denomination in promoting language or in linking congregants to ethnicity. Adding a third denomination (Mennonites) to these questions could prove fruitful, but preliminary research and secondary sources suggest that such an approach would not fundamentally change the main findings of this book. The case of German-speaking Catholics also contributes to an important yet overlooked aspect of the history of education in Ontario: this denomination had control of state-funded separate schools, and this group of German speakers struck a different balance between language, community, and the state.

Many inhabitants of Ontario of German birth and heritage spoke a great deal about and engaged in activities related to their ethnicity, while thousands of others reacted with varying degrees of indifference. That indifference has often been the bane of nationalist community leaders.[8] Children fit somewhere in between indifference and active involvement in communities. In particular, they had different ideas about language, which attracted much concern from parents, teachers, and religious leaders. When studying ethnicity and ethnic groups, it is important to note, in the words of historian Hernán Otero, that an ethnic community "is an element to test and not an *a priori* fact, justified by the mere presence of people of a common national origin."[9] Otero stresses that historians typically study an ethnic core while not always reflecting on "the proportion of people who make up that core."[10] It is also often a set of community leaders or insiders who produce the lion's share of documentation that historians later analyze.[11] Historians Jeffrey Lesser and Raanan Rein assert that "the study of ethnicity must include people other than those affiliated with community institutions" and that "unaffiliated ethnics" who are not part of formal institutions and who have exogamous marriage patterns should not be overlooked.[12] Tobias Brinkmann highlights the fact that "group," "heritage," and "community" are often used imprecisely for those who by and large are "passive members of the *organized* part of an immigrant group in a specific place."[13]

Rather than analyzing *ethnic identity* and how an identity would lead to a clear adherence to a community, it seems more helpful to examine the relational and constructed understanding that many German speakers had about their ethnicity and that other people had about "Germans." People's linguistic behaviour, religious participation, and the attitudes and discussion of children born in North America show the fluidity of people's understanding of ethnicity, even if they could all claim a single German ethnic identity. As Rogers Brubaker and Frederick Cooper write, "Conceptualizing all affinities and affiliations, all forms of belonging, all experiences of commonality, connectedness, and cohesion, all self-understandings and self-identifications in the idiom of 'identity' saddles us with a blunt, flat, undifferentiated vocabulary."[14] The concept of identity, they add, "is ill suited to perform this work, for it is riddled with ambiguity, riven with contradictory meanings, and encumbered by reifying connotations."[15] Indeed, the focus on ethnic difference and groupness masks how people do not fit into such categories or fall into overlapping or competing groupings. Brubaker and Cooper argue that categories based on ethnic identities erroneously impose an idea of "internal sameness" and "bounded groupness."[16] They warn that "group boundaries are considerably more porous and ambiguous than is widely assumed ... This categorical code, important though it is as a constituent element of social relations, should not be taken for a faithful description of them."[17]

Ethnic Boxes and the First World War

Two assumptions dominate both popular memory and most scholarly studies of German speakers in Ontario, and both are related to space and the impact of the First World War. Waterloo County, which lies approximately 100 kilometres west of Toronto, and its main city, Berlin, have been said to be the centre of all things German, and the renaming of that city as Kitchener in 1916 is taken as proof that the war did away with that Germanness. That same thinking seems to implicitly suggest that no previous forces could have also had a damaging impact on the public and private transmission of German culture and language to Canadian-born generations. This book takes aim at both assumptions (Waterloo and war), not only as a corrective for German-Canadian history, but also with broader implications for how scholars write about cultural pluralism and the forces of cultural change in North America.

Drawing almost exclusively from sources produced in one place, research about Germans in Ontario has been reduced to the study of Waterloo County.[18] It is a striking historiographic error. In 1911, only 19 per cent of the residents of Ontario of German heritage lived in that county.[19] People and institutions in Waterloo County do appear in this book, but their connections to the broader Ontario and North American context remain part of my analytical perspective. Provincial education policy – made in Toronto – was applied to several counties where the Education Department controlled "German schools." Lutheran leaders from across the province met regularly in Berlin as well as other cities such as Toronto and Hamilton, and they interacted frequently with German speakers in Pittsburgh, Philadelphia, New York, and St Louis. Federal orders-in-council and laws during the First World War took aim at German speakers all over the province and the country, with little specific interest in a single county.

There are some noteworthy consequences of the narrow interest in Waterloo County. Evidence from a single case study is extrapolated to represent the history of a much larger group of people who interacted with German ethnicity, and it has led scholars to overlook a large body of sources produced outside the porous boundaries of a county. It converts the history of the second-largest group of immigrants in Canadian history (outnumbered only by the British) in the most common destination for international migrants (Ontario) to a local history, with little interest in showing the broader resonance.

This tendency to box ethnicity into specific spaces such as Waterloo County and then imagine the surrounding territory as homogeneous and non-ethnic is a common phenomenon in scholarly studies and popular understandings of cultural pluralism in the Americas. Similar examples can be found in writings about Chinatowns and Little Italies from New York to Buenos Aires. Such simplifying assumptions and labels are a way that cultural pluralism, citizenship, and belonging are reconciled by people of distinct backgrounds. In the case of German speakers and Waterloo County, the historiographical myopia may be a product of these popular perceptions. The region has a broader public interest, at least in the last half century, of fostering that distinct ethnic heritage. It has certainly proven easy to write dozens of studies based on documents from this one county. Yet there are plenty of other documents from elsewhere in both German and English that redraw the boundaries of ethnicity.

The idea that the First World War played a decisive role in provoking a cultural eclipse of German ethnicity across North America used to be a central argument in much of the historiography.[20] A handful of more recent studies of Waterloo County and American cities such as New York, Buffalo, and Philadelphia have largely refuted this point, instead pointing to a long process of cultural change between the 1890s and 1914.[21] In the words of Peter Conolly-Smith in his study of New York City, "America's entry into World War I, traditionally and all too conveniently identified as the moment of the 'eradication' of German-American culture, was, in my view, less a pivotal moment for America's Germans than the culmination of a decades-long process of cultural negotiation and accommodation."[22] In an oft-referenced book sponsored by the Canadian Historical Association and published in 1985, Kenneth McLaughlin erroneously claims that during the war "German-language services were halted ... German schools were immediately closed."[23] Statements such as that one were part of a broader narrative about the crushing impact of the war on German communities in Canada. Yet German-language religion continued throughout the war, most German-language teaching had stopped before 1914, and other German instruction at Lutheran and Catholic colleges in Ontario continued.

Assumptions about the importance of the war places great weight on a four-year period and seems to minimize what were in fact decades of change. Indeed, one can find plenty of examples of decreasing participation in German-language activities before the war began – whether church services, classes at school, newspaper subscriptions, or clubs and other social activities – and one can find many other examples of continuity during and after the war. The wartime context accelerated some transitions to English, but it was nowhere near complete, nor the only cause. At the same time, this book approaches the study of ethnicity and the making of Canadian pluralism as a question of *practice* rather than *fate*. To focus on the abrupt changes brought by war or culminating in war is to not focus on the role of ethnicity, language, and community in people's everyday lives and in the making of a pluralist society in late nineteenth and early twentieth-century Ontario.

Two commonly used examples about the negative impact of the First World War on Germans in Ontario unfortunately will not go away: the name change of Berlin to Kitchener in 1916 and how people reported their ethnic heritage on the 1921 Canadian census. Yet in reality, both examples reduce complicated histories to war-centric narratives. Moreover, these two cases could be read as compelling examples of almost the opposite points they are meant to prove.

In May 1916, the city of Berlin held two plebiscites. The first was over the question of keeping the current name, and, based on the result of that vote, a second one was held on what to replace it with. It is true that the residents of one city made a concerted effort to distance themselves from a marker of German ethnicity. Yet the residents of Hanover, Mannheim, Zurich, Baden, New Hamburg, New Germany, Hespeler, Heidelberg, Schwartz, and Breslau – all in Ontario – did not feel compelled to do the same. That should tell us something about how Germans experienced the First World War as well. What is also worth stressing is that in the middle of the First World War, 49 per cent of the town's adult male residents voted to keep the name Berlin.[24] The vote and name change do not point only to an anti-German and highly British nationalistic situation, but a situation in which ethnic heritage and Canadian belonging were more complex for about half the population of Berlin and being German and belonging in Canada were not as antithetical as has since been assumed.

Figure 0.1 appeared in the city of Berlin's long-standing German-language newspaper, the *Berliner Journal*. The weekly existed between 1859 and 1918 and had a circulation of approximately 4,500 on the eve of the First World War.[25] The paper took a public stand against the name change. In this announcement in the paper, the committee opposed to the name change wrote in German, "For patriotism, they say, we should support the movement [to change the name]. But it is more patriotic and more useful for the British Empire to gain a single recruit or raise a single dollar." The announcement concluded, "Show your trust in the City of Berlin and the loyalty of its citizens by voting on Friday, May 19 and answer with a decisive ‚Nein'"[26]

This No campaign illustrates how a significant group of German speakers, ultimately supported by almost half the voters, navigated between ethnic and civic interests. As Anne Löchte notes, some English speakers also opposed the name change, and the *Berliner Journal* published statements made by anglophone supporters or in other English-language newspapers.[27] They sought to cast attention on winning the war itself, argued that the name Berlin was in fact loyal, and believed that ethnicity and civic belonging could coexist. The very fact that space for such arguments existed in the public sphere in the spring of 1916 suggests the need for a more nuanced reading and memory of the name change and German experience during the war.

Sind Sie dafür,

daß der Name dieser Stadt geändert werde?

Dies ist eine Zeit, in der die Dominion- und Provinzial-Parlamente, sowie munizipale und öffentliche Körperschaften Wahlen, und das aufregende Besprechen anderer Angelegenheiten verschieben, damit alle gemeinsam in der Verteidigung des britischen Reiches zusammenwirken.

Die Namensveränderung hätte nicht zu dieser Zeit vor das Volk gebracht werden sollen.

Wir möchten diejenigen nicht kritisieren, die diese Agitation in Scene gesetzt haben, aber bemerken, daß ihre Argumente nicht stichhaltig sind und des Geistes der Gerechtigkeit ermangeln, der jedem Briten innewohnen sollte.

Wir leben in einer der loyalsten, friedlichsten und blühendsten Städte der Dominion, aber die Diskussion dieser Angelegenheit hat viel böses Blut erregt, ja, Ursache zu ungesetzmäßigen Handlungen gegeben, und dafür sind die Urheber dieser Bewegung verantwortlich.

Aus Patriotismus, heißt es, sollten wir die Bewegung unterstützen. Einen einzigen Rekruten zu gewinnen oder einen Dollar für patriotische Zwecke zu opfern, ist patriotischer und dem britischen Reich förderlicher.

Man sagt, die Weigerung, den Namen zu ändern, würde zu finanziellem Ruin führen, aber heute sind unsere Geschäftsleute so beschäftigt, wie nie zuvor, ja, manche sind gezwungen, Ueberzeit zu arbeiten. Manche sind sogar außer Stande, die Aufträge auszuführen, die ihnen zugegangen sind. Jeder Handwerker, der im Stande ist zu arbeiten, arbeitet heute für einen guten Lohn. Unsere Arbeiter fertigen die besten Waren für den canadischen Markt an, und so lange sie sich den Ruf bewahren, wird der Name „Berlin" weder für sie noch für die Fabrikanten ein Hemschuh sein.

Die Bürger, die sich um die Namensänderung bemühen, maßen sich das Recht an, jeden als disloyal und proreaktionär zu verschreien, der nicht mit ihren Ansichten übereinstimmt. Die Gegner der Namensänderung sind ebenso loyal gegen das britische Reich und loyaler gegen die Stadt, in der sie leben und prosperieren, als die heftigsten Agitatoren, die den Namen der Stadt und ihren guten Ruf untergraben wollen.

Wer zu Gunsten der Namensänderung stimmt, bekennt sich des Mangels an Loyalität schuldig, den diese Agitatoren Euch und Eurer Stadt zur Last zu legen bemüht sind. Beweist Eure Vertrauen auf die Stadt Berlin und die Loyalität Eurer Bürger dadurch, daß Ihr am Freitag, den 19. Mai, am Stimmkasten antwortet mit einem entschiedenen

„Nein!"

Das Komitee.

0.1 Sind Sie dafür, daß der Name dieser Stadt geändert wird? Nein!

A second example that could be read in two very different ways is how people reported their ethnic heritage to Canadian census takers in the aftermath of the First World War.[28] In the 1911 census, 192,320 people in Ontario reported German as their ethnic origin.[29] Yet in 1921, that number fell to 130,545 while the number of people reporting "Dutch" increased from 35,012 to 50,512, and many others probably latched onto their mixed ancestry and reported "English," "Scottish," or "Irish."[30] A 32 per cent reduction does show a clear distancing from German affiliation. However, it also means that the other 68 per cent of people of German origin in the province did not do the same. What is more, in the 1931 census, the number increased to 174,006, which includes both new immigrants and others more willing to reveal their German origin.[31] While the 1921 census reporting has been read as an example of the rejection of things German in Ontario society, it in fact could demonstrate a general retention of an ethnic label for the vast majority. This second example does show the reduction of a public expression of German ethnicity at one specific moment, but a 32 per cent reduction is not – in my view – as totalizing as the war-centric narrative would suggest.

German Migrants and the Making of a White Ontario

This is a story of how a privileged group of European immigrants and their descendants carved out a bigger space for cultural and linguistic pluralism in Canadian society. This story is part and parcel of a history of exclusion. It coincided with the displacement of Indigenous peoples from access to not only land and resources but also the generational transmission of language and culture. As Laurie Bertram notes in her study of Icelandic immigration to Manitoba, this group's "relations with local Indigenous people and technologies were complex and diverse, and they changed over time, but they are essential to understanding the history of the community."[32] David Roediger writes that immigrants to the United States in the second half of the nineteenth century found and sought "their places in the white supremacist US social order."[33] The efforts of German speakers to construct or maintain ethnicity are also an effort to make Ontario a more European and white place.

The evolving place of German ethnicity in Ontario was linked to the ebb and flow of Germanophone migration. German speakers came to Ontario in sizeable numbers beginning in the 1780s and 1790s from the United States, and in the 1840s and 1850s directly from the areas of Central Europe that would become Germany.[34] Alongside people of British and other backgrounds, Germans were among the first European settlers in Upper Canada in the 1780s and 1790s. They moved in particular from New York and Pennsylvania to the Niagara Peninsula and the area east of Kingston.[35] This early migration had a lasting presence. According to the 1871 census, almost a quarter of the inhabitants of Dundas and Stormont Counties in eastern Ontario were of German heritage.[36] In these early decades of German-speaking migration from the United States to Upper Canada, the main denominations were Lutheran, Reformed, and Mennonite.[37] In the early nineteenth century, Niagara continued to be a destination for German-American settlers, as was the area around the Grand River (in what became Waterloo County) and near Markham Township (north of Toronto).[38] Yet by the mid-nineteenth century, Niagara and Markham did not draw many new German speakers, and Waterloo and new settlements in western Ontario grew rapidly.[39]

These early German migrations were deeply enmeshed with the rising land dispossession of Indigenous peoples in southern Ontario. The Grand River settlements in what became Waterloo County were built on Block 2, organized by the German Land Company starting in 1807, which had acquired land from a speculator who had in turn acquired it from the Haudenosaunee Six Nations. The earliest land "purchases" offered annuities and created reserves, but especially after 1815 the colonial government set out to systematically take control of almost all land in southern Ontario and to dole it out to white settlers.[40]

By 1800, 350,000 acres of the already established Grand River reserve were alienated and another 250,000 were taken away in the 1830s. At this point, the remaining 50,000 acres made it the biggest reserve in southern Ontario, but its redistribution to German- and English-speaking settlers in Waterloo County is a telling example of how non-dominant immigrant groups played a crucial role in settler colonialism.[41] Over the course of the first half of the nineteenth century, the government of Upper Canada worked to reduce the amount of Indigenous-controlled lands and sell it

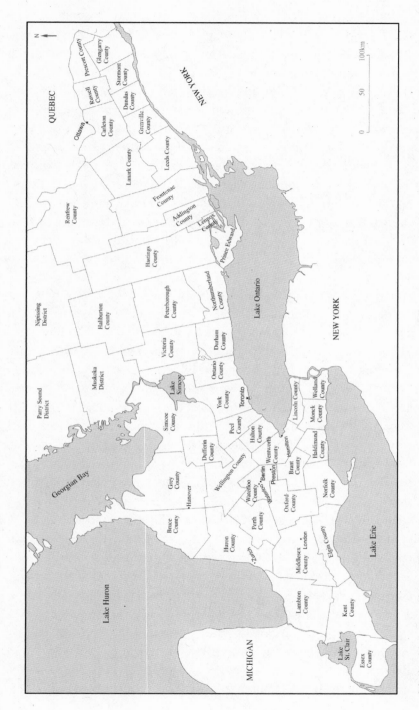

0.2 Map of the counties of Ontario, 1880.

at very low prices.[42] As J.R. Miller notes, "In seven treaties between 1815 and 1827, the Crown secured access for non-Natives to almost all of the remaining arable land in southern Ontario."[43]

Further German immigration in the 1820s and 1830s into western Ontario drew settlers onto the newly acquired Huron Tract (Crown Treaty 29). The new land was cheaper than older settlements around the Grand River, which in turn attracted even more settlers. This led to other German-speaking communities in Perth and Huron Counties in the 1820s and 1830s.[44] This push continued in the 1850s and the 1860s, with German-speaking immigrants arriving in Waterloo County and then moving onward to Bruce and Grey Counties.[45] The process continued throughout the nineteenth century, and German speakers joined anglophones and later francophones as settlers on the frontiers of an expanding Ontario and Canada.

Starting in the 1840s, migrants from Germany began arriving in significant numbers in Canada West. This coincides with a spike in German emigration, which mainly headed to the United States. Table 0.1 illustrates total emigration from German lands from 1820 to 1914, and the increase in the 1850s and 1860s had a noticeable impact on German immigration to Canada West. A direct shipping route between Hamburg and Bremen and Quebec City opened in 1846, but most German-speaking immigrants to Canada in this period still transited through New York, which was faster and more comfortable.[46] As German emigration steadily rose into the mid-1850s, the Canadian government made special provisions to attract this preferred group of settlers. It hired German interpreters in Montreal in 1851 and then two more in Berlin and Hamilton, Ontario in 1854. The government also sent German-Canadians to Germany to serve as information agents.[47] It was in this period that Lutheran and Catholic German speakers began to predominate in areas that until then had been a mix of Lutheran, Reformed, Mennonite, Amish, and other Protestant groups.

German speakers were amongst the first settlers in Waterloo, Perth, Huron, Bruce, and Grey Counties, and they developed into local elites – alongside anglophones – in all of these places. In the words of Werner Bausenhart, a large proportion of early German migrants were "high skilled and well-educated members of society."[48] This was a socio-economically stratified group, but a stratification that mirrored closely

Table 0.1 German overseas emigration by decade

1820s	1830s	1840s	1850s	1860s	1870s	1880s	1890s	1900s	1910–14
22,500	145,100	418,900	1,100,300	767,800	627,900	1,362,500	604,600	276,500	104,300

Source: Reinhard Doerries, "German Transatlantic Migration from the Early Nineteenth Century to the Outbreak of World War II," in *Population, Labour and Migration in 19th- and 20th-Century Germany*, edited by Klaus Bade (Leamington Spa, UK: Berg Publishers, 1987), 128.

people of British heritage. This relative affluence – alongside other ideas about the hierarchies of European cultures – shaped the perception that English-speaking Canadians had of German speakers, and it enabled German speakers to distinguish themselves from other groups from eastern and southern Europe that began to arrive in greater numbers around the turn of the twentieth century.

People of German heritage were involved in the increasingly industrialized economy of the province. They were elected to local school boards and as local mayors and members of Parliament. A large number of people who produced the sources at the core of this study were immigrants to Ontario in the 1850s and 1860s or, by the 1910s and 1920s, the children of those migrants. That German speakers were among the earliest European settlers in the province was a crucial factor behind the entrenched rights that the German language had in Ontario's elementary schools throughout the nineteenth century.

Three telling examples of the success of people of German heritage in joining both local and provincial elites are William Euler, Adam Beck, and Daniel Knechtel. William Euler, the child of German immigrants, was born in 1875. He was mayor of Berlin/Kitchener between 1914 and 1917 and then elected to federal Parliament in 1917. He was a cabinet minister between 1926 and 1940 and then a senator until his death in 1961. Adam Beck was born in Baden, Ontario in 1857, the child of two German immigrants. He became mayor of London, Ontario in 1902 and member of provincial Parliament in 1903. He played a leading role in developing hydroelectric power in the province, and he led the provincial power company between 1906 and 1925.[49]

Finally, Daniel Knechtel was born in 1843 in Waterloo County. His parents had immigrated there in 1830 from Landstuhl in Rhineland-Palatinate. He moved to Hanover, Ontario in Grey County and began working as a carpenter. He married Christiana Stadelbauer, an immigrant from Bavaria, in 1866. Knechtel, alongside thousands of other people in the final third of the nineteenth century, played an important role in the province's industrialization. By 1899, Knechtel's factory had four steam-powered elevators and 150 machines. By 1911, Knechtel was employing 275 woodworkers in a four-storey factory in Hanover.[50] In that year, 70 per cent of the town's inhabitants were of German heritage, and, according to historian Joy Parr, this concentration then drew more German-speaking migrants from elsewhere in North America and Europe.[51]

By the 1870s, the influx of German speakers from both the United States and Europe had slowed significantly. The 1880s saw another spike in emigration from Germany, but the United States attracted the over-whelming majority of these people. A revealing example is that in 1882, of the almost 250,000 people to leave Germany, 37,004 landed in Canada. Yet of those people, 36,059 moved on to the United States, while 584 moved to Ontario and 361 to Manitoba.[52] Between 1862 and 1891, approx-imately 18,000 German speakers settled in Ontario while approximately another 410,000 entered Canada en route to the United States.[53] In the 1920s, there was again a spike of German-speaking migration to Ontario, much of which came from regions in central and eastern Europe, east of the newly redefined borders of Germany and Austria.

Canadian immigration policy has typically looked favourably upon German speakers.[54] In a hierarchical system that preferred British immigrants, Germans did not find themselves in the non-preferred category except during the two world wars when immigration from anywhere ground to a halt. The fact that German speakers were among the largest groups throughout the nineteenth century and that there was a spike in new German-speaking immigration in the 1920s illustrates this preferred status. Paying too much attention to temporary restrictions or the supposed fall from grace into a non-preferred group of immigrants risks being myopic and masks the general privilege of German speakers. For example, taking aim at an increasingly discriminatory practice of the BC government, the Japanese-Canadian leader G. Shimono complained to federal officials in 1922 that three naturalized British subjects of Japanese birth who had fought in the First World War had been denied a fishing license, but there was no reduction in the number of licenses issued to white, "naturalized British subjects even if they are of German, Austrian or Swedish origin."[55] By the early 1920s, deeply embedded ideas about where German speakers fit in the Canadian racial hierarchy trumped wartime concerns.

Counting Ethnicity

One can make a rough estimate of the total number of people of German cultural heritage in Ontario. It becomes much more complicated, however, to ascertain how many had an advanced proficiency in the German language, or how many affiliated with other people in their towns, cities, and regions under the auspices of a common ethnicity. The numbers provided by censuses and by the self-proclaimed leaders of any given community hint at the maximum number of people with some connection to a given ethnicity. However, in the case of German ethnicity, those numbers include and exclude in different ways those who were born in the Americas or in Europe outside the boundaries of the German nation-state and people who thought about ethnicity in different ways.

As table 0.2 shows, German speakers made up almost 10 per cent of the total population of Ontario in 1881. While the total number remained relatively constant, it consistently shrank as a percentage of the total population. Until approximately 1905, German was a more common origin than French in Ontario. Table 0.2 also shows a province growing more diverse. As a percentage of the total population, people not of British, French, or German origin rose from 4 per cent in 1901 to 12 per cent in 1931. In that year, 35 per cent of the province's population was not of English, Scottish, or Irish origin.

Ontario was by far the province with the most German nationals and German speakers in this period. According to the 1911 census, 49 per cent of people of German "origin" in Canada lived in this province (192,320 people). And of the 39,577 people in Canada born in Germany, 15,010 (38 per cent) lived in this one province.[56] Yet as those numbers indicate, only a small portion of "Germans" had actually immigrated from Germany.

Table 0.2 Ethnic groups in Ontario, 1881–1931

Year	Population Ontario	Population Canada	Ontario residents of German origin	Ontario residents of English, Scottish, and Irish origin	Ontario residents of French origin	Ontario residents of other ethnic origins
1881	1,926,922	4,324,810	188,394	1,541,633	102,743	94,152
1891	2,114,321	4,833,239	n/a	n/a	n/a	n/a
1901	2,182,947	5,371,315	203,319	1,732,144	158,671	88,813
1911	2,527,292	7,206,643	192,320	1,927,174	202,457	205,341
1921	2,933,662	8,787,949	130,545	2,282,015	248,275	272,827
1931	3,431,683	10,376,785	174,066	2,539,771	299,732	418,114

Sources: Census of Canada, 1880–81. Recensement du Canada. Volume IV (Ottawa: Printed by Maclean, Roger and Co. Wellington Street, 1885), 10–11; Sixth Census of Canada, 1921. Volume I. Population (Ottawa: F.A. Acland, Printer to the King's Most Excellent Majesty, 1924), 354–5; Seventh Census of Canada 1931. Volume I. Summary (Ottawa: J.O. Patenaude, I.S.O., Printer to the King's Most Excellent Majesty, 1936), 348–9; Seventh Census of Canada 1931. Volume II. Population by Areas (Ottawa: J.O. Patenaude, I.S.O., Printer to the King's Most Excellent Majesty, 1933), 294–5.

In 1881, 23,270 people in Ontario had been born in Germany while most other "Germans" had been born in Canada and the United States.[57] By 1911, the number of people born in Germany who lived in Ontario had declined to 15,010.[58] By 1931, that number had declined to 10,662, while the number of people born in Austria, Czechoslovakia, and Russia had also declined or increased only slightly over the previous decade.[59]

Many discussions about ethnic categories in the early twentieth century were highly influenced by ideas of race.[60] The references to European groups as different "races" in documents from before the 1960s, in the words of Matthew Jacobson, are "too conveniently passed over simply as misuses of the word 'race.'"[61] He adds that "American scholarship on immigration has generally conflated race and color, and so has transported a late-twentieth-century understanding of 'difference' into a period whose inhabitants recognized biologically based 'races' rather than culturally based 'ethnicities.'"[62] It is important to pay attention to the use of racial language. A belief that ethnic traits, primarily language, were inherited ran through educational philosophies and experiences throughout this period, and motivated repressive policies towards people of German heritage during the war. It also motivated several community activities as adults strove to ensure that "German" children learn the German language.

Language was a fundamental component of these racialized under-standings of people's difference. For example, the 1901 Canadian census instructions stipulated that "mother tongue is one's native language, the language of his race; but not necessarily the language in which he thinks, or which he speaks most fluently, or uses chiefly in conversation."[63] In the 1931 census the definition changed slightly. It wrote that the mother tongue is the "language of the home whether the person has learned to speak it or not." It added that, "except through intermarriage (the race of a person is that of the father), there is no way of acquiring mother tongue ... Again, mother tongue (as distinguished from official language) is not, or should not be, a matter of preference by the person but something that is inherited by him.[64] This belief that language was inherited shaped all sorts of adult behaviour towards children, people's ideas about schooling, and the labels that were applied to religious institutions.

We can count ethnicity in Ontario in other ways. The 1871 School Act that began the modern public educational system in the province allowed local school boards to decide to teach in English, French, or German. No other language enjoyed this status. In 1892, twelve of the thirteen German-language newspapers in Canada were published in Ontario.[65] In the same year, two of the one hundred religious publications in Canada were bi-weekly, German-language Lutheran periodicals published in Ontario, the *Kirchen-Blatt* and *Lutherisches Volksblatt*.[66] There were 129 Lutheran congregations in Ontario in 1900 that operated predominantly in German.[67]

Although difficult to count precisely, a wide range of actors constructed their own and other people's ethnicity in different ways. Generational differences, denominational identity, varying degrees of bilingualism, and the perceived sense of minority status vis-à-vis the linguistic and denominational surroundings of Ontario created multiple, overlapping, or competing definitions of German ethnicity. A belief that ethnicity, language, and religion mattered drove thousands of people to create institutions. Through these ethnic spaces, many thousands of German speakers in Ontario reproduced ethnicity. In so doing, they raised large groups of Canadian children to be proficient in German alongside English. Moreover, making ethnic space meant carving out a place for another Protestant denomination (Lutheranism) or a greater place for the Catholic Church in Ontario society. Many adults' efforts to reproduce ethnicity, in turn, shaped the nature of the cultural pluralism that emerged.

If we contrast official statistics with the much smaller numbers of people involved in German-language education or organized religion, we may begin to question how helpful statistics are. As Bruce Curtis has shown in the case of the Canadian census in the mid-nineteenth century, the science of statistics was heavily dependent on political concerns about ethnicity and language.[68] Information on people of German heritage in these Canadian censuses was influenced by a series of deceptive factors that twenty-first century readers ignore. According to the methodology outlined in the introduction of each census between 1881 and 1931, European ethnic origin was defined by one's paternal line of ancestry, regardless of the number of generations a person was removed from migration, and regardless of the ethnic heritage of an enumerated subject's mother or grandmother.[69] As a result, census takers would count as "Scottish" the child of a Canadian man of Scottish heritage and a German immigrant woman, but count as "German" the child of man whose great-grandfather immigrated to North America from German-speaking Europe and whose mother was born in Ireland.

German Immigration and the Language of Belonging in Ontario

Focusing in particular on education, religion, and language, the chapters of this book analyze the efforts of German-speaking immigrants and Canadians to carve out a place for community, family, and ethnicity in Ontario society. Schools and churches were of course only two kinds of institutions among many, such as business associations, newspapers, clubs, and sports associations. Other than newspapers, which have been sources rather than my objects of analysis, most other kinds of organizations where people could have come together along ethnic lines have left little documentation. Conversely, educational institutions offer a wealth of materials from individual schools, local school boards, and provincial records, and religious institutions offer abundant materials from local congregations, Lutheran synods, and Catholic orders or religious congregations.

More fundamentally, schools and churches were very large institutions with tens of thousands of participants (whether parishioners, laypeople, and leaders, or schoolchildren, teachers, and politicians). These two kinds of institution – more than business and sports associations, newspapers, and ethnic clubs – cut across social class, gender lines, and generational differences in revealing ways. Moreover, as Roberto Perin points out, church leaders in this period went out of their way to creatively integrate rebellious teenagers and to foster relationships between wealthy patrons and workers.[70] These institutions included enthusiastic people who wanted to foster the German language and culture, but also those who were more indifferent to it. Finally, a focus on religion and education uncovers the relationship between ethnicity, the surrounding society, and the state, while other kinds of institutions often remained more separate from the state.

Chapter 1 examines the changing place of German in schools and the transition away from local control (through school boards) and to central authority in Toronto. It charts the efforts of the provincial government to ensure that children would be educated in English. A series of regulations in the 1880s and 1890s undid the previous status that both German and French enjoyed as alternate languages of instruction in Ontario's public and Catholic separate schools. The ideas driving these cultural politics and the goal of linking one language with civic belonging in Ontario grew from the previous context in which English, German, and French all had special privileges. While local school boards technically had the power to decide the language of instruction, rising central control over curriculum, textbooks, and teacher training enabled the government to assert its control, particularly over German speakers.

Chapter 2 turns its attention to a topic that appears through the book: the experience of German speakers in Ontario during the First World

War. While the war did not stop people from being German – as chapters 3 to 6 will show – it did limit the way that many people could publicly express German ethnicity. An important place where the war's impact was felt was through a series of orders-in-council and laws that grouped together people with various degrees of connection to either Germany or Austria-Hungary and labelled them subversive threats to Canada and the war effort. As the result of wartime paranoia, certain ethnic backgrounds became increasingly incompatible with civic belonging. In the early years of the war, a series of federal orders-in-council targeted non-naturalized immigrants, but later in the war the federal government stripped most naturalized immigrants born in Germany and Austria-Hungary, as well as German speakers born in Russia, of the right to vote, and ultimately banned all publications in German. These policies slowly expanded the net of who would be mistreated during the war, and the policies had a broader ripple effect on things associated with some form of a German community.

Returning to the topic of education, chapter 3 shifts the focus to two colleges that taught several subjects in German and catered to Catholics or Lutherans of German and other backgrounds. Looking beyond the state, this history of education shows how religious communities promoted the German language at a time when other schooling did the opposite. At these institutions, the German language and culture coexisted with a strong interest in fostering religious education. While both colleges slowly became less German and more clearly only Catholic or Lutheran, they nonetheless retained their bilingual character throughout the 1920s. St Jerome's and Waterloo Lutheran Colleges in Berlin and Waterloo were male-only colleges, which in turn shaped how language and religion were used in German-speaking communities over time. Compared to the steady marginalization of German at Ontario's elementary schools documented in chapter 1, these colleges illustrate the autonomy of religious institutions and, in contrast to local school boards, proved important in the promotion of German to Canadian youth. It shows how language and religion were two elements within many people's understanding of German ethnicity.

Continuing with the study of organized religion as a central anchor of German-speaking communities in Ontario, chapter 4 charts the networks that bound Lutherans in the province into a larger North American world. It argues that these ties played an important role in creating and maintaining German-language communities in Ontario and across Canada. Some of the largest German-language institutions in the province were connected to ideas and people that transcended Canada's political boundaries. Connections to other German speakers in large US cities helped keep the German language ingrained in the fabric of the Lutheran churches in Ontario into the 1920s. This religious focus seeks to show another fundamental aspect of community, yet one which diverged greatly from the case of education.

The final two chapters continue with religious sources to analyze the nature of German-English bilingualism in Ontario. Chapter 5 focuses on children and argues that their language practices and adults' responses to children's behaviour shaped the transition from German-language Lutheran and Catholic congregations to bilingual ones. Yet the chapter also shows significant differences in the importance that Lutherans and Catholics gave to the German language and how they offered German-language education to young people. While children of German heritage increasingly chose English over German in the early decades of the twentieth century, this was not a linear progression, and denominational rather than generational differences were important. Lutherans placed greater weight on the German language for their denomination, and the institutional support that this Church offered played a central role in the ongoing vitality of German and bilingual congregations throughout the 1910s and 1920s.

Chapter 6 asks what the language of religion was for congregations across the province sometimes defined as German, and it shows how religious institutions and denominational identity moulded people's understanding of language and ethnicity. Pastors, elected lay leaders, and the female and male members of different church groups (such as aid societies and social committees) did prefer German. However, they did not create isolated or unilingual spaces. Instead, adults, youth, and children struck a balance between both languages and made German and English together the language of religion. This linguistic history proposes that children's language choices and adults' concerns reveal much about how communities form and how people understand their ethnicity.

As the chapters that follow show, the definitions of German ethnicity slowly evolved, as did the nature of the linguistic and cultural pluralism of Canada. Yet throughout this period, German immigrants and their children successfully claimed a space for bilingualism and religious diversity within the national body. They made and remade the boundaries of ethnicity.

ONE / The State and Ethnicity

The relationship between the state and ethnicity in Ontario changed significantly between 1880 and 1930. The period begins at a time when the Ontario government actively worked to expand the elementary school system, train teachers, and reduce illiteracy. In this moment, with the government most concerned with creating a school system, German, French, and English could be used in the province's public and separate schools as languages of instruction. Yet that trilingual system was a vestige of a pre-1880 world, and things soon began to change. By 1900 and even more so on the eve of the First World War, English-speaking nationalists in Ontario (and the Canadian Prairies) had increasingly come to see the linguistic pluralism brought by decades of migration – whether from Europe or Quebec – as a problem. The previous rights of local communities to teach in other languages came under fire. Over the course of the war, concerns about the use of other languages in schools expanded into other domains, and several linguistic minorities were suspected of disloyalty. A series of orders-in-council targeted German speakers and others, and it forced many to register with local authorities or to prove that despite their linguistic abilities they were naturalized British subjects. Weeks before the end of the war, state concerns about multilingualism culminated with the closure of newspapers and the banning of other publications in many languages.

Several scholars have demonstrated that German speakers were a preferred group in Canada in this period, and occupied a place of privilege in the ethno-racial hierarchy of European immigrants alongside British and Scandinavian immigrants.[1] While that did afford

German speakers several benefits, especially compared to other groups from eastern and southern Europe and from Asia, it did not exempt them from a growing ideology in which politicians and bureaucrats sought to reduce the place of ethnic and linguistic diversity in Ontario society. Before delving any deeper into what politicians and bureaucrats thought and did, it is worth stressing that government policies coexisted with the actions and wishes of German speakers and other ethno-linguistic groups in Ontario. The state mattered, but as parts II and III of this book show, people and communities also shaped the nature of cultural pluralism.

The growing linguistic ideology in this time period was dominated by what Yasemin Yildiz calls the "monolingual paradigm." She contends that starting only in the nineteenth century, monolingualism came to be seen as "a key structuring principle that organizes the entire range of modern social life, from the construction of individuals and their proper subjectivities to the formation of disciplines and institutions, as well as imagined collectives such as cultures and nations."[2] Indeed, as Benedict Anderson notes, language and nation became interwoven concepts for many European nationalists in the nineteenth and early twentieth centuries.[3] According to Eric Hobsbawm, the concept of *nation* had not been a particularly ethnic or linguistic category in western Europe until the late nineteenth century.[4] Yet from the 1870s to the First World War, "ethnicity and language became the central, increasingly the decisive or even the only criteria of potential nationhood" across Europe, and this change marked a significant shift away from the previously open relationship between cultural and political subjectivity.[5]

These international ideas had a significant impact on the relationship between ethnicity and the state in Canada. Rogers Brubaker contends that twentieth-century state builders have believed that "polity and culture should be congruent: A distinctive national culture should be diffused throughout the territory of the state, but it should stop at the frontiers of the state. There should be cultural homogeneity *within* states, but sharp cultural boundaries *between* them." Increasingly, governing elites came to believe that "cultural nationality and legal citizenship should be coextensive."[6] James Scott argues that the modern state and its officials seek to create a population with the standardized characteristics that will allow the state to monitor and manage its citizenry and resources. The builders of a modern nation-state attempt to create a landscape and population that will further facilitate efficient management. Central to Scott's analysis is the concept of "legibility." The more legible and standardized a population and its social space are, the more amenable they are to the techniques of state officials.[7] The educational system of Ontario displayed many characteristics of this will to standardize and make legible in such areas as its pro-English language policy and the regulation of textbooks. Chapter 1 turns its attention to the growing authority of the Education Department in Ontario and how it slowly removed the special privileges of German as a language of instruction in the province's public and Catholic separate schools. Chapter 2 then focuses on a series of federal policies during the First World War, which took aim at immigrants from Germany and Austria-Hungary and ultimately more broadly at German speakers and other linguistic groups. Combined, the chapters show an evolving linguistic ideology and state efforts to manage and ultimately limit ethnic diversity in Ontario and Canada.

1. MAKING ENGLISH CANADA
French and German Schools in Ontario

In regard to teachers in French or German settlements a knowledge of the
French or German grammar respectively may be substituted for a knowledge
of the English grammar.

> **EDUCATION DEPARTMENT OF ONTARIO**, *Regulations and Correspondence*
> *relating to French and German Schools* (1889), 12.

I come next to consider that most disturbing of all questions – French and German
schools – and I bracket these two because every objection that applies to one applies to
the other. From an Anglo-Saxon standpoint they are both foreign languages, and national
characteristics have very little to do with the question.

> **GEORGE ROSS,** minister of education of Ontario. "Report of a Speech Delivered by the Minister
> of Education at the Reform Demonstration, Toronto, June 29th, 1889," in Ross,
> *The Separate School Question and the French Language*, 12.

There are no French or English provinces in Canada, and there cannot be any, all
provinces being British. The provinces must recognize the necessity of a complete
knowledge of both the official languages, unless narrow provincialism, which is
detrimental to progress and good understanding, is desired and promoted.

> **ASSOCIATION CANADIENNE-FRANÇAISE D'ÉDUCATION D'ONTARIO,**
> *Bi-lingualism in Ontario* (1912), 4.

When anglophones and francophones debated bilingual education in Ontario from the 1880s to the eve of the First World, they often spoke of German schools. Beginning in the mid-nineteenth century, German stood alongside French and English as one of three possible languages of instruction in the public and separate schools of the province. French and German were at two points on the same spectrum facing off against a growing English linguistic ideology. Ideas in English Canada that linked the singular usage of English to the definition of the nation excluded not only French but all languages.[1] German retained its special status until 1912 when the Education Department attempted to eliminate French as a language of instruction under Regulation 17. With this new regulation, both were removed as alternative languages of instruction, a status that German never regained.

The multilingual nature of Ontario's school system in the mid-nineteenth century gave rise to a series of cultural policies starting in the 1880s that aimed to ensure that all schools in Ontario taught English, even if it was alongside French or German. With these policies, government officials and politicians increasingly sought to merge cultural and political definitions of belonging, and they embraced the idea that all citizens should share a common language in a way that was atypical until the 1880s. By 1912, provincial regulations, textbook and curriculum policies, school boards, and parents had long since replaced German with English as the language of instruction in every locality in the province, even where German had been heavily used until the 1890s. The case of German in Ontario, as well as that of Polish or Ukrainian in Manitoba, provides important insights into language politics and the evolving ideas about cultural and civic belonging in Canada. These questions have often been reduced to struggles between English and French. However, a broader linguistic landscape existed.

Focusing on the efforts to make the Ontario school system monolingual, this chapter argues that a dialogue with both French and German speakers formed English speakers' ideas about national and civic belonging. Ideas about linguistic difference and assimilationist nationalism marked the boundaries of ethnicity and state efforts to remake the nature of Ontario's linguistic pluralism. The spotlight on the German language and German speakers reveals the process by which an

English-Canadian civic culture arose and the strategies that German and French speakers developed to maintain their languages as instructional ones. The educational projects aimed at making a monolingual society played a crucial role in the emergent idea of "English Canada." Yet the changing nature of language education in the province did not only result from bureaucrats and politicians but also from the goals of families and communities, something seen by the different responses of German and French speakers.

While French speakers in Ontario benefitted from certain rights (whether perceived or constitutionally explicit), Germans seemed to receive a similar status because of a relatively privileged socio-economic status and their early presence in the province. They also benefitted from a certain settler privilege. The Ontario government created space for locally controlled schools teaching in one of three European languages (English, French, and German) between the 1850s and 1870s, at the same time that officials from Canada West or the federal government were laying the groundwork for Indian day schools and residential schools. J.R. Miller notes that while missionaries running schools in the mid-nineteenth century often learned Indigenous languages to help with their proselytizing goals, as early as the 1850s both government and central church bureaucracy sent directives to missionary educators to use only English, and this was the start of "increasing pressure in the schools to end the children's use of Aboriginal languages."[2] It is worth stressing, then, that the space allowed for bilingual education in Ontario coexisted with the eliminationist ideology of settler colonialism. The space created for German schools in the nascent system of compulsory education after 1871 in Ontario also coexisted with the creation of segregated schools for African Canadians. As Robin Winks underlines, this system traced its origins to the early nineteenth century and was the result of active efforts of whites to exclude.[3]

Although historians have often framed French Canada as the counterpoint to British imperial identity in Canada in the late nineteenth and first half of the twentieth century, in many ways that Britishness was subsumed within the idea of English Canada.[4] Much of the interest in Britishness and the British Empire was grounded in the local and national contexts rather than a bold assertion of a global identity.[5]

English Canada – like French Canada – was something that politicians, intellectuals, education bureaucrats, and families actively constructed. As both a reflection of this vision of the nation and a way in which the vision was implemented, schools in Ontario and in western Canada set out to ensure that every citizen spoke English.

The efforts of anglophones to make Ontario and western Canada English-speaking at the turn of the twentieth century competed with another idea that emphasized that Canada was made up of two founding peoples and the two groups could be at home anywhere in the country's territory.[6] Propounded in particular by Henri Bourassa (a prominent federal and provincial politician for almost four decades[7] and founder and editor of the prominent Montreal newspaper *Le Devoir*, 1910–32) and Lionel Groulx (Catholic priest and historian of French-Canadian history), this vision of French Canada lasted until the 1960s when a new vision of the nation was mapped onto a smaller territory, the province of Quebec.[8] Marcel Martel and Martin Pâquet have described the policies of anglophone governments and provincial elites in Ontario and Manitoba as efforts to "homogenize" the population living within their territories.[9] They examine the promotion of unilingualism, through schooling in particular, arguing that "the years 1848 to 1927 were characterized by a state activism in language policies."[10] They contend that anglophones and francophones often tried to "nationalize language" and to create unilingual political spaces.

Such policies were part of an international trend. In the United States, Progressive Era school politics starting in the 1880s and lasting until the First World War were characterized by the centralization of authority at the expense of local variation, and alternative languages of instruction were slowly eliminated as a consequence.[11] According to Paul Ramsey, bilingual schooling in the US Midwest began in the 1840s as public education took off and lasted until the 1880s, when the Progressive Era "brought forth a new tone to American society. The centralization of schools, particularly in urban areas, challenged the localism that allowed bilingualism to flourish in America's public institutions."[12] As Frederick Luebke notes, between the 1870s and 1890s, legislators in many states began to craft legislation that ensured that English was the sole language of instruction while allowing other languages to continue as subjects. In the final decade before the First World War, "a fairly consistent pattern of legislation emerged ... [which] obliged teachers to use English exclusively in their instruction."[13]

Making German Schools Bilingual

In promoting compulsory education after the School Act of 1871, bureaucrats and politicians in Ontario articulated a linguistic ideology. Universal and compulsory attendance was accompanied by a project of universal literacy, which soon evolved into a focus on English literacy. The Education Department began to require specific textbooks, to increase the number of certified teachers, and in general to work to ensure that all children attending Ontario's public and separate schools learn English even if alongside French or German.

The most salient feature of the language policies of Ontario's Education Department between 1880 and the First Word War – even during the conflict over Regulation 17 and when Canada was at war with Germany – was not conflict between linguistic groups, but rather a firm fixation on English grammar, composition, spelling, and pronunciation. These were all separate subjects, and together they formed the cornerstone of the curriculum in public and separate schools. In 1900, English composition, literature, grammar, and writing were four of the nine subjects tested on the high school entrance exam.[14] These multiple language classes made English one of the defining experiences of the Ontario school system, even at French and German schools. Through this focus on English, the French and German schools of the 1870s became bilingual schools by the turn of the twentieth century.

The changing position of German in Ontario schools illustrates a crucial cultural component of what Bruce Curtis has called the "educational state."[15] The Education Department and local school boards had jurisdiction over separate domains within a single state apparatus. Parental lobbies and elected trustees could influence the implementation of provincial policy in their local public and separate school boards, and they were the ones who ultimately decided whether to teach German or French. The local school board was in charge of administrative matters, infrastructure, and hiring the teachers who had been trained by the province. The majority of the funding for public and separate schools came from municipal school grants and assessments raised through local taxation rather than by the central state, and local boards also had the power to ensure the proper use of locally raised funds. The domain controlled by the Education Department, however, played an important role in fostering the use of English, which in turn fundamentally influenced the nature of French and German schools. In particular, in the 1880s and 1890s, the department took on a near monopoly on matters of curriculum, textbook selection, and teacher training. The province also had a powerful agent in the form of school inspectors who took great interest in key matters that fell under provincial rather than local control.

French-language education in Ontario often took place under the auspices of Catholic separate schools, but it was the regulations about language of instruction, not the fact of their being separate schools, that enabled parents and school trustees to teach in French. Public schools in Ontario (meaning secular, non-Catholic schools) could also be "French schools" or "German schools," and German was the language of instruction in some Catholic separate schools. While section 93 of the British North America Act did give Catholics in Ontario and Protestants in Quebec rights to separate schools, and while section 93 has been invoked in the defence of francophone rights, provincial language policies were also important.[16] Constitutionally protected religious rights have been a helpful way to claim language rights, but in the late nineteenth century, the language policies of governments in both Ontario and Manitoba sought to separate language and religion (and remove other languages and Catholic autonomy).

The official legislation that permitted the existence of French and German schools evolved over time. It began in the nineteenth century in the absence of legislation and was codified and revised between 1851 and 1871.[17] In the 1850s, the Council of Public Instruction for Upper Canada allowed local school boards to grant certificates to French-speaking and German-speaking teachers, which enabled them to teach in those languages. By the 1870s, this had developed into more formal support. The province allowed "French and German Public and Separate Schools in the French and German settlements of Upper Canada."[18] George Hodgins, a leading education official in Ontario between 1844 and 1890 and close ally of Egerton Ryerson, the architect of this school system, stated that this policy approach led to the "evolution ... of the various nationalities among us into a homogeneous Canadian nationality."[19] That is to say, it allowed on a temporary basis institutional support for a trilingual school system.

A changing provincial discourse about French and German reflected the status that these two languages had in relation to English. By 1883, French and German schools were allowed to exist through a regulation that stated: "In regard to teachers in French or German settlements a knowledge of the French or German grammar respectively may be substituted for a knowledge of the English grammar ... The County Councils, within whose jurisdiction there are French or German settlements, are authorized to appoint one or more persons (who in their judgment may be competent) to examine candidates in the French and German language."[20] By the time of Regulation 17 (1912–27), a failed attempt started by James Whitney's Conservative government to eliminate French from Ontario's schools, the provincial approval of the use of French or German as alternative languages of instruction to English had become Regulation 15.[21] In what had been "French and German Public and Separate Schools" in the 1870s, by 1912 the two languages were used as alternatives to the main language (English) and permitted by a regulation.

Despite the openness to French and German in the mid-nineteenth century, a series of provincial policies in the 1880s and 1890s turned French and German schools – whether public or Catholic separate schools – into "bilingual schools." George Ross, the minister of education, summed up the state of the province's language policies succinctly in 1889: "in dealing with the question of two languages in our Public and Separate Schools, the Department has held constantly in view the following considerations: (1) It is indispensable that English should be thoroughly taught in every school, Separate or Public. No objection, however, is taken to the study of the French language so long as the Inspector is satisfied with the efficiency of the school in English. (2) It is also indispensable that every teacher engaged in a Public or Separate School should be able to teach English."[22]

The status that German and French had enjoyed as alternative languages of instruction in Ontario changed fundamentally in 1885. In that year, the government made English compulsory in every school where it was not already the language of instruction. A single textbook series, the *Public School Readers*, became obligatory in all schools. The Education Department required every school to teach English writing, spelling, and composition, as well as translation into English. These four separate English subjects advanced the linguistic ideology in schools where French or German remained the language of instruction.[23] In a speech defending provincial policy towards French schooling, Ross lauded the 1885 policy change and emphasized that this marked an improvement over the previous lack of obligatory English-language instruction in French or German settlements.[24] In 1889, he asserted that "the right to a good, thorough English education is recognized by the Constitution of the Province of Ontario as a birthright of every citizen, irrespective of creed, and, as I understand public sentiment, no Government could long exist that ignored, much less repudiated, this right."[25]

In 1890, the imposition of English in what remained French or German schools solidified. Throughout this period, the province did not change the legislation that stated that instruction could be given in French or German "in school sections where the French or German language prevailed."[26] In 1890, however, two new regulations modified this law. One stipulated that the English abilities of children at French or German schools should be the same as the language skills of children at English schools.[27] The second authorized French or German to be taught *in addition to* English, instead of the 1885 regulation that added English to the curriculum of French and German schools.[28] These incremental policy changes subtly undid the previous trilingual system. In so doing, the provincial government took an important step toward a new linguistic ideology where all citizens of a given territory (Ontario) should share a common language (English).

These policy changes did not lead to instant implementation. Indeed, historians of education have demonstrated the disjuncture between policies and their actual implementation in Ontario even in the early twentieth century.[29] In studies of francophones in Ontario, scholars have emphasized resistance to these policies and the inability of many francophone teachers in rural schools to teach in English. For example, in 1889, Ross happily reported that English was taught in every public school in Ontario.[30] Yet three commissioners who carried out a study of "French-English schools" that year commented on the poor English abilities of some teachers, and they recommended that "teachers not familiar with the English language should apply themselves at once to the study of English."[31]

Local school boards could push back by failing to hire teachers capable of teaching English in addition to French or German. Nevertheless, the push for English reveals much about the linguistic ideology of the emergent school system that attempted to make English necessary and German and French supplementary. The policies also mark a rupture with mid-nineteenth-century thinking that allowed the use of state resources – most of which were raised and controlled by government officials at the local level – to support a multilingual society. In the case of schools where German was taught, trustees accepted the inclusion of English, and thereby ensured that German-speaking children would become proficient in English even as the same schools taught German.

In 1889, in the face of growing concern over French schooling in eastern Ontario, the Education Department commissioned studies of both French and German schools. The commissioners, Alfred Reynard, D.D. McLeod, and J.J. Tilley, reported on fifty-eight schools in eastern Ontario. They wrote, "We conversed with all classes of the French people, and they invariably expressed themselves not only as *willing*, but as *desirous* that their children should learn the English language. They are also desirous that they shall learn to read and write in French – their mother tongue."[32] Yet the commissioners, rather contradictorily, also found that the vast majority of school boards continued to hire many teachers who struggled with English, which in turn undermined the government's efforts to advance its vision of an English-speaking citizenry. The commissioners found a variety of situations, and in some instances were pleased with the amount and level of English taught. Nevertheless, many of those fifty-eight schools taught in English for only one hour per day, and in those schools, the commissioners recorded: "pupils understood easy sentences, but could speak very little English"; "Only very young pupils present and these knew simply the names of a few objects in English. English was taught this year by order of Inspector"; "pupils very backward in English."[33]

Textbooks and the Language of Instruction

Textbooks greatly preoccupied bureaucrats in the Education Department in the 1880s and 1890s. Between 1882 and 1892, the number of authorized textbook series for all subjects decreased from fifty-three to ten, and Minister George Ross happily reported in 1893 that the standardizing project that he had begun upon taking office ten years earlier had been accomplished.[34] Authorities in the provincial capital rather than local school boards controlled textbook selection, and in so doing they could assert their authority over local language politics. In the case of German-language education in particular, this act of standardization limited the materials that teachers and school boards could use to teach the language. In this period, the shrinking list of authorized textbooks included mainly books published in Canada.

As part of their 1889 report on French and German schools in Ontario, commissioners Reynard, McLeod, and Tilley reported that seven different German textbooks or series were being used in Ontario public schools, six of which were published in the United States and one in Canada.[35] The commissioners noted that these textbooks, "though not authorized, have been introduced by the trustees or teachers as the most suitable they could find."[36] However, the commissioners also noted that the English readers made obligatory in 1885 were used in all of the German schools they visited, something that attests to the implementation of language policies promoting English.[37] The commissioners recommended that a single series of German readers be authorized and all others be discontinued. They also noted that "as only a small proportion – about one fourth – of the German children learn German in the schools, and as a large majority of these on coming to school understand simple English sentences, we do not deem it necessary to recommend any special provision, such as a bilingual series of readers, to facilitate elementary instruction in English."[38] That is to say, the commissioners found no reason to prescribe additional materials to teach English beyond the *Public School Readers* from 1885.

In 1890, the Education Department asserted its authority over local school boards as it began to follow through on the commissioners' recommendation to authorize a single German book. The clerk of the executive council, John Cartwright, wrote that the minister had ordered "that where the German language prevails, and the Trustees, with the approval of the Inspector, require German to be taught in addition to English," a single series entitled *Ahn's German Books* was to be used alongside the *Public School Readers*.[39] Beginning in 1890, therefore, the only vehicle for promoting German in schools where German had once been the language of instruction was this series along with one other book (to be discussed shortly). Before 1890, German could be taught in the absence of codified textbook regulations, but after this point central state authority rather than local decisions played a decisive role.

If unauthorized textbooks were used, the province reserved the right to withhold its legislative grant to local school boards.[40] In the 1890s, teachers could be fined $10 for using unauthorized textbooks.[41] Controversies over Regulation 17 prompted greater consequences. Teachers could be suspended and the school boards could deduct from their salaries a sum equal to the grant withheld from the school board.[42] Teacher training was another way that the Education Department in Toronto could usurp some of the school boards' autonomy. By moving towards provincially run normal schools and away from county-run model schools in the three decades before the war, the province selected and trained its workforce according to its standardizing requirements, ones that did not reflect local interests. The rise of normal schools in this period was a way that central authorities could implement a set of cultural policies. Unlike French speakers in Ontario who could recruit teachers trained in Quebec, by the turn of the twentieth century German-speaking teachers had overwhelmingly been educated in the English-language institutions of Ontario. Model schools gave temporary, third-class teaching certificates whereas a normal school granted a teacher a second-class and permanent certificate to teach in the province.[43]

Individual school boards did not appear to reject the prescribed German textbooks in the 1890s, although several historians have found that francophone parents and communities did indeed resist the imposition of central state authority during the conflict over Regulation 17.[44] In 1890, George Ross reported to the legislature that "it appears that the *Public Schools Readers* are used in every [German] school, and that on the whole, substantial progress is made in the study of English," and that when "the Trustees and Inspector consider the study of the German language desirable," the four *Ahn's German Books* were to be used.[45] The *Ahn* series was imported from New York City, and this is one example of the connections that streamed into Ontario from several nodes in the United States. As was the case for the production of religious texts, American cities with much larger German-speaking populations played a crucial role in supporting German in Ontario.

For any German-speaking parent, educator, or community leader dreaming of a bilingual school system in specific localities in Ontario, the provincially prescribed textbooks represented a pedagogical nightmare. *Ahn's German Books* were clearly intended for the children of anglophones and would have been a disservice to any child who spoke German at home. The readers explained everything in English, and it seems that such grammars would have contributed to cementing English as the dominant written language for children from German-speaking households, with questionable benefits for promoting bilingualism. The reader for the first class began by teaching German handwriting (*Sütterlin* script) as well as German sounds by comparing them to English ones. For example, the short German "i," explains the book's author P. Henn, is pronounced like the "i" in the English word "bit," and the long "i" like the "ee" in "meet."[46] Henn further explained that the "ch" sound did not exist in English and that it needed to be learned from the teacher, suggesting that the intended pupils would not already be orally proficient in German. The most advanced fourth book sought to give the pupil "a fair mastery of German in speaking and in writing,"[47] which again suggests that children from German-speaking homes were not the target group. The book introduced pupils to more advanced aspects of the language compared to the previous three books, but the level was still relatively basic. It taught the use of auxiliary verbs, prepositions governing the dative and genitive cases, and conjugations of strong and weak verbs. It included conversational exercises and a vocabulary section that translated German words into English.[48]

In addition to *Ahn's German Books*, the province continued to authorize what was known as "Klotz's German Grammar" after considering the commissioners' recommendations in 1889. The book had been widely used for two decades in many schools in the absence of state regulation. Unlike the other authorized German readers, Klotz's grammar was clearly intended for native speakers and would have been helpful in promoting a written proficiency in German among children who arrived at school already capable of speaking it. In 1898, however, and driven by the search for legibility, provincial bureaucrats removed Klotz's textbook from the authorized list.[49]

Otto Klotz published *Leitfaden zur deutschen Sprache oder kurz gefasstes Lehrbuch der deutschen Sprache in Fragen und Antworten* in 1867 in Preston, Ontario. He was the school superintendent in Preston and a member of the Waterloo County school board.[50] Just two years before, as Bruce Curtis has written, Klotz was engaged in conflict with Egerton Ryerson and the Education Office over the English textbooks and readers used across Canada West. In 1868 Klotz's resistance to central authority led to a new series replacing the Irish textbooks that had been introduced in the 1840s.[51] Curtis has argued that Klotz's demands forced the province to modernize its school readers.

Within this context of disapproval of outdated books, Klotz also produced an advanced German grammar for use in Ontario's elementary schools. It resembled a classical grammar written in German-speaking Europe. However, Klotz wrote that such grammars were too philosophical and that the local youth could not understand them sufficiently.[52] He added, in German, that "the lack of a textbook to teach the German language has been mentioned so often and felt even more so by everybody who has been involved with teaching German that it would be completely redundant to justify the need for such a schoolbook."[53] His reasons for writing the grammar were that "teachers using English with few exceptions also teach English grammar. However, a teacher using German usually limits himself entirely to reading and writing. Therefore, his knowledge of grammar remains almost completely unused."[54] Finally, he noted that "certainly the book will be helpful if German parents express their desire that their children learn the mother tongue alongside English so that they do not just speak German but also can read it and write it."[55] Klotz's grammar contained no texts and it was exclusively in German. He discussed several linguistic and grammatical issues such as sounds, spelling, pronouns, verbs, conjunctions, and sentence structure. It was clearly to be used in schools with German-speaking teachers and pupils, and it was not intended to teach German as a second language.

After the elimination of Klotz's grammar in 1898, the only textbooks that local school boards in Ontario could use (*Ahn's German Books*) were designed for anglophones. German could be the language of instruction according to legislation created in 1871, but the authorized textbooks, along with the imposition of English alongside German and the financial penalties for failing to follow these requirements, ensured that German could not be taught in a meaningful way to the children of native speakers. As a result, the textbooks used in the elective and infrequent German language classes were of the utmost importance. Yet all of these books taught German grammar in English, and they explained German sounds with the assumption that the student had a better mastery of English phonemes.

The Education Department's stance on French-language textbooks greatly resembled its approach to German books. In 1887, Théodule Girardot sent a list of possible textbooks to the minister of education, George Ross, commenting that until then the province had too many authorized textbooks. Those previously authorized in 1868 included French-language books on arithmetic, geography, and English grammar (explained in French). Seeking to influence the nature of provincial standardization, Girardot proposed a series of French-language readers by Monpetit and Marquette as well as *Histoire du Canada, Histoire d'Angleterre, Géographie illustrée, Algèbre intermédiaire, Arithmétique commerciale*, and *Géométrie*. He also suggested two books aimed specifically at teaching English to francophones (*Nouveau cours de langue anglaise selon la methode d'Ollendorf* and *Dictionnaire Anglais et Français et Français et Anglais*).[56]

As was the case with German and following the same goal of standardization, George Ross disagreed. In 1889 he removed all previously authorized French books. In their place, the province authorized a series of readers called *The First Reader, The Second Reader*, and *The Third Reader*, published by the Toronto publisher Copp and Clark. Because this series only covered the first three of five forms in the province's primary schools, Ross authorized Louis Figuier's *Les grandes inventions modernes* in circumstances "where the use of an advanced reader is considered desirable by the trustees and inspector."[57] The 300-page book from France included chapters of approximately fifteen or twenty pages on topics such as telephones, railways, steam engines, electricity, photography, weapons, lighting, telescopes and microscopes, and gas.[58]

In an effort to standardize, the Education Department imposed textbooks on German and French schools that were ill-suited to teaching the children of German and French speakers. In a system where centralized state authority coexisted with the power of local school boards, textbook selection became a new frontier that undermined the ongoing local autonomy to teach in languages other than English. After the late 1880s, schools in Ontario did more to undermine balanced bilingualism than they did to promote it.

The Place of German in the Curriculum

German did not occupy a prominent place in the curricula of Ontario schools while English became a language of instruction in districts that had previously used German. Between 1880 and 1914, German occupied a relatively marginal place in an overall educational experience organized firmly around several separate English subjects. Although provincial authorities and francophones continued to speak about German schools in the same context as French schools, provincial policies in the 1880s and 1890s in fact undermined the language's privileged position. Considerable variation existed at Catholic separate schools (teaching in German) and in different regions of the province, but a common pattern emerged whereby German was a subject rather than a medium of instruction.

The previously mentioned 1889 commissioners' report of French and German schools found that German was not being used as a language of instruction in any public school in Waterloo, Perth, and Bruce Counties, where German speakers lived in relatively high concentrations (see figure 0.2). The commissioners wrote that

> as the surrounding districts became occupied by English-speaking people, the German language gradually gave way to the English, so that now the schools, though attended by German children and making some use of German, are practically English schools and the German language is no longer used as the medium of instruction in any of them, except for as may be necessary to give explanation

to those pupils who, on coming to school, know little English. In the districts visited the population continues to be almost wholly German, but the people can generally speak English. Their children, therefore, on entering school, though speaking German at home, have in almost all cases some familiarity with the English language so that they can be taught by English-speaking teachers. While the German people recognize the necessity of having their children learn English, many of them desire that some instruction in the German language shall also be given.[59]

The commissioners' observation of the teachers' dominant use of English reflects the fact that the provincial workforce was increasingly trained in centralized normal schools and that qualified teachers were brought into (partially) German-speaking areas. This report suggests that the dominant spoken language of these young children when they first began attending state-controlled schools remained German. Even by 1901, census takers in Waterloo County reported that 9 per cent of five- and six-year-olds of German origin did not speak English.[60] This 1889 bureaucratic report illustrates an anglophone's perspective on cultural change, but it also likely provides an accurate assessment of the overwhelming presence of English despite many children's proficiency in German when they began school. In addition, this assessment reveals an important divergence between German and French speakers. Schools in eastern Ontario continued to use French as the primary language of instruction in 1889, whereas these commissioners found that German was taught "in every case as a separate subject."

Beyond finding that German was not a language of instruction, the commissioners found that "of the 2,412 German children on the roll in the schools visited, only 602 were learning German, and of the 483 English children only 56 were learning German. The time given to the teaching of German averages 4 1/3 hours per week, or 52 minutes per day. The teaching of German consists almost entirely of reading and writing with some translation. German grammar is only taught in four schools."[61] Despite the legislation and regulations permitting "German schools" until 1912, by 1889 German was no longer the language of instruction in any public school in the province. This absence of German-language instruction demonstrates the limited space that the Education Department and school boards that comprised a mix of English- and German-speaking trustees gave to this language.

Influenced by emerging ideas about the English language and citizenship in Ontario, concerns about the place of French and German in the educational system were the cause of commissioners Reynard, McLeod, and Tilley's entire project. They noted whether any language other than English was used partially or wholly in teaching at these schools. In every single "German" school, they reported that no language other than English was used or they explained that German was taught as a subject and never as a language of instruction.[62] Inspector Thomas Pearce reported that in the town of Berlin and in neighbouring villages of Preston, New Hamburg, Wilmot, and Woolwich, the small number of children who took German used the authorized *Ahn's Grammar* and *Ahn's Readers*. Pearce added, "These pupils study English also. Arithmetic, Geography and History are taught in English only." Scholars have noted that it was a common complaint of inspectors and a frequent accusation by Conservative members of the legislature that teachers in French schools were unable to teach in English.[63] However, the commissioners found that teachers at schools where German was a subject were completely capable of teaching in English.[64]

The commissioners based their report on the in-depth study of eighteen "German" schools in Waterloo, Perth, and Bruce Counties, areas where in the mid-nineteenth century the majority of the local population was German-speaking. Describing them as "German" in 1889, however, reveals more about the anglophone gaze than the linguistic reality. Of the 2,895 pupils registered at these schools, 2,412 were described as "German."[65] Yet only one-quarter of the "German" pupils actually studied German, two of the eighteen "German schools" did not even have a German teacher or assistant, and none of the schools that did had more than one German teacher.[66] While a single teacher sufficed for many small rural schools with between thirty and fifty pupils, the public school in the town of Waterloo employed one German teacher for the 371 pupils the commissioners labelled as "German," and the town of Berlin had one teacher for 745 "German" pupils. The public school in Berlin taught twelve and a half hours of German per week, but the

1.1 Group of children and school in Waterloo County, ca. 1910.

school in Waterloo taught only three hours per week. At thirteen schools, instruction hovered around two or three hours per week, and three other schools taught German for between ten and twelve hours per week, albeit to a small portion of their student body.

The commissioners' report also revealed that rural schools with a single teacher often taught the language to one-third or one-half of all "German" pupils, while schools in Berlin and Waterloo taught only 10 per cent of "German" children.[67] This does not suggest, however, that families in these two towns were less interested in the language than rural families, or that children in urban areas were less capable of speaking German. Other factors external to people's identity and personal choices were also in play. For example, a lack of provincially certified and linguistically capable teachers played an important role, as did the decisions of the school board that also had English-speaking trustees. At the public school in the town of Waterloo, Inspector Thomas Hilliard informed the commissioners that only fifty of the 371 students took German. Nevertheless, he also added that students had to be in the junior fourth class before they could even begin studying the language.[68] Therefore, if approximately one-quarter of the students at this school were in or above the junior fourth class, the fifty students studying the language were

54 per cent of eligible children. When given the choice, more than half of the "German" children of a certain age group studied the language.

At the same time, and to again highlight the overall English environment of this schooling, Inspector Hilliard also noted that students who studied the language in the town of Waterloo did so for just two hours per week. He was also quick to note that "English is the vehicle of instruction throughout," and that those who did study "take the full course in English."[69] Based on the subject matter found in the textbooks used, along with the few hours of instruction that the educational system offered, it is apparent that most children were not being educated to acquire a balanced proficiency in German and English.

The information in the commissioners' report reveals two important facts that have received little historiographic attention. First, German was taught in many places beyond the town of Berlin (it became a city in 1912), both elsewhere in Waterloo County and more widely in Ontario. Second, despite the bureaucratic discussion of German schools in many sources, the linguistic reality on the ground reveals that there was very little that was German at these Ontario schools.

In their findings, commissioners Reynard, McLeod, and Tilley used the term "nationality" to describe the ethnic origins of children born in Ontario. This usage, combined with applying the label "German schools" to institutions where English was the language of instruction and where there was not necessarily a German-speaking teacher, indicates a racialized understanding of ethnicity, or a permanence of ethnicity defined by lineage or biology. The category of analysis for these commissioners was the genetics of the inhabitants of the area, and this did not allow for any variation in the commissioners' view of the culture children practised or the language they supposedly preferred to speak. Contemporary ideas that interwove race and ethnicity led many to believe in the intractability of ethnicity despite the obvious linguistic markers to the contrary.

Catholic elementary schools followed a slightly different path. In his 1882 report on Roman Catholic separate schools in western Ontario, J.F. White reported that "in Waterloo County there are many sections where German is the language of both the teachers and pupils. Generally, in those schools, one half of the day is devoted to teaching in the mother tongue and the other part to English studies."[70] In 1887, Inspector

Cornelius Donovan reported that at the "German" Roman Catholic separate schools, the teachers, "while instructing in reading, spelling, Christian doctrine, and sometimes other subjects in the mother tongue of their pupils, faithfully follow the departmental programme of English studies. In spite of the additional labor involved, these schools, taken all around, are as successful as most, and more successful than some of their confreres where no language but English is used."[71] By 1888, Inspector White wrote that in the Roman Catholic separate schools in western Ontario, German was taught in addition to English at nineteen different schools, before shifting his description to the strong English abilities of the pupils who arrived at school knowing "only their mother tongue."[72]

Writing in 1916 amid the tensions of the First World War and Regulation 17, Theobald Spetz, a prominent priest in Waterloo County, spoke about the bilingualism of Catholic schools in Ontario. He praised the government for allowing German because of the initial scarcity of English-speaking teachers. He added, "The government allowed time and common sense to prevail. As a result German gradually gave way to English, so that there are now scarcely any schools where it is taught, though it is a pity that such is the case."[73] He also stated that at the Berlin separate school, English had been the main language from the beginning "though German was also taught efficiently alongside."[74]

Despite the official label of "German schools" applied to dozens of public and separate schools in Ontario, the language occupied a minor place in a highly English-language curriculum. The persistence of the label was, in part, tied to the ongoing presence of French schools. The same legislation governed both, and the existence of the latter in some ways depended on the former. This relationship was largely pushed aside after 1912 when politicians and anglophone nationalists shifted their tactic from pushing for English at French (and German) schools, seeking instead to remove French as a language of instruction.

Implementation at the Local Level

In several studies of German speakers in Ontario, the teaching of German in the public schools of Berlin, Ontario and its cessation in 1915 has been taken as representative of the rise and fall of the German language in

Ontario.[75] Nonetheless, the focus on Berlin conflates the decision of a single public school board with provincial language policy. It can be helpful to zoom in on this important region, but its relationship to the broader provincial context should not be forgotten. Indeed this historiographic focus reflects the broader trend of boxing ethnic and linguistic pluralism into specific spaces and imagining homogeneity elsewhere. It has also led to incorrect conclusions about English-Canadian nationalism and German-Canadian experience during the First World War, for a lot changed before 1914 and things persisted differently outside the public school board of Berlin.

From 1900 to 1915, local leaders created and ran the German School Association (*Deutscher Schulverein*), and it has since attracted significant scholarly attention.[76] The *Schulverein* served as a lobby group to the public school board in one town, and it successfully encouraged parents to enrol their children in German classes taught at Berlin's public schools. The creation of the association accompanied a broader restructuring of the curriculum and the educational state in Ontario where German became a subject. The very efforts of the leaders of the *Schulverein* demonstrate one of the ways that concerned parents, educators, and local school promoters acquiesced to the changing space afforded to German in state-controlled elementary schools.

Several prominent men in Berlin were involved in the association's leadership. In 1915, members included the town's mayor, Dr J.E. Hett, along with former mayors J.L. Breithaupt and W.H. Schmalz.[77] Emil Hoffmann, one of the most central figures in the leadership of the German Lutheran Canada Synod, was one of the honorary German inspectors. Eleven members were clergymen and six of the eleven, all Protestants, were active members and served as honorary German inspectors.[78] No Mennonite pastors were involved with the *Schulverein*. Moreover, only a single Catholic priest was a member, and he was not involved in the leadership or inspection. It is telling that while there were many German-speaking Catholic priests in Berlin, just one became a member of the *Schulverein* while leaders of most German-language Protestant congregations in the town were members and many took leadership roles.

The minutes of the Berlin Catholic School Board reveal that the *Schulverein* was not involved with the local Catholic separate school, although this institution taught one-quarter of Berlin's pupils and had a much higher proportion of ethnically German children. The absence of Catholic priests in the German School Association is also understandable. German-speaking priests, parents, and school promoters managed to attain a majority on many Catholic school boards. In 1897, four of the eight public school trustees in Berlin were ethnically German whereas all five Catholic school trustees were ethnically German, and all five were members of the Resurrectionist congregation that ran St Jerome's College.[79] In 1904, six of seven members of the Berlin Catholic School Board had a German last name.[80] In 1912, all of these men had a German last name, and six of seven trustees were laymen.[81] Equipped with their own school board and St Jerome's College that offered secondary and post-secondary education, German-speaking Catholics had little need to lobby the public school board to increase the space allotted to German.

Beyond Berlin's public schools, there existed other relationships between language, school boards, and state regulation. The effects of the German School Association's lobby were not far-reaching. In nearby regions that were described as "German" by the Education Department, the pre-1900 subordinate position of German continued. In 1910, just a few kilometres from the German School Association in the Waterloo County rural schools, all children studied the separate subjects of English literature and English composition, and all children in certain grades learned English grammar while fewer than 3 per cent took German.[82] In nearby Hanover, Grey County, all children studied English literature and composition, but just over 7 per cent of pupils took German.[83]

The most notable aspect of the *Schulverein*'s activities is the impact that it had on enrolment. As table 1.1 shows, enrolment grew steadily in the decade before the war, but German classes stopped in 1915.[84] W. Böfe, a leader of the school association, commented on the early growth, writing in the *Berliner Journal* that "people have begun to recognize that it is good to learn German."[85]

There was a strong interest in German as a subject in the adjacent town of Waterloo, but, as table 1.2 shows, that had existed since the 1880s. In 1916, ministerial reports showed that 100 per cent of all pupils in Waterloo's public school were studying the language, and this included children from both German- and English-speaking families. I have not

Table 1.1 Pupils in Berlin
public schools studying
German as a subject

Year	Pupils
1903	150
1904	528
1909	1055
1913	1355
1915	1619

Sources: Report of the Minister of Education,
Province of Ontario, for the Year 1909 (Toronto:
L.K. Cameron, 1910), 10-13; Report of the
Minister of Education, Province of Ontario, for the
Year 1913 (Toronto: L.K. Cameron, 1914), 12-13;
Report of the Minister of Education, Province of
Ontario, for the Year 1915 (Toronto: A.T. Wilgress,
1916), 99; No author, "Erfreuliche Fortschritte,"
Berliner Journal, 4 January 1905, 6.

Table 1.2 Pupils in Waterloo
public schools studying
German as a subject

Year	Pupils
1889	447
1909	520
1913	571
1916	632

Sources: Regulations and Correspondence
Relating to French and German Schools, 114;
Report of the Minister of Education, Province
of Ontario, For the Year 1909 (Toronto: L.K.
Cameron, 1910), 18-21; Report of the Minister of
Education, Province of Ontario, for the Year 1913
(Toronto: L.K. Cameron, 1914), 21; Report of the
Minster of Education, Province of Ontario, for the
Year 1916 (Toronto: AT Wilgress, 1917), 157.

found any evidence that the German School Association influenced the local school board and the strong presence of German instruction, but the continued enrolment would suggest that the *Schulverein* played a role in maintaining the number of children who learned German.

Viewed in its Ontario-wide context, the *Schulverein* was limited in scope. The enrolment boom in Berlin's public schools found no resonance at the Catholic elementary school in the same town, in rural schools of Waterloo County, or elsewhere in the province. Moreover, while local knowledge and expertise could have improved the nature of the German lessons, this renaissance took place strictly within the confines of provincial regulation and used books intended for anglophones. Finally, by considering the textbooks used between 1890 and 1915 and the number of hours of German lessons, little changed in the German classes in Berlin after the foundation of the *Schulverein* in 1900 other than enrolment.

From 1900 to 1902, German instruction in Berlin's public schools took place outside regular school hours.[86] Louis Breithaupt, one of the leaders of the *Schulverein* and a prominent figure in the Berlin business community, inquired of the Education Department about the Berlin school board's autonomy to change this, and the deputy minister informed Breithaupt that where French or German prevails, the "trustees have full power to require instruction to be given in either of these languages to pupils, so far as may be directed by their parents or guardians."[87] The department also told Breithaupt that the school board could determine the number of hours and that "the question of promotion [exams] is a matter also that rests with the local authorities, and a knowledge of German may be taken into consideration in determining what pupils may pass to a higher class."[88] What could be perceived as total freedom, however, masks provincial requirements to use authorized textbooks designed for anglophone students and to teach German only in addition to English – an important deviation from the 1871 School Act that allowed German to be a language of instruction in settlements "where German prevails."

Inspector Thomas Pearce provided a good overview of the *Schulverein*'s activities in 1904, writing:

> Since the beginning of the present term, the arrangements for giving instruction in the German language are on a better and more satisfactory basis than they have hitherto been. There is now one room at each of the four schools [public schools in Berlin] used exclusively for the German classes. These classes are drafts from the other departments of the school. The lesson given to the fourth class pupils lasts 45 minutes, that to all other classes 30 minutes. Some classes have four, some three and others two lessons in the week. The daily time schedule is arranged in such a way as to reduce the disturbance to the rest of the school to a minimum. A very important detail of the scheme is the decision to give German a place and a value at the annual promotion examinations. It is to take the place of Art (new curriculum) and to be given the same

value as penmanship. Two teachers are employed to teach German, one takes the classes at the Central and Margaret Ave. schools, the other the classes at Agnes St. and Courtland Ave. schools. The time of the former is nearly fully occupied, the time of the latter is about two-thirds occupied ... The instruction given comprises Reading, Spelling, Writing, Conversation, Translation and Composition.[89]

That German instruction was afforded such limited hours, and that the language was on equal footing with art and penmanship rather than with English spelling or grammar, reveals how the status of German had shifted over the two preceding decades. Moreover, in 1889, the commissioners reported that the 10 per cent of children taking German in the town of Berlin devoted 12 hours per week to it, whereas under the auspices of the German School Association after the turn of the twentieth century, a large majority of children studied the language between 2.5 and 4 hours per week. Pearce also noted that thirty-five teachers worked at the public schools of Berlin, and that two of these instructors taught German. In other words, 94 per cent of teachers in the town of Berlin taught subjects in English while only 6 per cent taught in German.[90] From the 1870s into the late 1890s, the Berlin high school dedicated much more attention to the study of German.[91] That the German School Association did not play any role in secondary education at a moment when secondary education was becoming increasingly important in Ontario suggests that the *Schulverein* had to take advantage of the vestiges of nineteenth-century legislation that permitted German in elementary schools while remaining silent about the language's place in secondary schools.

In Berlin, the rising enrolment in the pre-existing German classes took place firmly under the watch of provincial authority. Every year, Inspector Thomas Pearce reported on the number of children enrolled and other details on the growing German-language instruction, which suggests that he was monitoring the program fairly well. That he did not complain about the use of unauthorized textbooks or any other matter that would violate provincially defined regulations, a matter the province took increasingly seriously, suggests that the activities of the German School Association promoted German within the confines of a provincially prescribed program.

Although inspectors' reports have been a rich source for the study of French schooling in Ontario, the reports for the Waterloo region are not. The evaluations were of the teacher and not the school or the instruction of German. Had the teacher only been semi-proficient in English, the inspector would have complained about the language of the school and informed the trustees about this "problem." In any given year, the inspector surveyed a sampling of teachers. He rated the categories of "teaching power," "governing power," and "manner," and provided information on years of experience. He gave some brief remarks about the teacher. Thomas Pearce's reports about public schools in Berlin and parts of Waterloo County show that a disproportionately high number of teachers had English names compared to the region's ethnic make-up. In addition, Pearce described the work of the teachers with German names in a positive light.[92]

The case of Catholic separate schools reveals other aspects of a complex history. Although Catholic separate schools represented just one-tenth of all schools in the province, in specific areas and for German-speaking minorities they should not be overlooked, because many were important sites of German-language instruction. At the Bruce County rural Catholic separate schools in 1910, 49 per cent of the pupils learned German.[93] In the Waterloo County rural Catholic separate schools, 85 per cent of children studied German in addition to the separate subjects of English literature and composition.[94] Similarly, 68 per cent of the 1,794 children at the Berlin public schools studied German under the leadership of the *Schulverein*, but 100 per cent of the 603 children at the Berlin Catholic separate school in 1910 did so without the *Schulverein*.[95] At the same time, and to complicate matters further, in 1910 none of the 174 children at the Catholic separate school in the town of Waterloo studied German,[96] whereas 100 per cent of the 526 children at the public school in the town of Waterloo did so.[97] That is to say, the Catholic separate schools in rural Waterloo County taught much more German than the public equivalents, but the Catholic separate school in the town of Waterloo taught much less than the public equivalent.

German persisted relatively well in Catholic separate schools until the end of the war across the province. At the Catholic separate schools of Bruce County, 214 of the 671 enrolled pupils studied German in 1918,[98] and 182 of the 472 pupils at the rural Catholic separate schools of Waterloo County studied the language in that year.[99] Of the 918 pupils attending the Catholic separate school in the city of Kitchener (formerly Berlin) in 1918, 736 studied German, which is a noticeable increase from the 603 that studied the language at that school in 1910.[100] Many rural schools, despite the religion of their trustees and children, remained in the public system because of better funding.[101] The lack of enrolment in German classes in the 1890s in some places, and then an increase in some localities after 1900, did not depend solely on the linguistic abilities of children and the identities of parents. Local decisions to hire teachers and to accept the provincially authorized textbooks also played a decisive role.

At the close of the war, the province removed German as an elective subject from elementary schools, and this element of state authority is far more significant than the potpourri of decisions made by individual school boards that removed or kept the language during the war. Starting in 1919, German was not taught in any public school in Ontario.[102] Similarly, in that year almost no German was taught in the Catholic separate schools of the province.[103] While that is a similar outcome and shows the effect of the war, it decentres the overwhelming interest in the history of Berlin, Ontario and the decision of its public school board in 1915. The changes in 1918 also coincide with the ramping up of anti-German language policies at the federal level and the September 1918 "Order Respecting Enemy Publications" that banned newspapers in several languages for two years, which I will discuss in chapter 2.

Regulation 17, German, and the Natural Rights of Francophones

Bilingual education became the centre of a major political crisis in Ontario starting in 1912. The Education Department attempted to limit the use of French as a language of communication to the first form (i.e., the first two years of primary education), and required that all public and separate schools teach only in English after that; it also limited the teaching of French to one hour per day.[104] In the face of public protest, the next year the province did allow the continued use of French as a language of communication beyond the first form for those unable to understand English.[105] Regulation 17 was a clear act of anglophone nationalism and a prime example of the linguistic ideology that advanced a monolingual paradigm in Ontario. As Jack Cecillon notes, this policy was part of a broader trend dating back to the 1870s in New Brunswick and the 1880s in Manitoba that sought to assert the country's British character.[106] The 1912 policy took aim, in particular, at the growing populations of French speakers in eastern Ontario, in the border region of the province around Ottawa and eastward in Prescott and Russell Counties, and in northern Ontario in the area west of Lake Nipissing and east of Lake Superior.

The vestiges of nineteenth-century language policies remained, and German became a topic of debate for anglophones and francophones alike. For James Whitney's Conservative government and his minister of education, Robert Pyne, German speakers were an enviable model that francophones should have emulated. In their eyes, German speakers slowly welcomed the presence of English in their schools, and by 1910 German was not used as a language of instruction anywhere in the province. Conversely, French-speaking teachers, hired by French-speaking trustees, continued to struggle with English, and much of a child's daily experience at a bilingual school involved the extensive use of French and the limited and accented use of English. French speakers were aware of the official status that German enjoyed in provincial regulations regarding language of instruction as well, but they insisted that they had natural rights as one of Canada's two founding peoples. Francophones brought up Germans as a way to explain the special rights that others did not have.

In 1914, Canadian senator Napoléon-Antoine Belcourt represented the board of trustees of the Roman Catholic separate schools of Ottawa before the Supreme Court of Ontario. He argued that the province recognized parents' "right to demand that the French (or German) language be the language of instruction and communication in the schools attended by their children."[107] The new government legislation, in his view, "violates natural law and natural justice because it seeks to take away the right to have one's money applied to one's own purposes, so long as such is not immoral ... That is a right, similar to other rights of property, the taking away of which constitutes a violation of natural law."[108] He argued that "the right to speak one's mother tongue is a natural right which every human being has ... The enactment of Regulation 17 constitutes the only attempt ever made in the British Empire to deprive British subjects of the use of their mother tongue."[109] In making his argument, Belcourt appeared entirely oblivious to the language politics and school policies in Ontario and elsewhere in Canada toward Indigenous peoples; he was participating in the assimilationist settler colonialism of Canada while lamenting his own mistreatment by the British Empire. In contending that the French and the English were the founding peoples of Canada, he also erased the presence of Indigenous peoples on the land claimed by the Canadian state.

Other French speakers in Ontario, incensed by their mistreatment by the anglophone majority, made similar statements that seemed to overlook the language politics directed toward Indigenous peoples in Canada. C. de la Légalité claimed, "We are being submitted to the same treatment in this matter as are the Maoris of New Zealand, the native population corresponding to our Indians, with the exception of the miserable pittance which we have to beg for each year."[110] De la Légalité expressed concern about the mistreatment of the Maori while not recognizing the parallels in the treatment of Indigenous populations in Canada and New Zealand. Jules Tremblay argued that because the first explorer of Ontario was Étienne Brûlé in 1611, francophones have certain rights alongside anglophones but in distinction to German speakers. He argued, "In fact, the use of our ancestral language and its teaching by our teachers is supported by the right of first occupation of land, by the law of nations (*Jus gentium* or *le droit des gens*), by the custom, by the constitutional right and even by the statutes of the Province."[111] He concluded, "French Canadians are at home in Ontario, like everywhere in Canada, because they are the first to arrive, because the law of nations protects their mother tongue and their traditions."[112] Tremblay advanced a common French-Canadian idea of the time which proposed an overlapping geography for both French and English Canada, one that the language policies of Regulation 17 disputed.

Napoléon-Antoine Belcourt took aim at the special rights of francophones in relation to Germans. In his view, "the natural right of the French-speaking subjects of His Majesty in Canada in the matter of language is entirely different from the right of Germans and all others."[113] Despite his previous assertion about the rights of all to speak their mother tongue, he argued that "the Germans and other people who have emigrated, or will later on come to Canada to reside, they have no such right. On the contrary, it is manifest that by coming voluntarily to settle and live in Canada they abandoned, renounced and waived their natural right to speak their native language."[114]

In a call to arms against the recent policy changes, the Association canadienne-française d'éducation d'Ontario (ACFÉO) took a similar tack and distinguished their rights from those of German speakers. Its leaders argued that "we do not claim it [the right to teach our mother tongue] as a privilege, as would be the case with the German-Canadians, but emphatically hold that we have a right to this tuition, even if Ontario were, as is wrongly claimed by some, an exclusively English province."[115] The association's leaders added: "To assimilate the status of [the] French and German languages in Ontario is not justified by the Constitution. To deprive the French population of Ontario of French tuition is an illegal and unjustifiable infringement upon natural and official rights of the French minority."[116] Both Belcourt and the ACFÉO spoke of natural rights, but neither believed that that legal concept was universally applicable. To save French in Ontario schools, francophones distinguished themselves from German speakers. The triad of English, French, and German as possible languages of instruction had already disappeared, and it was in francophones' interest to stake out a new position in the face of anglophone nationalism.

Conclusion

French was not the only language on the minds of anglophone elites in the late nineteenth and early twentieth centuries. The presence of other linguistic groups in Ontario and elsewhere in Canada was a part of the linguistic space shaping ideas, discourse, and politics about the nation and citizenship. Understanding the changing position of German in Ontario is an important aspect of the changing educational system. The assertion of English over German through a series of incremental policies was certainly less abrupt than the approach taken by the government of Manitoba towards predominantly French-language Catholic schools in the 1890s. Nevertheless, there appear to be many parallels between the two cases, and these linguistic and educational histories reveal much about the ideas of language and the meaning of citizenship held by many English Canadians in positions of power.

From the moment German was no longer used as a language of instruction, there were no German schools in Ontario. While legislatively possible until 1912, provincial requirements about English, authorized textbooks, individual school boards, and even German-speaking parents turned them into English schools with a certain bilingual focus by the 1890s. Starting in 1885, provincial regulations required English to be taught in all schools, and after 1890 German could only be taught in addition to the dominant language in the province. In the 1880s, schools in many localities in Ontario with similar concentrations of German speakers taught the language to varying degrees, and by the time of the 1889 commissioners' report, German occupied a position secondary to English in all "German schools." This was partially the result of an emerging linguistic ideology that blended the meanings of language and nation and that could, therefore, not permit local variation.

Although German speakers were not passive subjects, state bureaucrats and anglophone politicians were active promoters of the English language. Many German speakers did not push back to anywhere near the same extent as many francophones in the same period in Ontario. By the 1890s, state regulation along with local trustees' decisions and parents' desires ensured that English was the language of instruction at all German schools in Ontario. Nevertheless, as this transition took place, German remained a subject in the curriculum of many schools in the province, and German remained present in elementary and high schools largely because of its historical presence in the educational system.

By focusing on specific domains within the multi-layered state apparatus, the case of the German language in Ontario has demonstrated how both local control and central authority coexisted and often ruled over separate spheres. Through a series of cultural policies, the Education Department ensured that schooling in Ontario undermined German more than it promoted a balanced bilingualism among the children of German speakers. Finally, there was little that was German about the educational experience for the majority of "German" children in Ontario from the 1890s onwards. Rather, the experience was largely an

English one. The next chapter turns its attention to the First World War, highlighting in particular external pressures and state policies during wartime society. It continues the study of anglophone perceptions of German speakers and state efforts to undo the linguistic pluralism of nineteenth-century German immigration to Ontario.

2. BEING GERMAN DURING THE FIRST WORLD WAR

How did German speakers in Ontario experience the First World War? The answer to this question has often been reduced to the following: during the war, things German on the home front took on an enemy status and there was a great cultural decline. Yet that answer finds many contradictions. At one level, it presupposes the rigidity of ethnic categories, and stating it today replicates assumptions about ethnic difference that were created a century before. During the war, many Canadians of British heritage equated German ethnicity and the German language with German nationality and foreign loyalties. But to take that as the answer to the question I pose above is to ignore concrete examples of how things German continued through the war and flourished after it, or how other things German declined before the war began. For example, as part III will show, German-language religious practice continued throughout the war and into the 1920s. And as chapter 1 showed, it was not the war that removed German from Ontario's public schools, but rather anglophone nationalism and a linguistic ideology that developed between 1890 and 1912.

This chapter focuses in particular on the boundaries drawn by outsiders and government policies. It argues that over the course of the First World War, the federal government merged various meanings of being German and increasingly associated them with the enemy. This started with non-naturalized immigrants, expanded to most German-speaking immigrants, and by the close of the war included all German speakers, including those born in North America. In the wartime context and in the eyes of outsiders, the boundaries of ethnicity became sharper. Ethnicity, citizenship, and political loyalty became more entangled categories, and the Germanness of some – in the eyes of the Canadian state – was not fully compatible with Canadian belonging. This is only one side of the story, and parts II and III of this book show that German speakers in Ontario experienced the First World War in a variety of ways.

The war did lead to a number of discriminatory policies and more far-reaching popular interpretations of government policies. In particular, a series of federal policies took aim at "Germans," which lumped degrees of connection with Germany or Austria-Hungary into a single Other. While these policies affected only a portion of people of German heritage in Ontario who are at the core of this study, the anti-German context did have a ripple effect on others who did associate with (or were associated with) some sort of German community. However, in many other ways, the war did not stop people from "being German." For bilingual people born in Canada, the war may have led to a reduction in public expressions of German ethnicity while not fundamentally altering the books they read, the language they spoke with other members of their families, or their feelings about German culture. And while it is important not to overlook the pressure to lessen public expressions of German ethnicity, such pressure was felt differently by children with one or two German-speaking parents, Canadian-born adults educated in a bilingual context, and people who immigrated to Canada after reaching adulthood in central Europe.

The four years of the war did not stamp out all institutions, personal identities, and linguistic abilities, but they did change the ways that German ethnicity was expressed and transferred to younger people in the 1920s and 1930s. As Royden Loewen writes, the war demanded new levels of political and cultural integration into Canadian society.[1] Wartime did lead to a decrease in German-language institutions across the province. The German School Association of Berlin, which encouraged parents to enrol children in language classes, ceased activities in 1915. Some clubs and singing societies closed and many lost members. The last remaining German-language newspaper in the province lost some readers during the war and was closed by the federal government in late September 1918; the war years must have influenced the paper's publishers in their decision not to restart publication in the 1920s.

This focus on the treatment of German immigrants and German-Canadians during the First World War has broader implications for understanding how the rights of citizenship interacted with Canadian cultural pluralism at the turn of the twentieth century. At the start of the war, internment camps were created to imprison German and Austro-Hungarian citizens (immigrants not naturalized as British subjects domiciled in Canada) who were suspected of subversive behaviour or intention. A number of other orders-in-council were passed in the first year of the war that similarly took aim at "enemy aliens." These other orders were also significant in the state attack on approximately 85,000 non-naturalized immigrants. In 1917, the Wartime Elections Act stripped the right to vote from all immigrants to Canada from enemy nations (e.g., Germany and Austria-Hungary) and German speakers from Russia who had naturalized as British subjects after 1902. That law simultaneously gave the vote to women who were relatives of Canadian soldiers serving overseas. This legislation affected far more German speakers in Canada, even more so because it included men who had arrived years before 1902 but who naturalized after this date. Finally, just seven weeks before the armistice, a federal order-in-council banned publications in "enemy languages." The "Order Respecting Enemy Publications" affected to some extent every person of German heritage in the country, including Canadian born. Although not everybody of German heritage read the news in German and even fewer relied solely on this language, the order labelled German an enemy language. In so doing, it expanded the state definition of the wartime threat from non-naturalized immigrants to a language spoken by hundreds of thousands of Canadians.

Most policies during the First World War targeted immigrants rather than Canadian-born people, and this difference is worth stressing. According to the 1911 census, there were 161,007 people in Canada who had been born in Germany or the Austro-Hungarian Empire (39,577 German and 121,430 Austro-Hungarian subjects).[2] Austro-Hungarian emigration was more recent.[3] Of these 161,007 people, 15,010 Germans and 15,555 Austro-Hungarians lived in Ontario (38 per cent and 13 per cent of the total of each group).[4] At the same time, there were 393,320 people, according to the definition of the Canadian census, of German origin (half in Ontario) and 129,103 of Austro-Hungarian origin. That is to say, 90 per cent of "Germans" in Canada were born in Canada, while 94 per cent of people of Austro-Hungarian heritage were born in the Austro-Hungarian Empire. As a result, the policies that focused on immigrants affected Austro-Hungarians more than Germans while the final policy that focused on language did the reverse, all the more so because only a portion of Austro-Hungarians were German speakers.

Internment and Fears of Subversive Immigrants

At the outset of the First World War, concerns emerged in Canada about the loyalty of some immigrants and the potential threat posed by "aliens of enemy nationality." Three days after Britain's declaration of war against Germany, an order-in-council (PC 2085) called for the arrest of "all German officers or reservists attempting to leave Canada at any port on the Atlantic or Pacific."[5] That policy was revised slightly a week later with a new order-in-council (PC 2150) that gave the police the power to arrest suspected enemy aliens, and the government published the *Proclamation Respecting Immigrants of German or Austro-Hungarian Nationality*. It gave the state the power to arrest and detain officers, soldiers, or reservists attempting to leave Canada and anybody attempting to engage in espionage or share information with the enemy. Another order-in-council approved on 28 October 1914 formally created the system of internment camps under the authority of the minister of justice.[6] The new order added that "no alien of enemy nationality shall be permitted to leave Canada without an exeat from a registrar."[7]

At the same time, as a result of half a century of high rates of European immigration, the Canadian government recognized that "many persons of German and Austro-Hungarian nationality [were] quietly pursuing their usual vocations in various parts of Canada" and that it was "desirable that such persons should be allowed to continue in such avocations without interruption."[8] The government made enemy aliens register with authorities, and it obliged them to sign an undertaking pledging to observe the laws and abstain from taking up arms as a way to earn an "exemption from detention as a subject of Germany (Austria-Hungary)."[9] Those who did not sign the undertaking could also be detained as prisoners of war.[10] As Bohdan Kordan notes, the label "enemy alien" branded a huge group of people as foes, and both the undertaking and the proclamation "implied that such individuals were naturally inclined to do harm."[11]

German speakers in the public sphere in Ontario pushed back against this label, and they emphasized the Canadian government's second goal of allowing such immigrants to "continue in such avocations without interruption." In response to the first order-in-council, the *Berliner Journal* wrote:

> The dice have been cast, the two biggest empires of Europe have taken up arms against one another. We Germans, whether immigrants or Canadian-born, feel the gravity of this conflict doubly. The love of the old fatherland is innate to us and the reverence for our new homeland should not create a conflict in our feelings. Canada, the grand Dominion, a part of the enormous British Empire, invited us to build our home here. We must not forget the years of peace and prosperity that we have lived under the British flag. The Union Jack has flown above us and our children were born under it. Germany's victory or defeat changes nothing in terms of relations with our adoptive father and new homeland.[12]

A detailed analysis of the *Journal* shows a German-language paper that toed the British patriotic line throughout the war.[13]

All told, almost 8,300 German and Austro-Hungarian immigrants were interned as prisoners of war and some 85,000 others were required to register and report monthly to state authorities.[14] Internment placed immigrants in work camps in the Canadian hinterland. Their tasks included clearing and stumping land and raising barns for "experimental farms." Many internees in British Columbia built roads and cleared land for national parks.[15] The economic criteria of these projects undercut the stated security goals of internment.[16] At all camps, internees were forced to follow orders and disciplined when they did not, and they could be shot if they attempted to escape.[17] According to the government's official report, ten men were shot when trying to escape, six of whom were killed.[18] At least five died in work accidents and three by suicide. A total of 107 men died in custody; some deaths were surely the result of internment, such as the twenty-six deaths from tuberculosis.[19]

German-Canadians took a keen interest in the treatment of non-naturalized immigrants who were interned. The *Berliner Journal* published relevant orders-in-council in the English original and a German translation.[20] It also reported on the conditions of internment. In early December 1914, for example, it informed readers about internees in Toronto. It drew its information from the American consul, who served as a neutral observer. The paper reported that food and treatment were reasonable, and tobacco, games, and books could be sent to prisoners. However, it spoke somewhat critically about how the wartime context affected non-naturalized German nationals. It reported about a Dr Kohlmann who had been working as an engineer for the city's waterworks. He lost his job because of his status as a "reservist," and he was forced to leave the country.[21]

There was an important gendered component to internment.[22] All 8,579 enemy aliens to be interned were men, and the legal justification for internment required all internees to be soldiers or pseudo-soldiers so as to incarcerate them as prisoners of war. Yet in addition to the 8,579 internees, eighty-one women and 156 children were interned at two camps with special accommodations (in Spirit Lake, Quebec [see figure 2.1] and Vernon, BC), and another forty women and eighty-one children were left at home and given financial support for rent, food, and fuel.[23] None of these women and children were counted as internees, and according to the official government report, they were taken into custody or supported financially at home because they depended upon interned men as breadwinners of their families.[24] If espionage or sabotage was a real threat to the Canadian war effort, presumably the 60,042 German and Austro-Hungarian female immigrants or some naturalized German and Austro-Hungarian immigrants (men and women) could have been suspected.[25] However, the 1907 Hague Convention that outlined the rules of war made it difficult to intern women and children as prisoners of war. As a result, the Canadian government followed the legal rationale that permitted the internment of men and made other arrangements for women and children. The Hague Convention did allow for civilians to be interned and treated as prisoners of war, but only those who were somehow directly implicated in the hostilities.[26] The Canadian practice of forcing these civilians to engage in heavy, manual labour

2.1 Women and children at Spirit Lake Internment Camp, Abitibi, Quebec.

under armed guarded was, in the view of several international observers, a contravention of the convention.[27]

Internment in Canada followed a broader pattern in the British Empire.[28] However, the specifics of who was targeted and how interned enemy aliens were treated differed in different colonies and dominions. Just three days after the war between Britain and Germany began, the secretary of state for the colonies in London sent a message to governments across the empire, and this is what provoked the first Canadian order-in-council on 7 August 1914. The message asked local authorities – whether in Canada or Kenya – to "arrest and detain all German officers or Reservists as prisoners of war. Watch Austrian officers or reservists." The Canadian Committee of the Privy Council noted, however, that "having regard to the fact that many immigrants of German nationality are quietly pursuing their usual avocations in various parts of Canada, it is not considered either feasible or desirable to attempt to arrest and detain all German officers and Army reservists in the comprehensive manner set forth in the despatch [from London]."[29] Unlike most other parts of the empire, in Canada there was a much higher proportion of Austro-Hungarians than Germans. And unlike other dominions and colonies in the British Empire which similarly interned German nationals, Canada used these interned enemy aliens as a form of forced labour.[30] This was despite the concerns of British imperial officials, protestations of the German government, and observations of neutral American representatives who noted the "continuing use of compulsory internment labour."[31]

The imperial and Canadian concern that there were thousands of military personnel in Canada ready to return to enemy service (perhaps a decade after leaving central Europe) reveals more about wartime paranoia than the actual employment and retention practices of the German and Austro-Hungarian militaries. Historians should not accept at face value the claims in government reports that there were "officers, soldiers or reservists" eager to re-enlist in the militaries of the Central Powers. Very close to zero men in Canada were currently employed as German or Austro-Hungarian soldiers, while almost all German and Austro-Hungarian nationals in Canada had done some military service earlier in their lives. This would have included some naturalized British subjects who managed to keep their German citizenship.[32] If the definition of a reservist is somebody with military training who is ready to be called into active duty, being thousands of kilometres away from central Europe disqualified any German or Austro-Hungarian national in Canada from being a reservist, despite what Canadian officials asserted. In August 1914, it was also not a priority for the German and Austro-Hungarian militaries to enlist people who had left their countries years or decades before. These militaries had no real way of notifying former soldiers and officers of the call to arms (neither Canadian mail nor German-Canadian newspapers were possible forms of communication between the Central Powers and emigrants), and they had no means of forcing emigrants to abandon work, family, and lives to return to Europe to fight.

Austro-Hungarians were interned as prisoners of war in significantly higher numbers, but for a shorter period of time. Of the 8,589 men to be interned in twenty-four camps across Canada, 5,954 men were Austro-Hungarians (69 per cent) and only 2,009 were German nationals (along with ninety-nine Bulgarians and 205 Ottoman subjects).[33] It is worth noting that 10 per cent of these people (nationality undefined but mainly German) were not immigrants to Canada, but brought to the country as internees from Jamaica, Barbados, Bermuda, Saint Lucia, and Newfoundland.[34] Over the course of 1916 and 1917, as more men enlisted or were conscripted and labour shortages emerged in Canada, almost all of the Austro-Hungarian detainees were released after signing a parole pledging loyalty and obedience.

German nationals were not similarly released. In contrast to the early release of Austro-Hungarians, 2,009 German nationals were interned, and at least 1,644 remained in custody at the close of the war who were then deported to Germany.[35] A much higher portion of German nationals (82 per cent) were interned for the duration of the war and then deported, and that should not be erased from the Canadian memory of wartime repression. William Otter, the major-general in charge of internment operations, reported that some "6,000 of Austrian nationality were released from confinement," and he stated that "this system proved a great advantage to the organizations short of labour, and save with very few exceptions, all those given freedom complied with the terms of their undertaking."[36] That number of 6,000 was a slight exaggeration: of the 5,954 interned, at the end of the war there were still 302 Austro-Hungarians in custody who were repatriated in 1919 and early 1920.[37] Among the 1,946 Germans and Austro-Hungarians who were deported were almost all of the 817 men brought to Canadian camps from the British Caribbean and Newfoundland.[38]

In Canadian historiography, Ukrainian internment dominates as a topic, but almost to a point of overlooking Germans and any other ethnic group born in the Austro-Hungarian Empire. Bohdan Kordan writes the vast majority of those interned were "peasants hailing from Ukrainian ethnographic territories within the ramshackle Austro-Hungarian Empire."[39] In a book about civilian internment writ large, Rhonda Hinther and Jim Mochoruk write that "during the Great War (1914–1918), over 5,900 eastern Europeans, primarily from the Austro-Hungarian Empire, were interned ... Approximately 80,000 more were forced to register with, and report on a regular basis to, local authorities."[40] In so doing, Hinther and Mochoruk efface German nationals' internment altogether (only referring to the 5,900 eastern European internees) while using a statistic on registration that included both Germans and Austro-Hungarians

2.2 Two male prisoners at Spirit Lake Internment Camp, Abitibi, Quebec.

(80,000). Gregory Kealey summed up the data as follows: "2009 Germans, 5955 'Austrians' (Ukrainians), 205 Turks, 99 Bulgarians."[41] Jeff Keshen, in the same issue of the *Canadian Historical Review*, wrote instead that "public hysteria as well as employment surplus prompted authorities to intern thousands of Galicians," while making no reference to Germans.[42] John Herd Thompson writes, "Legally, the only 'enemy aliens' were those who had not yet naturalized: about 20,000 Germans and some 60,000 Ukrainians."[43] Thompson labels 100 per cent of non-naturalized, male, Austro-Hungarian immigrants Ukrainians. These all seem like overstatements, and certainly fail to capture the ethno-linguistic diversity of Austro-Hungarian immigrants to Canada.

Ukrainian was a complex ethno-national category in 1914. As Kate Brown notes, before projects to homogenize multiethnic populations in borderland spaces, denominational difference (Catholic, Orthodox, or Uniate) often split peasants who spoke the same dialect and lived in the same area into the national categories of Polish and Ukrainian.[44] Ukrainian became a more homogeneous category in Europe as the result of interwar Soviet nationality policies, and post-1945 community mobilization in Canada has played a role in shaping the memory of how ethnically diverse groups hailing from Ruthenia, Bukovina, and Galicia were treated during the First World War.

Canadian authorities did not classify internees by ethnicity or language, so it is difficult to determine how many Ukrainians were interned, and it is curious that other scholars write with such confidence. All records that do exist point to an ethnically diverse group of people interned based on citizenship or imperial subjecthood. For example, in his final report, William Otter wrote in one instance: "Austro-Hungarians, covering Croats, Ruthenians, Slovaks, and Chzecks [sic]."[45] Aware of Austro-Hungarian ethnic diversity, he listed Ruthenians, some of whom would have identified as Ukrainians, alongside other groups that would not have. German-speaking Austrians, Croats, Poles, Hungarians, and Czechs probably did make up a noteworthy portion of the Austro-Hungarian internees, even if Ukrainian speakers were the single largest group.

In prewar Canada, the government's use of geographic and not ethno-linguistic categories regarding Austria-Hungary has added to the ambiguity about ethnic groups interned. The 1911 Canadian census, for example, divided the 121,430 Austro-Hungarian-born immigrants in Canada into the following categories: Austrians (56 per cent), Galicians (26 per cent), Hungarians (9 per cent), Bukovinans (8 per cent), and Bohemians (1.4 per cent).[46] The label of Austrian could have been used by Canadian bureaucrats either to refer to Austrian provinces in the empire, which would include German, Italian, and Slovenian speakers, or to refer to people from anywhere in the Austro-Hungarian Empire, which would include many more linguistic groups. The category "Hungarian" was likely political-spatial and would have included Croats, an ethno-linguistic group that appears in other Canadian sources regarding internment. Ukrainians would have come from both Galicia and Bukovina, but so too did Poles and Jews.

Internment was not the only way that popular and government fears of subversive immigrants were put into policy. In September 1914, order-in-council PC 2283 prohibited any enemy alien from using or possessing "fire-arms, ammunition, dynamite, gunpowder or other dangerous explosive[s]." The penalty was a $500 fine or up to three months in prison. All enemy aliens were required to deliver any such items to a justice of the peace within ten days of the order's announcement. The order authorized the police to search an enemy alien's premises without warrant. It also placed the onus on the accused to prove that he was not an enemy alien (i.e., demonstrate his status as a naturalized British subject in Canada).[47] This reverse onus with respect to guilt could also be found in the War Measures Act (1914).[48] While the order put security concerns ahead of the goal announced three weeks earlier of allowing enemy aliens to carry on their "avocations without interruption," it also played a role in lumping all German and Austro-Hungarian immigrants into a single category that disregarded the legal value of naturalization. It placed the onus on naturalized British subjects to prove their status. Since the order included ethnicity and linguistic abilities as the point of departure (until a suspected immigrant could prove otherwise), it also gave authorities the ability to search and confiscate items from Russian immigrants who could be confused with Austro-Hungarian or German nationals such as German speakers, Ukrainians, Poles, Ruthenians, Bukovinans, Galicians, and others.

An important clause in the order-in-council issued on 28 October 1914 (PC 2721) that formalized internment authorized the government to incarcerate those without sufficient means to support themselves.[49] That order spoke to the difficult employment situation in Canada in the first year of the war, exacerbated by the fact that these same German and Austro-Hungarian nationals could not leave for the United States to seek work because of the exit restrictions placed on enemy aliens.[50] It was this clause in particular that turned a tool aimed at enemy agents (particularly German nationals) into a mechanism that interned ethnic minorities such as Ukrainians, Poles, Croats, and Czechs. This clause about destitution is one reason why Austro-Hungarians rather than Germans were interned in high numbers. W.H. Bradley, an American diplomat in Montreal who served as the diplomatic liaison for Austro-Hungarian interests once the war started, reported in late 1914 that 4,000 Habsburg subjects in the city, mainly Ukrainians, Poles, and Croats, had sought assistance. He noted that 2,000 of them were without work and hundreds relied on a community relief kitchen for daily sustenance.[51] The *Berliner Journal* reported on similar difficulties facing German nationals in Toronto. It noted that a committee made up of the American consul and two German-Canadians "have the difficult task of looking for work opportunities for those out of work. In some cases, they manage to find at least temporary jobs. But the difficulties are great in Toronto where the municipal office has over 9,000 unemployed who registered."[52]

In the first year of the war, at least a quarter of all internees found themselves in camps as the result of requests made by municipal authorities seeking to lessen the number of destitute people drawing on local support.[53] William Otter was aware of this practice, writing in his 1921 report that "it is also suspected that the tendency of municipalities to 'unload' their indigent was the cause of the confinement of not a few."[54] The prevalence of mental health issues amongst the internees was, according to Otter, further evidence of how municipalities sought to offload burdens on their social welfare system onto the federal government. For a time, the 116 interned men who were labelled "insane" were placed in asylums at the government's expense, and in all but three cases they were subsequently deported to their countries of origin.[55]

The question of labour continued to influence the policies of internment. In June 1915, order-in-council PC 1501 undermined the policy of allowing enemy aliens to continue working without interruption, as laid out at the start of the war and as part of the original policy of internment. The government claimed that when "aliens of enemy nationality are in common employment with others" there was a "serious danger of rioting, destruction of valuable works and property and breaches of the peace." As a result, the order authorized local authorities "to direct the apprehension and internment of aliens of enemy nationality who may be found employed or seeking employment or competing for employment in any community." In these instances, these interned aliens of enemy nationality would be "kept and maintained in all respects as prisoners of war" but subject to release by the minister of justice.[56] Through these orders, competing for work turned recent immigrants into candidates for prisoners of war.

As Kordan notes, this order came in part as the result of local pressure. In August 1914, a group of waiters in Montreal "complained to the major local hoteliers that over 400 individuals of German and Austro-Hungarian origin held remunerative jobs which could easily be occupied by men currently unemployed and 'belonging to the Allies.'"[57] In the same month, the city of Calgary "gave instructions that single men of Austro-Hungarian and German birth working in the city's street-cleaning department were to be replaced by Britishers, since [in the words of commissioner A.J. Samis] 'it would be monstrous to employ members of a nation at war with the British Empire while men of the British race were unable to find employment.'"[58] In May 1915, a group of British waiters in Toronto complained to authorities that "the management of the King Edward Hotel continued to retain Germans in their employ 'in spite of our Canadian boys being bayoneted when lying wounded.'"[59] According to John Herd Thompson, "in almost every Canadian city at least once during the war, a frenzied mob smashed and looted the property of real or imagined German-Canadians after rumours that an 'alien' had been employed in preference to a veteran."[60] The lack of employment opportunities in general led to a particularly harsh treatment of German and Austro-Hungarian immigrants. While internment only targeted non-naturalized immigrants, these popular protests and some hiring practices were surely not as nuanced.

Denying German and Austro-Hungarian nationals employment opportunities added incentives for them to try to leave for the United States. In some cases, this led to arrest and internment.[61] According to research done by Peter Melnycky on first-person accounts, most former Ukrainian camp inmates reported that they were arrested when trying to enter the United States in search of work.[62] Cognizant of this growing issue, the federal government did issue some orders-in-council to allow emigration. In April 1915, one addressed the case of "a considerable number of aliens of Austro-Hungarian or German nationality at Vancouver who have been employed upon construction works which are now completed or suspended." Because they had no intention of returning to Europe, order-in-council PC 858 authorized these and other workers in Vancouver to go to the United States "because otherwise their maintenance is likely to be a charge upon the country." In November 1915, this policy was expanded to empower the chief constable in both Victoria and Toronto to similarly enable the emigration to the United

States of those enemy aliens who agreed not "to engage in hostilities or to otherwise assist the enemy."[63]

Internment during the First World War became a legal and conceptual precedent that played a role in enabling far more repressive state policies towards Canadians of Japanese heritage, whether citizens by birth or naturalization, during the Second World War. Yet in that case, the concept of enemy alien was expanded to include British subjects by birth. The internment of German and Austro-Hungarian nationals in the First World War and of German and Italian nationals starting in 1940 were not the only precedents for Japanese internment, and a long history of racial discrimination also led to the internment and dispossession of people of Japanese birth and heritage. But decisions to intern in the Second World War were clearly influenced by decisions taken in the First World War, all the more so because over the course of the war the enemy threat grew from some foreign nationals to eventually target the German language. There are important differences between German and Japanese experiences in Canada, fundamentally shaped by race and racism. While – in the eyes of Canadian law – the German language became a threat at the close of the First World War, and while naturalized Canadians of central European birth lost the right to vote in 1917, no naturalized immigrant from Germany or Austria-Hungary was interned and absolutely none of the approximately 360,000 people born in Canada who were of German heritage were ever considered for internment.

Citizenship, Voting, and Naturalization

Another step in state repression of some German speakers came after three years of war. Robert Borden's Conservatives passed the Wartime Elections Act in September 1917, largely out of concerns that the government would lose support in the upcoming federal election because of its recent decision to begin conscripting men into military service. It provided women in the military as well as the wives, mothers, and sisters of serving soldiers the right to vote in federal elections while also using the law to take aim at more immigrants than previous orders-in-council had done. The act targeted "every naturalized British subject who was born in an enemy country and naturalized subsequent to the 31st day of March, 1902. A person shall be deemed to have been born in an enemy country, within the meaning of this paragraph, if he was born in a country which forms part of the territory of any country with which His Majesty is at war."[64] It made an exception for those who had a son, grandson, or brother in the Canadian military. According to John English, "the Act was designed to create legions of new voters who were likely to support the Unionists [the coalition government to be headed by Borden], and to disenfranchise voters who would likely be opposed to conscription."[65] Like internment, the law targeted people born in both the German and Austro-Hungarian Empires, but it took aim at a different group: naturalized immigrants.

German-speaking immigrants were a particular target of this legislation. The act made specific reference to Germany and "Austria" (not the Austro-Hungarian Empire), while it did not mention the Ottoman Empire or Bulgaria.[66] In addition to the clause that disenfranchised based on country of birth, another clause focused specifically on language. It took aim at "every naturalized British subject who was born in any European country (whether or not the sovereign or government thereof is in alliance with His Majesty in the present war) whose natural language, otherwise described as 'mother tongue,' is a language of an enemy country, and who was naturalized subsequent to the 31st day of March, 1902."[67] With that language clause, the act went out of its way to also disenfranchise German speakers in Canada born in the Russian Empire (it made an exception for Mennonites) and Swiss Germans. It did not include German-Americans in Canada because it stated "any European country." The reliance on the concept of mother tongue to categorize people who grew up in multilingual spaces in central and eastern Europe was more fraught than the English-speaking authors of the legislation probably realized. Bilingualism was prevalent, and a person's dominant language did not always align with their first language, the language of their mothers, or the language of their childhood home.[68]

The definition of a language of an enemy country could have been open to debate, but the bill's proponents clarified their anti-German intentions. Dozens of languages were spoken in the multiethnic German and Austro-Hungarian Empires, but some of those were also spoken in Allied countries. In this period, political borders in Europe did not correspond to ethnic boundaries. If the intention of the clause was to target foreign-born people in Canada who spoke any language of the German Empire, it would have included Polish, Yiddish, and French speakers born in Allied nations. Polish, Ukrainian, Romanian, and Serbian were all languages spoken in Austria-Hungary but also in Russia and in the kingdoms of Serbia and Romania, which were at war with the Central Powers.

The Liberal MP Frank Carvell from Carleton, New Brunswick, pressed the government on the language clause. He asked, "I cannot understand why you should disfranchise a man who is a naturalized British subject, who was born in an Allied country but whose mother tongue was that of an enemy country ... I presume there may be Russians of that class who might speak the Austrian language [German, the dominant language of the Austro-Hungarian Empire]." Prime Minister Borden responded curtly, "German or Austrian." Arthur Meighen, a cabinet minister (secretary of state for Canada) who played a large role in proposing the act, followed up, "there is no distinction in sympathy whatever between those foreign people, provided they speak the enemy language, whether they are born in Austria or across the border [in Russia]."[69] In Meighen's assessment of his bill, in the case of German speakers from Russia, a person's dominant language was more important than his citizenship or the residence of his ancestors (Russia) for more than a century. With the clause and the government's clarification in parliament, the xenophobic tone of the Wartime Elections Act becomes even stronger.

The government was further pressed on the issue by two other Liberal MPs, and in both cases they questioned the implications of this clause on German speakers from either Russia or Belgium.[70] Confronted with the issue of Polish speakers born in Germany and Russia, Meighen explicitly stated, "if born in Russia, [and if] they speak Polish [they] do not come under the Bill at all."[71] Though the government seemed to be deliberately vague by referring to "the Austrian language" in some instances and playing ignorant about how this legislation could possibly affect Belgians, in this specific exchange Meighen seemed to make clear that the language of an enemy country did not refer to all languages spoken in central Europe but rather the language of the governments of the Central Powers (German and perhaps Hungarian).

Disenfranchising naturalized British subjects was an important rupture with the legal understanding of citizenship as spelled out in the

1914 Naturalization Act.[72] The 1917 Wartime Elections Act treated some naturalized subjects as different from others and from Canadian born. The 1914 legislation specified that naturalization entitled people "to all political and other rights, powers, and privileges, and [made them] be subject to all obligations, duties and liabilities, to which a natural-born British subject is entitled." Most importantly, it specified that a person "from the date of his naturalization have to all intents and purposes the status of natural-born British subject."[73] The new electoral legislation did not, however, respect the supposed equality between people who naturalized after 1902 and natural-born British subjects. Internment, the result of orders-in-council approved soon after the War Measures Act, targeted only non-naturalized immigrants born in enemy countries. Yet as the war dragged on and the authority of the federal government became more robust, the Wartime Elections Act did not reflect the same concerns and also focused on British subjects.

Because of wartime censorship and anti-German sentiment, the largest German-language newspaper in Ontario, the *Ontario Journal* (previously named the *Berliner Journal*), was careful in how it mounted its disapproval of the election law. During the war, it added a new section entitled "Views of the Press" and cited English-language newspapers such as the *London Free Press*, the *Weekly Sun*, and the *Toronto Star* that expressed views similar to its own. Aligning itself with the criticism levelled by these papers, the *Journal* wrote in German that "the removal of the rights of naturalized citizens is a violation of confidence that cannot be justified."[74] It quoted the *Toronto Star*, which called the law "a large danger for Canada's free institutions."[75] In a longer editorial that it translated into German from the *Star*, the paper told readers, "we have invited them and promised them the rights and privileges of citizens … if they keep their part of the contract, we are obliged to also uphold ours."[76] The criticism of the policy in the *Toronto Star* is noteworthy, as is the strategy of the German-speaking editors of the *Ontario Journal* to shield themselves from censorship.

The parliamentary debate about the legislation in September 1917 sheds light on the contours of the thinking behind disenfranchisement. Arthur Meighen stated that because those born in enemy countries were exempted from conscription, "it is also unfair to them that in the midst of such a war they should be called upon to determine by their vote the vigour, or the direction, which that war should take, while their next of kin and their brothers, or their sons, are fighting in the armies against us. That argument has been advanced to us by some of this class themselves."[77] He also added, "those who cannot in the nature of things be absolutely divorced in sympathy or sentiment from the peoples from whom they come should not be permitted, in justice to the rest of the population, to exercise a measure of control over the destinies of the war."[78]

The opposition Liberals took exception in particular to the disenfranchisement of naturalized British subjects. In debates, they seemed especially concerned about how constituents – those born in Germany and Austria-Hungary as well as German speakers born in Russia – would lose the right to vote and the implications of disenfranchising British subjects. Charles Murphy, a Liberal MP from Russell County, Ontario, shot back at Meighen's claims about the purposes of the proposed law, stating, "This Bill is directed not against the Kaiser and kaiserism, but against the German people themselves, who are resident within the boundaries of Canada. Once this game of disfranchising the foreigner whom we bring to our shores and to whom we guaranteed equal citizenship and equal rights with ourselves is begun, where, I ask you, is it likely to stop?"[79]

Another Liberal MP, Georges Henri Boivin, from Shefford, Quebec, asked: "if the Government wish to be consistent, why do they not disfranchise every man who is too old to fight? These aliens who have been in this country since 1902 have done their share in this war. They have contributed very generously in certain cities of Canada to Patriotic and Red Cross Funds and to the Belgian Relief Fund ... After paying directly and indirectly for several years their share of taxation for the carrying on of the war, they are told that they have not the right to vote."[80]

It is worth noting that these defences of Germans were inconsistent with other instances where British subjecthood did not guarantee groups the right to vote. Indeed, citizenship and voting in this period should not be conflated.[81] A series of laws and judicial decisions in this era denied women, Asian Canadians, and Indigenous people the franchise, and they were all British subjects. Indeed, one act of Parliament in 1881 defined naturalization (the Naturalization and Aliens Act) and a distinct one in 1885 defined voting (the Franchise Act). The 1881 Naturalization and

Aliens Act in fact allowed Asian immigrants to naturalize in Canada, but court cases such as *Cunningham v. Tomey Homma* and *Quong Wing v. The King* restricted both voting and labour rights for naturalized persons from Asia.[82] Moreover, Peter Price notes that legal conceptions of nationality were "rooted in assumptions about gender and the capacity of women to identify as members of a political community ... A married woman's nationality was contingent on that of her husband," and she would gain or lose British subjecthood depending on the nationality of her husband.[83] Indigenous people in Canada, like colonized people all over the British Empire, were British subjects, even if their relationship with the Crown was different than European settlers'. In fact, the 1876 Indian Act – notably passed around the same time as these other acts that gave form to evolving notions of citizenship – included the concept of "voluntary enfranchisement" which pitted status under the Indian Act against voting rights. An Indigenous man could vote if he gave up his status under the act. That relationship was only redefined with the Canada Elections Act (1960).

In the parliamentary debates, some Liberals labelled the proposed legislation "German" or "Kaiser-like" – meaning draconian, undemocratic, or not in line with British/Canadian legal and civic values – in an attempt to remove its disenfranchising elements. Rodolphe Lemieux, a Liberal MP for Rouville, Quebec contended that the provision aimed at naturalized British subjects made "of the most solemn pledges and of our naturalization laws so many 'scraps of paper' so that, at the next general election, Hun-like, yes, Kaiser-like, they [the ruling Conservatives] may hack their way through the constituencies of Canada."[84] With "scraps of paper," Lemieux was making reference to a commonly discussed statement made by the German chancellor in 1914. In a final discussion before the start of the war, Theobald von Bethmann-Hollweg told the British ambassador that Germany did not have any real obligation to uphold Belgian neutrality because the Treaty of London (1839) was a mere scrap of paper.[85] Lemieux's assertion that the ruling Conservatives had a similar approach to their own naturalization law was a stinging criticism.

Wilfrid Laurier, the leader of the Liberal opposition in Parliament, called the bill a repudiation of British values, noting, "This is not a Liberal measure, it is not a Canadian measure, and it is not a British measure. It is a retrograde measure and a German measure."[86] He warned that when the war ended and when Canadian immigration policies again sought workers and farmers in Europe, the country would have to turn to "Galicians, Bukowinians, and Rumanians" because there would be little interest in Britain, France, and Belgium to emigrate to Canada. In light of the treatment of naturalized immigrants in the proposed bill, he doubted that "these different races will be disposed to come to this country, when they know that Canada has not kept its pledges and promises to the people from foreign countries who have settled in our midst."[87] Laurier's complaints about the future success of immigrant recruitment was a reference to his own policies between 1896 and 1911, when many of the immigrants now under attack with the Wartime Elections Act came to Canada.

The 1917 law was a continuation of the legal attack against some immigrants that had begun with internment and other orders-in-council in the first year of the war. Combined, the orders and the new law affected most immigrants in Canada who had been born in Germany or Austria-Hungary as well as German speakers from Russia. They also created a general atmosphere in which the legal weight of the state was thrown behind the anti-German sentiments widespread in wartime Canada. This is despite the initial proclamation that it was "desirable that such persons should be allowed to continue in such avocations without interruption."[88] The electoral law was in fact more clearly anti-German than internment because of its language clause and the government's insistence that the clause was intended to disenfranchise German-speaking immigrants from Russia but not Polish-speaking immigrants from Russia. In disenfranchising some naturalized subjects, it also expanded the legal understanding of enemy alien and legitimized public concerns about subversive immigrants. It was an important step in the cultural war on the home front, which would continue in the final year of the war.

From Nationality to Ethnicity

A final step in the anti-German policies of the federal government came just seven weeks before the war's end. An order-in-council passed on 25 September 1918 (PC 2381, the "Order Respecting Enemy Publications") prohibited publishing, importing, mailing, delivering, receiving, or possessing books, newspapers, magazines, periodicals, pamphlets, tracts, circulars, leaflets, handbills, posters, or other printed matter "in the language of any country or people for the time being at war with Great Britain."[89] The order included fourteen languages. In addition to German, it also banned Austrian, Hungarian, Bulgarian, Turkish, Romanian, Russian, Ukrainian, Finnish, Estonian, Syrian, Croatian, Ruthenian, and Livonian.[90] The inclusion of Austrian in addition to German – especially for published rather than spoken language – seems to be a political statement about Canada's two main wartime enemies. Nothing was published in Canada in "Austrian." The naming of Livonian – by 1918 an almost extinct Finnic language spoken in coastal Latvia – was probably an error; the authors likely intended to take aim at Latvian or Baltic languages in general. The order made an exception for publications of literary, scientific, religious, or artistic character and anything used in education. With its focus on the languages of countries at war with Canada and also the languages in or bordering the Soviet Union, the order merged two concerns for the Canadian state, namely the subversive actions of people loyal to the Central Powers and of leftist organizations.

In studies of German speakers in Canada, the banning of German-language newspapers has been seen as an unnecessary act against a group overwhelmingly born in Canada and which did not behave in a subversive way during the war. Yet in light of previous orders-in-council, the publication ban should be read as an extension of other repressive policies fundamentally concerned with the German language. Werner Bausenhart has argued that the order "could also be seen as the Federal Government's contribution to the provincial legislation to abolish bilingual schools in the educational systems of Ontario, Manitoba, Saskatchewan, and Alberta."[91] Herbert Kalbfleisch calls the decision "hasty" and "unnecessary," but the result of an ideal in Ontario at the time "of conformity and homogeneity."[92] In light of the material presented in chapter 1 about a nascent linguistic ideology that sought to make Ontario an English-speaking province, this seems like a reasonable assertion. Yet as the now English-language *Ontario Journal* wrote in December 1918, "the war ended six weeks after the Union Government prohibited German papers in Canada. Why didn't they take action in 1914?"[93]

The answer may in fact lie in the strategies of the chief press censor, Ernest Chambers, and the length of the war. According to Jeff Keshen, Chambers worried primarily about foreign-language publications throughout the war while he largely assumed that editors of mainstream papers would remain loyal.[94] In 1916, Chambers wrote that the best way "to deal with foreign-language papers in Canada is to ban their publication altogether."[95] However, cabinet rather than the office of the censor had the power to close newspapers, and in Chambers's view the government was overly cautious.[96] The weight and length of the war enabled him and other authorities to turn a language spoken mainly by people born in Canada into an enemy threat.

According to Arthur Grenke, "newspapers and mail began to be censored as early as August 1914."[97] Yet the office of the chief press censor, created in June 1915, had a small budget and only a few people played important roles. A Miss E. Mercer, who normally worked for the Immigration Branch, was largely responsible for reading and translating all German-language publications, while E. Tartak, a professor of Slavonic studies at McGill University, did the same for a number of Slavic languages.[98] Canadian expenses on censorship were approximately $100,000 over four and a half years whereas the United States spent $9.7 million in nineteen months and the United Kingdom spent £2 million.[99] When calculated on a per capita basis and adjusted for the United States' later entry into the war, Canada spent far less on censorship.

In its last ever issue, the *Ontario Journal* published a letter from Ernest Chambers that it received in 1916, which congratulated the paper for complying with censorship rules.[100] It was a not-so-subtle strategy to denounce the order-in-council that labelled the German language a subversive threat. The paper also complained in its first issue in English on 9 October 1918 that German-language papers got their news by translating from English papers and therefore posed no threat.[101] A week later, it told readers, "Above all we must be good Canadian citizens and we are bound to work and pray for the success of our country in the present world struggle, so that our boys, many of them sons and relatives of those whom the prohibition of their accustomed home newspaper affects most seriously, may soon return victorious."[102]

This attack on German and other languages in 1918 in Canada had noteworthy similarities with other cases in the United States. The foreign-language press was seen as a source of immigrant disloyalty. The Trading with the Enemy Act of October 1917 required such newspapers to file a translation at the local post office of any articles related to the US government or any country currently at war, or to file for an exemption for this requirement.[103] For the following year, German- and other foreign-language newspapers stated either their exemption permit number or that they had filed a translation at the post office.[104]

This attack was also felt in matters of education. States such as Nebraska, Iowa, and Ohio passed laws that banned the teaching of German in schools (something that Ontario did not do despite other scholars' claims that it did). During the war, many restrictions (in the form of municipal ordinances or simple public pronouncements) were hastily applied and not legally enforceable, but after the war ended, state legislatures enacted laws.[105] According to Frederick Luebke, after the armistice was signed "the war against German language and culture in the United States continued with scarcely any diminution."[106] New state legislatures were elected in the closing days of the war, and the many new lawmakers came to power with the goal of imposing linguistic uniformity upon the American people.[107] Many of these bans were short lived and a 1923 US Supreme Court ruling ended an era of language restriction.[108] Yet while there was a similar attempt to push the German language out of the public sphere in the United States, this Canadian ban was on publications and not schooling. In the case of Ontario, German had already been largely pushed out of the school system by 1914. It remained a subject of instruction, and it was the individual decisions of local school boards to end classes; the provincial government did not ban it in elementary and high schools.[109]

From 1914 onwards, the *Berliner Journal* worked to stave off accusations of anti-Canadian loyalty. It, like German-Canadians themselves, found itself in new territory and had to walk a new line between ethnic interests and civic belonging. In late September 1914, it wrote: "We Berliners have been accused of lacking patriotism and loyalty since the beginning of the war. [But] our Berlin has always proven its loyalty and has always been proud to be a Canadian city."[110] The paper often sought donations for the

Patriotic Fund in order to provide extra support for the wives, children, widows, and mothers of soldiers. It told readers, "German-Canadians have always proven themselves to be loyal citizens and if the government had not known of their good qualities, it probably would not have produced so much propaganda for German immigration. We, with German names here in Berlin, have done no less than another city of Berlin's size, but we want to recommend warmly to our fellow citizens that they participate in the Patriotic Fund."[111] In a letter to the editor on 1 March 1916, in reference to the debate about the city of Berlin's name, a reader wrote, "We are not ashamed of our German heritage. We are descendants of Germans who came here. But although we come from Germans, we are neither German nor German-Canadian; nor hyphenated Canadians ... We are Canadian and are not inferior to anybody in terms of devotion to this country and the ideals of the British Empire."[112]

Although the Order Respecting Enemy Publications did not come until the fall of 1918, Chambers did have power to ban imported materials throughout the war and to temporarily punish newspapers in Canada. Of the tracts he prohibited, 222 came from the United States and 164 were not published in English or French.[113] During the war, sixty-five German, twenty-seven Russian, twenty Ukrainian, sixteen Finnish, and eight Yiddish publications were banned for at least a period of time.[114] Many of these came from the United States, and German-American publications were particularly scrutinized.[115] Chambers's concerns about German-language publications were not entirely without merit. According to Frederick Luebke, in the neutral United States, "German-American newspapers had indeed been immoderate during the first year of the war. Ethnocentric editors, who demanded fair play when they were unwilling to grant it to others, had been as blind in their pro-German partisanship as their pro-British detractors had been in theirs."[116] He adds, "German-Americans continued through 1916 to offend native Americans with their rallies and demonstrations, their fund-raising bazaars for the German Red Cross, their intemperate editorials and speeches against loans to the Allies, trade in war goods, and travel by American citizens on vessels of belligerent nations."[117] In 1915, after having accused the *Berliner Journal* of disloyalty but revising his decision, Chambers explained to the paper's editor, John Motz, that "the fact of your being of German extraction and publishing papers in a German language imposes upon you certain standards of carefulness which might not be expected of others."[118]

German-language publications may have also been a convenient foil, one that enabled Canadian lawmakers to take aim at the perceived postwar threat, namely the Soviet Union and leftist activism at home. The Order Respecting Enemy Publications (PC 2381) was accompanied by a second order-in-council (PC 2384) on the same day that made a number of organizations unlawful. This included the Russian Revolutionary Group, the Russian Social Democratic Party, the Ukrainian Social Democratic Party, the Group of Social Democrats of Anarchists, and the Chinese Nationalist League. The inclusion of Russian, Ukrainian, Ruthenian, Finnish, Estonian, and Livonian in the publication ban seems to complement the other order aimed at leftist organizations whose members spoke those languages. PC 2384 banned any association whose purposes were "to bring about any governmental, political, social, industrial, or economic change within Canada by use of force, violence, or physical injury." It further banned all meetings except religious ones "during the present war ... in the language or any of the languages of any country or portion of any country with which Canada is at war, or in the language or any of the languages of Russia, Ukraine or Finland."[119] In a single sentence, it lumped together German and several languages of what had been an allied empire until March 1918. This clause about language stands in sharp contrast to the Wartime Elections Act. Whereas that legislation made clear that it was targeting German speakers and not other central and eastern European languages, this order-in-council sought to include languages such as Polish, Yiddish, Czech, and Romanian, and it used the fact that they were languages in countries at war with Canada (Germany and Austria-Hungary) as the reason to target these organizations.

The Order Respecting Enemy Publications connected concerns about immigrants from central Europe (whether naturalized or not) with bilingual Canadians of German heritage. While by 1914 most German speakers in Ontario had been born there and spoke two languages on a regular basis, the ban on German-language publications in 1918 made their world black and white. In the case of Ontario, the federal order equated the province's third-largest linguistic group with an empire at war with Canada. That wartime context collapsed the space that many German speakers had carved out for cultural pluralism in the Canadian civic landscape. This focus on written language pushed German out of the public sphere in important ways, although it is important to stress that it had no effect on churches or on the teaching of German at schools and colleges in the province. Those institutions followed a different path into the 1920s.

Conclusion

How did German speakers in Ontario experience the First World War? Hundreds in the province got put in internment camps and most of them were later deported to Germany. Thousands lost the right to vote in the 1917 federal election. All of them were prevented from reading their news in German between late September 1918 and early 1920 when the Treaty of Versailles formally came into effect and Germany ceased to be an enemy country. Because the ban put the last remaining German-language newspaper in Ontario out of business, its impact lasted beyond 1920.[120] Yet while public expressions of German ethnicity lessened, people did not stop being German during or after the First World War. On one hand, schools in Ontario had already stopped being German in the 1890s. On the other, Lutheran churches continued to hold German services and operate Sunday schools that taught children in German long after the guns of August fell silent. Parents spoke German to their children in Ontario in both 1910 and 1920, but as a result of the war, Canadian parents of German heritage were probably more tolerant of children responding in English.

The ensemble of discriminatory policies aimed at "Germans," as defined by the Canadian state, linked together German speakers born in Germany, Austria-Hungary, Russia, the United States, and Canada in ways that not only were disputed by these German speakers, but also were contrary to many Canadian laws and social practices before August 1914. These policies lumped together various meanings of being German and worked to flatten the culturally plural landscape of Ontario. The citizenship rights that existed in the province and country before the war were greatly transformed after 1914. Naturalized and natural-born

British subjects did not have the same rights in 1914 and 1917 with the passage of the Wartime Elections Act.

Yet by the close of the war, the linguistic pluralism that had taken hold in Ontario over the previous century was changed as well. If in the 1880s and 1890s a linguistic ideology sought to ensure that all children in the province would be educated in English and pushed German and French to the margins, the 1918 ban on publishing, importing, mailing, delivering, receiving, or possessing printed matter in a number of languages took that linguistic ideology much further. Wartime laws and orders-in-council disappeared in 1920 when peace treaties formally came into effect, but their impact and the ideas that supported them were felt for the next two decades, before another war would further transform how immigration, citizenship, and cultural pluralism interacted in Canada.

In the next chapter, I turn my attention to two church-run colleges in Ontario. These bilingual institutions fostered the use of the German language for a small group of Catholic and Lutheran men at the same time as the province of Ontario worked to remove German from elementary schools. These colleges continued to create a space for German education during and after the First World War.

TWO / Making Ethnic Spaces

In the late nineteenth and early twentieth centuries, German speakers –
alongside people of many other backgrounds in North America – made
ethnic spaces. These spaces became sites where people of German
birth and heritage performed ethnicity, reinforced ethnic identities,
and fostered ties. In ethnic spaces, German rather than English was
commonly used, but they were nonetheless marked by permeable
linguistic boundaries. Beyond physical spaces such as churches, clubs,
charities, libraries, and schools that countered the pervasive presence
of English in most other aspects of people's everyday lives, newspapers
created portable ethnic spaces that met many of the same criteria of
fostering both community cohesion and the German language. Contact
with ethnic spaces profoundly influenced any child born in North
America. These spaces added points of contact with German and
extended bilingualism beyond the household, thereby giving children
greater linguistic proficiency in a number of other social contexts.

The degree to which there are ethnic spaces in a society both shapes
and reflects the nature of cultural pluralism. The efforts to make ethnic
spaces foster pluralism, but state policies, nationalist sentiments, media,
or consumer culture also limit that pluralism. The state in Ontario also
participated in making ethnic space by permitting German-language
instruction in provincially funded public and Catholic separate schools.
That the Education Department later moved to limit the use of German
in its schools in the 1890s meant that the state could also unmake
ethnic space and limit it to certain spheres such as the home or the
church. The move to limit the place of German in Ontario's education
system coincided with the growth of German-language Lutheran

Sunday schools in Ontario, which suggests that religious institutions in particular became another pole of power, alongside the state, in making cultural pluralism.

Part II focuses on religious institutions and analyzes the role of organized religion in making ethnic spaces. It embraces Nancy Christie and Michael Gauvreau's premise that "the church as an institutional form was not synonymous with religion as a broader cultural expression" and "the religious understanding and experience of ordinary people did not necessarily coincide with the prescriptions of clergy."[1] It contributes to that methodological point of departure by examining the ethnic culture and bilingualism connected to both formal religious practice and the communities organized along denominational lines. While casting light on the broader religious culture that deviated from the views of Lutheran and Catholic leaders, it is a social history of ethnicity, not of religion. Borrowing from the work of Robert Orsi, who asks what devotional practices meant for people's spirituality, values, and hopes, and how religion played a significant role in the lives of immigrants and their children, chapters 3 and 4 demonstrate how religious institutions and denominational identity shaped ethnic cultures in important ways.[2]

Religious institutions and networks have largely been overlooked in the historiography on German speakers in both Canada and the United States.[3] Nevertheless, Lutheran and Catholic churches were cornerstones of many German-speaking communities throughout Ontario. Through the Catholic and Lutheran colleges in chapter 3 and the Lutheran networks and institutions of chapter 4, part II explores how religious institutions gave meaning to ideas about being German in Ontario and North America. These institutions carved out a place for denominational pluralism in Ontario, and they show that ethnic culture and linguistic behaviour were often tied to religious cultures.

Chapter 3 focuses on both Catholic and Lutheran colleges, while chapter 4 focuses solely on Lutheran networks that connected German speakers to the United States, Germany, and missionary activities in India. German-speaking Catholics of course also developed cross-border ties. The Congregation of the Resurrection that ran St Jerome's College was active in Ontario, Illinois, and Kentucky, and priests and brothers in all three places had important ties to Rome. Canadian Catholicism was also deeply linked to the United States, Europe, and the Catholic world more broadly. Yet compared to German-speaking Lutherans in Ontario, the connections that German-speaking Catholics had with others in the United States did not seem to play such a fundamental role in shaping ethnic communities, particularly into the 1910s and 1920s. As chapter 4 will show, for Lutherans the boundaries of German ethnicity were reinforced because of cross-border networks. These ties were manifested in institutional structures, meetings among religious leaders from Ontario and the United States, the arrival of Lutheran pastors from Germany, Canadian and American funding of a seminary in Germany, and the Canadian use of American Lutheran seminaries to educate new, Ontario-born pastors. In contrast, German-speaking Catholics did not receive new religious leaders from Germany to the same extent, something which differs from the stronger transatlantic networks that Catholics in Germany did develop with German migrants elsewhere in the Americas.[4]

3. TEACHING LANGUAGE, TEACHING RELIGION

St Jerome's and Waterloo Lutheran Colleges

In the late nineteenth and early twentieth centuries, as the Education Department progressively removed the German language from the elementary schools of Ontario, two religious colleges successfully carved a German-language space into the upper levels of Ontario's educational system. St Jerome's, a Roman Catholic college in Berlin, and Waterloo Lutheran, a Lutheran college in Waterloo, promoted the German language in their curricula and extracurricular activities and were central nodes in two loosely defined ethno-religious communities. At many times, however, an interest in religious expansion rather than language maintenance drove this community-building. Linguistic concerns occupied a secondary place in the colleges' mission, which centred on offering a Christian education to a small group of young men. Language and other cultural representations of German ethnicity intermingled with the primarily religious focus in the programs of both colleges.

Weaving the history of education into broader debates about ethnicity and religion in Ontario, this chapter explores the ways that non-state educational facilities promoted the German language, but also how religious institutions rather than language made an ethnic community for many people of German heritage. These two church-controlled colleges add a final layer to the historiography of German-language education in Ontario that has, until now, focused exclusively on elementary schooling. Many community leaders were actively involved in these colleges, and the somewhat German character of both institutions offers a more complete view of how many German speakers participated in and experienced education in Ontario at all possible levels.

I argue that at these colleges German-speaking Catholics and Lutherans viewed both language and religion as central components of ethnicity. Over time religion took on greater importance, but throughout the 1920s, German retained a place in these colleges' educational mission. In this case, denomination rather than language marked the boundaries of ethnicity. Both colleges allowed a significant space for English in their teaching and daily activities, and the boundaries of linguistic difference were made porous from the inside, by German speakers themselves. St Jerome's also included Catholics of other backgrounds, which again reinforced denominational boundaries around an institution founded as a "German college."

Gender shaped this linguistic and religious educational project. The two educational institutions in Ontario that were most successful at supporting the German language were male-only colleges.[1] This discrepancy had implications for the reproduction of linguistic, religious, and ethnic communities over time. A group of male priests or pastors went to great lengths to educate a male-only student body for future careers in business or as clergy; through the education they offered, the two institutions maintained men's roles in those spaces. Not only did a group of men promote German as well as Catholicism or Lutheranism to a group of men, they also excluded women. If promoting German was important for the directors of St Jerome's and Waterloo Lutheran, it could be helpful to add that young people's genders as much as their ethnic backgrounds motivated religious leaders to ensure the promotion of an advanced proficiency in German.

The gendered nature of the colleges could be seen beyond the simple absence of female students or instructors. When describing the importance of discipline, the directors of St Jerome's told students and parents that the learning environment promoted not only "obedience, politeness, mutual respect, and kindness," but also "honor and manliness."[2] Infusing the college with a patriarchal hierarchy, the directors added that the college should be run "like a well regulated family."[3] The goals of promoting Christianity and German alongside other subjects at colleges that would lead to professional careers are examples of male institutions supporting the perpetuation and solidification of male roles in society as well. After all, the colleges' goals of creating moral citizens and "consistent" Christians could have been mirrored at a Catholic college for girls such as a convent school with a similar interest in German – yet this did not happen.

In this period in Ontario, there were no separate Catholic high schools but rather only public high schools and collegiate institutes. Yet the Catholic St Jerome's College offered high school training and accepted students directly after elementary schooling. The existence of Catholic colleges such as St Jerome's is a part of this history where Catholic elementary education existed within a state-controlled system but Catholic secondary education did not. St Jerome's had much in common with several *collèges classiques* founded by French-speaking Catholics in the same period. As Roberto Perin notes, "founded to prepare young men for the priesthood, these university-level residential establishments in fact became training-grounds for French Canada's professional élite."[4] Similar institutions could be found at the Oblate-run University of Ottawa, the Université Sainte-Anne in Nova Scotia, the Collège de St-Boniface in Winnipeg, and others in Sudbury, Ontario and Memramcook and Caraquet, New Brunswick.[5]

These two colleges were cultivating something other than an anglophone elite. In providing religious education beyond elementary school, they increased access for Catholics and Lutherans to cultural and economic leadership in society. They ensured that Anglicanism, Presbyterianism, and Methodism alone would not shape the emerging English-speaking society. In the case of St Jerome's, German speakers likely also modified the very nature of Catholicism in Ontario. As Kathleen Neils Conzen points out, linguistic heritage, demography, residential and educational patterns, worldview, and liturgical preferences distinguished German-speaking Catholics from other Catholics in the United States.[6] In creating Catholic yet German spaces in the nineteenth century, German speakers played a role in shaping the nature of Catholicism, in ways that both French Canadians and Irish Canadians did as well.

French-Canadian nationalists and religious leaders similarly drew connections between linguistic and denominational maintenance.[7] It was also an idea espoused by German nationalists in Europe as they worried about the threat of assimilation of German emigrants in the Americas.[8] The interest that the leaders of St Jerome's and Waterloo Lutheran expressed in language was less nationalist and more practical. They believed that their denominations and students had a natural relationship with German, and it was teachers' and directors' responsibility to support it. These ideas played an important role in the ongoing attention to German in the 1910s and 1920s.

Both religious colleges were free to infuse their curricula with German, whereas the state limited the German language in elementary education in Ontario. Paul Axelrod has noted that government involvement in universities in Ontario before 1945 was "minimal, informal, and irregular," and that only a few bureaucrats in the province's Education Department dealt with these institutions.[9] The state was not entirely absent, of course, and it defined its own hands-off control. These colleges received a provincial charter and had state permission to exist. However, in terms of setting their curriculum, choosing textbooks, and financing them, the state was relatively absent. The province did not issue regulations governing St Jerome's and Waterloo Lutheran, and provincial inspectors did not monitor them.

In the period between 1840 and 1890, the upper boundaries of secondary education in Ontario were not fully set.[10] D. Gidney and W.P.J. Millar discuss the shift away from classical education centred on Latin and towards a model focused on commercial training and greater attention to English.[11] They explain that in these decades, "Latin and Greek lost their exclusive claim to be the definitive studies of a liberal education. Science, English, and modern languages took a place within the charmed circle of studies that could discipline and culture the mind."[12] St Jerome's and Waterloo Lutheran fit into these broader patterns in the province. They did not draw a sharp distinction between secondary and post-secondary education, and they struck a balance between classical education and commercial training.

Students at these colleges came from many socio-economic backgrounds. Gidney and Millar have noted that students at high schools in Ontario in the late nineteenth century did not come solely from upper-class backgrounds.[13] Chad Gaffield, Lynne Marks, and Susan Laskin have also demonstrated that students at Queen's University at the turn of the twentieth century came from all social classes and that 16 per cent came from working-class families.[14] Information on the socio-economic status of the young men who attended St Jerome's and Waterloo Lutheran Colleges is not available, but it is likely that they too came from many social classes, including agricultural or working-class backgrounds. Nevertheless, St Jerome's and Waterloo Lutheran trained only a small part of the local population and prepared a small group of men to join the cultural, economic, and religious elite. As Michael Gauvreau notes in his study of Presbyterian and Methodist colleges, these institutions connected philosophical debates about creed and theology with "educating an Anglo-Canadian elite in the precepts of liberal culture."[15]

The Creation of German Colleges in Ontario

Through these colleges, German-speaking Catholics and Lutherans influenced the nature of the linguistic and denominational pluralism of the province. Even as German took a back seat to English over time, it remained a part of these initially bilingual colleges. Both language and denomination played an integral part in the community that formed around these institutions. By creating a space for Catholic and Lutheran secondary and post-secondary education, German speakers also broadened the religious landscape of the province.

St Jerome's College traces its roots to a small rural school founded in St Agatha, Ontario, in 1864. The founding priest, Ludwig Funcken, moved the college to nearby Berlin in 1866 where it rapidly grew. A new building was constructed in the 1890s (depicted in figure 3.1). It was located in downtown Berlin. The aim of the college was "to educate young men in the spirit of Christianity; to prepare them for higher professional studies in Seminaries and Universities; and to qualify them for Commercial life."[16] It also sought to provide young men with "the habits and principles of honorable living and to develop their natural talents in every respect. The religious and moral instruction of the pupils [was] consequently considered a matter of prime importance."[17]

The college offered a three-year commercial course to young men. Parallel to this, it had a five-year classical or philosophical course. This course's curriculum resembled the commercial course, but it also had

3.1 St Jerome's College, Berlin, Ontario, 1907.

a strong interest in German, other modern languages, algebra, Latin, and Greek.[18] In 1901, the classical course was divided into a three-year high school course and a four-year "college or arts course."[19] From this point onwards, the commercial and high school courses matched the secondary level of education in the province and the arts course assumed a post-secondary level.

St Jerome's was founded in the 1860s at a time when local cultural pluralism was acceptable to the state. The official petition to incorporate the Deutsch-Englische Collegium des Heiligen Hieronymus and the German-English College of St Jerome, submitted to state authorities of Canada West in August 1866, was in both English and German. Funcken wrote first in English and then identically in German to the English-speaking government officials that his college would be an institution "in which German and English are taught together, and from which young men may go forth, who whether as belonging to the learned professions, or as merchants or mechanics, may be enabled by a knowledge of the two languages to keep up free intercourse with us and promote immigration from Germany."[20] The petition also described the new college, even in the English version, as "the first German institution for superior education in the Province of Ontario."[21]

The college attempted to affiliate with the University of Western Ontario in 1909 and rekindled interest in 1927. In that year, a director of Western wrote to the leaders of St Jerome's that the university would need to observe the college's teaching for three to four years before allowing affiliation. He added, "We have no evidence that you have been doing Arts work apart from Theological work that would be acceptable to accrediting bodies other than theological," although the classical model of education St Jerome's offered did extend beyond theological training.[22] In this letter, the director told the leaders of St Jerome's that although he himself was Catholic, he felt that because of a growing amount of "unwarranted bigotry" it was better for the university to avoid new Catholic affiliations.[23] He also added that this matter of anti-Catholicism was not discussed with non-Catholic board members. Attempted cooperation with Western did not continue. The college finally affiliated with the University of Ottawa in 1947, which at that moment was run by a Catholic order (the Missionary Oblates of Mary Immaculate). St Jerome's federated with the new University of Waterloo in 1959, an institution that had grown out of Waterloo Lutheran College in 1957.[24]

In the period between Ludwig Funcken's death in 1890 and the 1920s, the priests that ran and taught at St Jerome's and who concurrently led a variety of other Catholic institutions in the area were marked by the college's strong German-language outlook. Most notably, much of the leadership in this early period had studied at St Jerome's under Funcken. In 1890, the college's superior, William Kloepfer, wrote about Funcken that "the German Catholics of this Province especially, own [sic] him a debt of gratitude for the interest he always took in their spiritual welfare and the untiring labors undertaken in [sic] their behalf. Perhaps it may not be generally known that all the German speaking priests in the Diocese, and some outside of it, owe their being to Dr. Funcken and his lamented brother, Father Eugene."[25] Yet into the early twentieth century, the initial influence of Funcken and his commitment to German waned.

In a speech commemorating the college's fiftieth anniversary in 1915, William Motz, editor of the *Berliner Journal*, claimed that virtually every Catholic priest in the Diocese of Hamilton had been trained at St Jerome's.[26] The college was not a seminary, but it served as the first step in training for the priesthood with its classical (post-)secondary education that it also offered to the broader lay population. Starting in 1908, the congregation ran a novitiate in Berlin as well.[27] Graduates of the college could be recruited into the Congregation of the Resurrection and receive their theological training at the congregation's institutions in Rome. Although receiving training in Europe was not typical for Catholic congregations in North America, it appears that this was the case for all young men in Ontario who joined the Congregation of the Resurrection until at least the 1920s.

Until the turn of the twentieth century, St Jerome's had a heavy German focus. James Wahl has argued that it was largely Funcken who promoted the language. In its foundational decades, the "thrust of the college was to be German even though the students were expected to learn both languages."[28] Nonetheless, writes Wahl, "several factors led to a gradual shift in the emphasis at St Jerome's so that by 1878 English was the primary language of instruction although, in the interest of preserving the German culture, the language of conversation was alternately German and English."[29]

Although Funcken had come from Germany and served a German-speaking population in Ontario, the congregation to which he belonged was not based in Germany. The Congregation of the Resurrection was mainly active in Polish-speaking Europe and it had mainly Polish-speaking priests.[30] Priests in exile from the Russian-controlled part of Poland founded the congregation in France in the 1830s.[31] Ludwig and his brother Eugen Funcken, who was also an active missionary in Ontario from the 1850s to the 1880s, were exceptions within this mainly Polish religious congregation. Ludwig Funcken did his higher education in Roermond, Netherlands. The large corpus of his papers, archived at St Jerome's University, reveals that he was proficient in Dutch. Nevertheless, in his correspondence with his brother, Ludwig wrote exclusively in German. Moreover, his professional life in Canada was in German and English, and not at all in Dutch. In 1886, Ludwig wrote to Eugen, who was temporarily in Rome, to ask him to convince the congregation to be more sympathetic to the importance of the German character of St Jerome's. Ludwig felt that the Rome-based Resurrectionists had little interest in his German linguistic outlook.[32]

Ludwig Funcken and the next generation of Canadian-born priests did their theological studies in Rome.[33] The Resurrectionists in Ontario, after Ludwig and Eugen Funcken, were institutionally bound to a congregation based in Rome that had strong ties to Polish-speaking Europe as well as the United States.[34] This had a profound impact on the degree to which St Jerome's strove to create a German-language space over time. Had a Germany-based Catholic congregation begun working in Ontario in the 1860s, St Jerome's would have likely received a steady trickle of German-speaking missionaries who blended ideas of religion with language, as was the case with Lutherans in Ontario and with German Catholics in other parts of the Americas.[35] Instead, after Ludwig and Eugen Funcken, the congregation running St Jerome's did not receive new priests from Germany. The larger, transnational network anchored in Rome and connected to Polish speakers that supported this college partially explains the declining support it gave to the German language.

Between 1890 and 1930, the college always had a noteworthy number of teaching priests with Polish names.[36] I have found little documentation about the arrival of priests' from Europe to supplement the locally recruited ones, but the new priests with Polish names who appeared over time suggest that when the congregation in Ontario received new priests, they came from Polish-speaking Europe. The Congregation of the Resurrection had a strong presence in Chicago and Kentucky as well, and it is possible that these priests of Polish heritage had come from the United States. The majority of the new members of the congregation in Canada were recruited from the local population in the Diocese of Hamilton. Ontario-born priests such as Theobald Spetz, William Kloepfer, and Joseph Schweitzer all spoke German. They corresponded with Funcken in German, but among themselves and with most others they wrote in English.[37]

Like St Jerome's, Waterloo Lutheran College occupied a shared space between secondary and post-secondary education. Founded as Waterloo Lutheran Seminary in 1911, it became a college with a seminary and high

3.2 Evangelical Lutheran Seminary, Waterloo, Ontario, 1911–24.

school stream in 1914. The high school stream was created "particularly to be a feeder to the Seminary, but it soon became evident that it filled a much needed want in providing a general education for our Lutheran young men and boys under churchly training and thoroughly Christian influence."[38] The seminary opened under a cooperative agreement between the German-language Canada Synod and the smaller English-language Synod of Central Canada, which had grown out of the German-language synod and was founded in 1909.[39] Figure 3.2 depicts the original building used to house the seminary.

With its later start, Waterloo Lutheran was considerably smaller than St Jerome's and this remained the case into the late 1920s.[40] Waterloo Lutheran Seminary began in 1911 with four students.[41] In 1913, there were six students, and five part-time teachers who worked concurrently as pastors.[42] In 1918, after the seminary expanded to include a high school stream, enrolment had grown to twenty-four.[43] In 1926, the college had thirty-six students.[44] In comparison, St Jerome's had eighty-seven students in 1895.[45] In 1908, there were 122.[46] In these decades, just over half of the students were from Ontario. Some came from other parts of Canada and many came from the United States, mainly Kentucky and Illinois. During the war and in the 1920s, a much larger portion of the students were from Ontario. In 1917, there were 115 students, and 79 per cent came from Ontario.[47] In 1930, there were 188 students, and 82 per cent from Ontario.[48]

The German-language Canada Synod had a long-standing interest in becoming more self-sufficient in questions of pastoral recruitment. In 1881, R. von Pirch, the pastor of the German Lutheran congregation in Toronto and president of the synod, met with several other pastors and lay leaders in the Canada Synod to discuss the idea of founding a seminary. They concluded that instead of a seminary, the synod should found a college "for the higher education of the youth of our congregations as well as for the Germans of Canada in general."[49] The committee decided that such a college should be located in Berlin, Waterloo, or New Hamburg, and it "should give our youth an academic training that matches our Canadian colleges (*Hochschulen*); the languages of instruction should be both German and English, Lutheran-religious education should receive particular attention, and the main goal of the institution should be to prepare students for theological study in one of our Lutheran seminaries."[50] Leaders soon shelved the project for practical and financial reasons, but it marked the beginning of a long process and demonstrates the connections between local communities and larger structures.

The German-language synod paid between two-thirds and three-quarters of the costs associated with the seminary between 1911 and 1925.[51] In 1925, the college received 46 per cent of the German-language synod's budget, and it was a major part of the synod's activities.[52] When the seminary's quarterly publication began in 1913, it printed 5,000 copies in German and only 2,000 in English, which suggests both that many Lutheran households in Ontario were interested in the small seminary and that of these Lutherans, more belonged to congregations in the German-language synod.[53] In 1925, the German-language Canada Synod and the English-language Synod of Central Canada merged, but the enlarged institution maintained its bilingual German and English outlook. The seminary noted in 1925 that "the language of instruction is German and English and all students shall be equipped to meet the bilingual needs of our church."[54] Compared to the subordination of the German language in the 1880s and 1890s in state-controlled elementary schools, the focus on maintaining bilingualism in the 1920s in this Lutheran educational institution reveals the role of autonomy in making ethnic spaces.

In 1923, Waterloo Lutheran began offering one year of education beyond high school, and in 1924 it affiliated with the University of Western Ontario at the moment when the nearby St Jerome's was struggling to do the same.[55] Waterloo Lutheran began offering a four-year arts program in addition to the high school and seminary streams. The first class in the new university stream graduated in 1928. The college became Waterloo Lutheran University in 1960. In 1957, the directors of Waterloo Lutheran College played a crucial role in founding the fully autonomous University of Waterloo, and in 1959 St Jerome's College affiliated with this new university.[56] Waterloo Lutheran University changed its name to Wilfrid Laurier University in 1973.

Supporting German, Supporting Religion

St Jerome's and Waterloo Lutheran Colleges sought to promote Catholicism and Lutheranism in Ontario society. For the leaders of both colleges, denomination rather than language was the cornerstone of the community they sought to construct. However, in both cases religion intermingled with language and other representations of German ethnicity. Both colleges taught the German language, and they did this to a much greater degree than state-controlled elementary and secondary schools. The colleges had a linguistically capable workforce to teach German, and particularly the Lutheran Church placed a special emphasis on the importance of German in religious practices. The nature of the churches that ran the colleges influenced the extent to which they remained German in the 1910s and 1920s. Waterloo Lutheran was only a single node in a much larger German-language Lutheran framework in Ontario, while St Jerome's was the main institution of a Catholic congregation surrounded by otherwise non-German Catholic institutions.

At St Jerome's College there was a relatively strong interest in promoting the language until 1901 and a continued but marginalized presence into the late 1920s. When it was founded in 1911, however, Waterloo Lutheran Seminary took as much interest in the German language as

St Jerome's had in the 1890s. Its German focus diminished during and after the war, but German remained relatively present throughout the 1920s. The fact that St Jerome's moved away from German long before the war, that Waterloo Lutheran renewed interest in the language in 1911, and that both kept some interest in the language during and after the First World War all demonstrate a non-linear history of German-language education in Ontario. They show the changing place of language in two denominational communities still linked to two distinctive ethnic backgrounds.

At the institutional level, St Jerome's was a bilingual German and English space in the 1880s and 1890s. However, in the classroom, English stood in the foreground. The annual catalogues in this period noted that all classes except German and philosophy were taught in English, adding that "the greatest attention is given to a thorough instruction in this all-important language [English]." The philosophy course was taught in Latin.[57] Nevertheless, despite the college's overwhelming attention to English in the curriculum, the annual publications also noted that "the conversational languages are English and German," and that "as the college is situated in a German district, and about one-half of the students being usually of German extraction, exceptional facilities for the acquisition of the German language, under German teachers, are offered in this institution."[58] This college's leaders drew their own boundaries of ethnicity.

Nevertheless, at the turn of the twentieth century, the college began to move away from its previous promotion of German outside the classroom. The directorships of John Fehrenbach starting in 1901 and Albert Zinger in 1905 mark a watershed moment for the place of the German language at St Jerome's. Until this point, the presidents of the college had been Ludwig Funcken and then Theobald Spetz, who was born in Canada West in 1850 to a German-speaking family, educated at St Jerome's, and was proficient in German. When the younger, Ontario-born priests, Fehrenbach and Zinger, took over the college after 1901, they implemented a greater interest in English while not removing German completely.

The shift away from German at St Jerome's can be observed in many ways. The college's description of itself as a place that taught German "under German teachers," and its description of Berlin as a "German district," ceased in 1901.[59] By 1909, the directors further distanced the college from an interest in fostering bilingualism. From this year onwards, the annual catalogues informed prospective students and their parents that the college sought to "cultivate the proper use of the English language," and these sources made no reference to German.[60] Whereas in the 1880s and 1890s German and English were described as the "conversational languages" of a college that taught the majority of its courses in English, by the early twentieth century the presence of German was limited to one of many subjects taught at the college. These linguistic changes could be found at other Catholic colleges in Ontario in the same period. After navigating a similar path for several decades, in 1926 the French-speaking Oblates who ran the University of Ottawa split their administrative structure into two linguistic sections. The separate, English-language St Patrick's College was created in 1929.[61]

The annual closing exercises at St Jerome's reveal both the German-English duality and the shrinking place afforded to German. In the 1880s and 1890s, these events featured speeches in both languages, and the college glee club sang several songs in German and English.[62] Towards the end of the century, the German speech remained, but it lost its status as one of two valedictories.[63] Starting in June 1900, the German speeches no longer formed a part of the pageantry at the closing exercises.[64] Moreover, the closing exercises in the late nineteenth century had always concluded with both a common Catholic song, "Großer Gott wir loben Dich!" (Te Deum or the Ambrosian Hymn), and then "God Save the Queen!" However, the singing of a German church song stopped in 1901.[65] It is worth noting that when German was used in song it was linked to religion, whereas English was linked to the state and civic belonging. Music was a central element of these year-end performances, and German songs and classical music written by German composers remained an important part of this spectacle. Similar to the case of German-language singing societies in Ontario and in many locations in the Great Lakes region, these annual events at St Jerome's College were an important site of performing German ethnicity.[66]

It is difficult to track the causes of the college's shift toward English, but it is worth noting that German remained present despite its diminished position. It appears that the shift was mainly the result of internal forces, and there do not appear to be pressures from the state or the broader society, or evidence of parents demanding greater attention to English. During the 1890s, the college became more multiethnic with a growing proportion of English- and Polish-speaking students. As a result of provincial language policies, the students who arrived at the college by the 1890s also had come through a largely monolingual, English-language elementary education. Nevertheless, by promoting both linguistic and religious pluralism, St Jerome's made ethnic space within the educational landscape of Ontario.

While German was a key aspect of this college's program, it was most importantly a Catholic college in English Canada. In the classroom itself, even in the 1880s and mirroring what one finds in Ontario's elementary and secondary schools, St Jerome's promoted English. The college offered five separate English courses (reading, spelling, grammar, composition, and penmanship) as well as arithmetic, bookkeeping, geography, history, natural philosophy, and religion. German, French, Polish, Italian, algebra, and some other subjects were optional.[67] The classical stream resembled the commercial course, but it lasted five years and had several additional subjects. Moreover, it had a strong emphasis on Latin. Similar to the commercial course, the classical stream taught "English in all its branches," as well as German, Greek, history, geography, arithmetic, algebra, geometry, natural sciences, music, religion, and professional courses such as penmanship, bookkeeping, shorthand, and typewriting.[68] When the classical course was split into a high school and four-year arts course in 1901, the arts course retained the classical educational model that focused on Latin, Greek, German, French, and philosophy.[69] German was taught in both the high school and college arts course that replaced the classical course. The strong emphasis on English for the business stream and the larger place allotted to German in the classical and later high school and arts courses reveal a somewhat diglossic situation between German and English. English alone was promoted for a career in business, while German was only promoted among those seeking a more philosophical training, often leading to the priesthood.

The overall goals of each level of instruction and the textbooks used reveal that St Jerome's promoted a higher level of German than that found in the elementary and secondary schools of Ontario. This institution was a far greater promoter of a balanced bilingualism between English and

German than the state-controlled elementary schools, which retained the title of "German schools" largely as vestiges of nineteenth-century legislation. Moreover, while provincial elementary schools had few teachers capable of teaching German, a large majority of the Resurrectionist priests teaching at St Jerome's were capable. The subjects that each priest taught rotated over the years, and numerous priests taught the German classes. This small, elite college created an ethnic space where the German language, along with Catholicism, was an important criterion for participation.

The textbooks used at St Jerome's College demonstrate that the institution had much more autonomy than the elementary and secondary schools of the province. In addition to textbooks that used English to explain German, the St Jerome's curriculum included a range of advanced texts. In 1887, the college used *Ahn's Grammar*, which I discussed in chapter 1, along with another grammar that used English to teach German and an advanced biblical history.[70] Throughout the 1890s, it used James Worman's *Elementary Grammar of the German Language*, a textbook produced in the United States that also used English to explain German.[71] Nevertheless, the curriculum also included a textbook exclusively in German, *Elementar-Sprachlehre*.[72] In the upper years of the five-year classical course, moreover, the college used a grammar written in Germany by Johann Christian August Heyse, which in many ways resembled Klotz's 1867 grammar examined in the last chapter. More important than the textbook selection is that the curriculum included not only grammar and translations but also syntax, composition, literature, and stylistics, which depended on additional literary texts and the knowledge of the college's teaching staff.[73]

That St Jerome's offered a high school course that included advanced German and followed with a four-year arts course in German meant that this institution, when instructing young men from German-speaking families, was capable of promoting a relatively advanced written proficiency in German in a way that the lower-level, state-controlled system discussed in chapter 1 could not. In 1907, the high school course at St Jerome's taught more advanced German than the publicly controlled high schools. While the first year included only grammar and exercises, the third and final year also included advanced grammar, prose, composition, and the study of German authors and special texts.[74]

The 1913 college course remained consistent with the classical course offered in the 1890s. Its curriculum included advanced grammar, German texts, composition, essays, and speeches, and it required participation in the St Ludwigs Literarischer Verein (the St Louis Literary Association).[75] Attendance in the German classes reveals that while the college was predominantly an English-speaking institution, a large majority of ethnically German students took the German language classes. In 1907, thirty-two students took high school German while fifty took high school English classes.[76] Because, particularly by this decade, many students did not come from German-speaking families, this data suggests that while everybody studied English, close to everyone who spoke German at home took these advanced German courses. However, during the boom in enrolment in German classes at Berlin's elementary schools with the support of the *Deutscher Schulverein*, students' interest in German at St Jerome's began to decline. In 1911, only twenty-eight studied German in the high school course while eighty took the English courses.[77] This difference reveals the importance of examining specific institutional practices rather group-level changes.

St Jerome's constructed a larger community in Berlin, but this community was defined more by denomination than language. In the two decades before the First World War, theatrical and music groups from the college gave annual performances in English at the Berlin opera house to raise money for the Catholic orphanage in St Agatha, which was run by the School Sisters of Notre Dame.[78] In 1895, the college was one of a few key groups that raised money for the secular Berlin-Waterloo hospital.[79] In both of these cases, St Jerome's supported a broader, non-linguistically defined community. A condition for accepting children at the orphanage was usually Catholic heritage, and the institution undoubtedly provided a Catholic upbringing. However, this was something that neither followed nor constructed linguistic boundaries. Moreover, the Berlin-Waterloo hospital, which received ample financial support from the surrounding community for decades beginning with its founding in 1895, had absolutely no German focus and did not speak of ethnic obligation in its calls for philanthropic support.[80]

The annual commencement activities were public events that garnered the attention of a larger community in the town of Berlin. The college's music teacher between 1905 and 1911, Theodor Zoellner, had been an active leader of the German musical movements at the German-language Concordia Club in Berlin and participated in many German-language singers' festivals in the Great Lakes region.[81] The fact that a leading figure in German-language activities was also involved with the college's public musical pageantry is noteworthy. However, when at St Jerome's, Zoellner was involved in English-language performances.

By 1900, St Jerome's was the local college of a rapidly expanding industrial town. It supported other community institutions and educated some of the male members of the business and professional elite. It infused its male-only education with Catholicism, the German language, and core subjects typical of a classical education such as Latin and philosophy. St Jerome's College, in many ways, was the foundation upon which many of the region's Catholic institutions were organized, and it was the main institution of the Congregation of the Resurrection. This congregation had a great deal of control in the nominally German-speaking areas within the Diocese of Hamilton. By 1900, many Catholic institutions – such as St Jerome's, Catholic social welfare institutions, and different school boards in Berlin, Waterloo, and Waterloo County – operated mainly in English, but the congregation retained its bilingual focus.

A decade after St Jerome's relegated German to classroom instruction only, Waterloo Lutheran brought a new balance between English and German for a different group of young German-speaking men in Ontario, one that was organized around a different denominational community. This reveals that other factors beyond generational change should be considered when examining the relational nature of English and German instruction. The church that supported Waterloo Lutheran played a role. The renewed attention to the language also reveals how Canadian-born German speakers maintained a dual interest in German and English. In the public school system where central state authority opposed German as a language of instruction, few parents, educators, and trustees struggled to carve out a greater space for German. However, when the Lutheran Church actively tried to maintain this duality, many people participated in a project of making ethnic space.

A first point of comparison with St Jerome's is that Waterloo Lutheran kept its records in both German and English between 1911 and 1915.[82]

St Jerome's stopped doing so by 1887. The annual catalogues between 1911 and 1915 were in both languages, and in the records of the Canada Synod the college was discussed in German. From 1915 onward, the Canada Synod's otherwise German-language documentation reported on the finances of the college in English.[83] Of the ten members of Waterloo Lutheran's board of directors, there was both a German and an English secretary to keep the college's records in both languages.[84]

Article 2 of Waterloo Lutheran's constitution stated that "the medium of instruction in the said Seminary shall be German and English and such other languages as may from time to time be approved of or be decided upon by the Board of Management."[85] This remained in the constitution in the 1920s, but the curriculum only included German language classes rather than a bilingual program teaching other subjects in German.[86] In 1912, the college's German secretary and the pastor of Toronto's German Lutheran congregation, Dr A. Redderoth, noted that Waterloo and its twin city Berlin "form the centre of Canadian Germandom and at the same time the centre of German-Canadian Lutheranism."[87] The seminary's curriculum included several courses in theology, philosophy, logic, and history in English as well as Hebrew, Greek, English rhetoric, and German rhetoric.[88] Upon entering the seminary, students had to pass examinations in Latin, Greek, and German.[89]

A shift away from German took place soon after the college's foundation, and this corresponded both with the First World War and the expansion of the college from a seminary to include a high school stream. In 1915, the college department taught German and French "as living languages to be acquired as a medium of communication and as treasure-houses of scientific, theological and literary material."[90] Although this indicates that German was not seen as parallel to English, but rather as a second language, the requirements of the German courses were noticeably higher than the French classes and higher than the level found at elementary and secondary schools as well.[91] The first two years of the high school course included translation, grammar, syntax, and memorization, but the third year included reading Luther's Catechism and "standard German authors."[92] The English level appeared more demanding than German with a focus on prose, poetry, and oratory.[93] Even in the late 1920s, the college continued to teach German at a relatively high level that included an emphasis on translation, reading, grammar, novels, poetry, and the provincially authorized *High School Grammar*.[94] When the college expanded to offer a university arts degree in 1924, it included German as one of the subjects.[95]

The key point to be drawn from Waterloo Lutheran's curriculum is that it was founded to promote German alongside English in 1911 at a moment when St Jerome's had already moved away from the language. Furthermore, Waterloo Lutheran continued to promote the language at a relatively high level and with linguistically capable professors (pastors of German congregations) during the 1920s. The overlapping interest in German and religion at these colleges indicates how both language and denomination constructed and supported ethnicity. A large number of the people who organized, worked at, or funded these colleges were ethnically German, but it was a community organized along denominational rather than linguistic lines that made these colleges. Both colleges carved out a German-language space in a small part of the educational system of Ontario, but fostering bilingualism was just one goal alongside denominational and economic interests.

Conclusion

In the decades between 1880 and 1930, St Jerome's and Waterloo Lutheran Colleges were close to the top of a pyramid that few people reached, while elementary schooling was an almost universal experience. Nevertheless, these two colleges were a part of the educational system of Ontario, and the fact that they were the only two that adequately prepared students with a balanced written proficiency in German and English makes them particularly important for the history of German-language education in the province.

Language and denomination intersected and constructed German ethnicity. In the case of these two colleges and particularly over time, religious goals came to assume a dominant position. Nonetheless, these colleges promoted the German language, and it is because of their autonomy from state regulation that they succeeded in doing so. The communities that supported them did not organize solely along linguistic lines. In their origins, the Catholic and Lutheran leaders involved in creating these institutions of higher education happened to be German-speaking. In many ways, they infused their Canadian colleges with important elements of their ethnicity. Yet religion was their primary interest, and over time the original and strong focus on German dissipated.

In the 1880s and 1890s, St Jerome's College actively promoted the German language in the classroom and in the social spaces of the institution. Although German was a subject rather than a medium of instruction, it was part of the institutional fabric. What had been a broad presence of the German language shifted, however, by 1901 to a focus specifically on German language classes. German remained a subject of instruction over the next three decades. The First World War had an impact on both colleges, but so did many other factors. The surging presence of English did not begin in 1914, and people's interest in German did not disappear by 1918, let alone in 1930. These colleges' curricula reveal that German had a weaker footing in 1920 than it did in 1910, but it also shows that Ontario society did not require the total elimination of German because of the war.

Both colleges were exclusively male spaces. They mirrored and reinforced the gendered values ascribed to higher education in this period. The fact the directors of these two colleges in Ontario created an institution solely for men implies that they removed half of the people necessary for constructing a sustainable German community over time, and as a result the creation of a linguistically defined community was not their goal. As the only two educational institutions in the entire province capable of promoting an advanced and balanced proficiency in written German and English, it is telling that only young men were eligible to attend. In many ways, this means that neither college sought the long-term maintenance or generational transmission of the language but rather sought to ensure that a small elite was capable enough to navigate between the traditional needs of German and the modern economic and professional benefits of English.

In the next chapter, I turn my attention to another way that ethnicity, language, and belonging coexisted well beyond the control of government education policies. Focusing on Lutheranism in Ontario and its deep connections to other German speakers in the United States, it shows important cross-border connections that supported German-language communities in Ontario into the 1920s.

4. THE BOUNDARIES OF RELIGION

German Lutheranism in Ontario and the United States

In 1886, a twenty-four-year-old Emil Hoffmann immigrated from Kropp, Schleswig, Germany to Wellesley, Ontario. A native of a small town in the Harz Mountains, he had studied in nearby Halle and did his seminary training in Kropp, 120 kilometres north of Hamburg. Hoffmann quickly became a leading figure in the Lutheran Canada Synod, the largest German-language institution in Canada in the early twentieth century. Between 1902 and 1920 he served as its president.[1] Over his career he led a number of the synod's most important congregations, such as the German Lutheran parish of Hamilton from 1889 until 1904, St Matthäus in Berlin from 1904 to 1912, and the Trinitatis congregation in Toronto from 1912 to 1920. In that year, Hoffmann moved to Waterloo to become the president of Waterloo Lutheran College, a position he held until soon before his sudden death in 1926.[2] Through his leadership in the Ontario-wide synod and his involvement in missionary activities in Manitoba, Hoffmann circulated within a large spatial network in Ontario and Canada.

At the same time, he also engaged in a larger North American network. Beginning early in his career in Ontario, he became a member of the German Home Mission Board of the US-based General Council, and in 1913 the Toronto pastor became the president of the board, making him a key figure in North American, German-language Lutheranism.[3] In 1911, Thiel College in Greenville, Pennsylvania bestowed upon him an honourary title of doctor of divinity.[4] A year before his death, Hoffmann briefly returned to Germany for the first time in four decades as a representative of the Canada Synod and the Philadelphia-based General Council to participate in the World Lutheran Conference in Eisenach.[5]

Emil Hoffmann lived in a transnational world. He came to Ontario because of institutional connections established in the 1880s between the Canada Synod, the General Council, and the seminary in Kropp. He met and corresponded with representatives of German Lutheran synods in the United States on a regular basis over his four decades as a pastor, synodical president, and leader of a loosely defined ethno-religious community in Ontario. As Hoffmann's case and this chapter show, German-language religious communities were linked together over a large space, transcending national borders. Those connections show how many German speakers in Ontario imagined and experienced their belonging in the province, country, and continent, and how both the local and the transnational shaped the practice of German ethnicity over the half century between 1880 and 1930. The nature of the connections changed over time, but there were also many continuities.

In this chapter, I argue that a large spatial network supported the creation and maintenance of German-language Lutheran communities in Ontario. German-language institutions were constructed and redefined in ongoing processes that crossed in and out of Canada's political boundaries, and this had a significant impact on the nature of the German ethnicity found in these institutions and the communities that organized around them. Ties to German speakers in large centres in the United States were one of the reasons that the German language remained ingrained in the institutional fabric of Ontario's Lutheran churches into the 1920s.

I focus solely on Lutherans for several reasons. Although German speakers in Ontario belonged to a number of denominations, Lutheranism was the single largest. In the competing Canada Synod and Canada District of the Missouri Synod, German speakers benefitted from complete autonomy in a way that German-language, Catholic parishes did not. The same lack of autonomy could be found among a variety of German-language, Protestant congregations in Ontario, such as Baptists or the Evangelical Association, that were part of larger English-language church bodies. Lutherans, like Mennonites, represent an important case study in how an autonomous ethnic institution was able to focus on language and reinforced ethnic ties. Organized religion formed a second pole – parallel to the state – that constructed ethnicity in Ontario society. However, whereas the provincial state played a dominant role in shaping the educational experience of children in Ontario, Lutheran church bodies pulled German speakers into a broader cross-border network and fostered the use of the German language.

A denomination – Lutheranism – centrally concerned with the ethnicity of its parishioners and one that kept its records in German rather than English complicates the narrative about the rise of organized religion in Canada. The emergence of Lutheran institutions coincided with the spread of organized Christianity in Ontario.[6] On the one hand, this reveals that within an institution that served as an anchor for language maintenance and a cornerstone of many local ethno-religious communities, the Lutheran Church joined in a process at a similar rate and to a similar degree as other English-speaking denominations in the province. On the other hand, organized Lutheranism in Ontario depended on ethnic ties and on strong connections with more developed institutions in the United States. In this sense, a theologically mainstream denomination did not match the late nineteenth-century centralization in Toronto of the Canadian Presbyterian, Methodist, and Anglican Churches.[7] The story illustrated by German-speaking Lutherans and Catholics is one that mirrored the experience of many immigrants. Any group whose denominational origins did not match the English-Canadian triad of Presbyterianism, Methodism, and Anglicanism established church structures more comparable to the case of Lutherans. Moreover, a fundamental aspect of the Catholic Church has been to offer a range of services to immigrants in their preferred language, and thus Catholicism shares aspects of the relationship between religion and ethnicity as well.

The General Council and the Missouri Synod were parallel Lutheran bodies that did not coordinate their activities. Lutheran congregations belonged to only one of these organizations. The Canada Synod was an important but single participant in the larger, US-based General Council, which grouped together many Lutheran synods in North America. The Canada District was a part of the Missouri Synod, a rival church body to the General Council, and these institutional structures likewise bound German speakers in Ontario to a North American world. Within the hierarchy of the General Council, there were synods, which were relatively autonomous church bodies that cooperated within an overarching organization. Synods, in turn, comprised individual congregations, which also had the power to leave the synod and to have a certain degree of local variation. By joining a synod, however, a congregation agreed to participate in the common goals of the people of other congregations. Still, the Missouri Synod was the highest body within its own structure, comparable to the General Council. Below the Missouri Synod, there were districts rather than synods, and below districts there were congregations.

There were theological differences between the General Council and the Missouri Synod, but in this period they both were deeply connected to their German origins and had similar views about the importance of the German language for their denomination. The Missouri Synod was more conservative, and its leaders sought to more closely follow two foundational documents for the Lutheran faith, namely the Augsburg Confession (1530) and the Book of Concord (1580). Its leaders were concerned about slippage between Lutheranism and other Protestant denominations.

There were other Lutheran bodies in the United States at this time. In 1867, the General Council had broken away from the General Synod (founded in 1820). Both the General Council and the United Synod of the South (formed in 1863) left the General Synod in part because of tensions over slavery and the Civil War. The General Council, with its new autonomy, could also refocus on German at a moment when the General Synod had begun to lose its initial linguistic focus. The three reunited in 1918 to form the United Lutheran Church in America, a predecessor to the Evangelical Lutheran Church in America (formed in 1988). In 1986, the Evangelical Lutheran Church in Canada also grew out of the United Lutheran Church in America.

German Lutherans in North America

Lutheran congregations in Ontario did not spring up organically from within the local German-speaking population, but rather emerged as the result of a concerted effort by other German-speaking Lutherans in the

United States. This relationship ignored national boundaries and drew German-speaking residents in Ontario into a North American structure. Pittsburgh, St Louis, Philadelphia, and New York – all cities with large, German-speaking populations in the late nineteenth century – stand out as important hubs that influenced how German-speaking communities in Canada developed and maintained themselves over time.

There was no direct correlation between the rise of Lutheran congregations in Ontario and the arrival of German-speaking immigrants in the province between 1800 and 1870s. The 1880s mark a crucial step in this process as the congregations in Ontario more firmly established their own institutional structure while still maintaining strong ties to the United States. The Pittsburgh Synod was the first Lutheran body to come to Ontario, and in the 1850s its pastors founded a number of congregations.[8] In 1861, these Ontario congregations amicably left the Pittsburgh Synod and formed the Canada Synod. In 1880, the Pittsburgh Synod continued to send delegates to the annual meeting of the Canada Synod.[9] As late as 1882, the president of the Canada Synod, Fr Veit, described Pittsburgh as the mother synod (*Muttersynode*).[10] In a similar vein, starting in 1901 fourteen congregations left the Canada Synod and joined the English-language Synod of New York and New England because these Ontario congregations had officially become English-speaking.[11] However, the reestablishment of institutional ties with American synods was short lived. In 1909 these English-language congregations formed the Synod of Central Canada, which maintained good relations with the German-language Canada Synod. In 1909, the two Ontario bodies began working together to found the Waterloo Lutheran Seminary, and in 1925 they merged and retained the name of the larger Canada Synod.

The Missouri Synod also began missionary work in Ontario in the mid-nineteenth century.[12] The Canada District's founder, A. Ernst, had come from the United States in 1867.[13] The congregations that its pastors founded formed the Canada District of the Missouri Synod in 1879.[14] The spread of districts was the standard practice for the Missouri Synod as it expanded across the United States and into the Canadian Prairies. By 1914, in stark contrast to the regional activities of the General Council that bound together many German speakers in the area around New

York and Pennsylvania, the Missouri Synod had twenty-two synodical districts in the Americas, as far south as Argentina, along with missions in Europe, Asia, and Australia.[15]

The missionary work of the Pittsburgh and Missouri Synods in the mid-nineteenth century followed ethnic lines. The members of the newly founded congregations were German speakers, and generally they were either "lapsed" Lutherans or Lutherans without a place of worship. In this early period and unlike most other Protestant churches in North America, two key criteria defined this Lutheran missionary work: missionary subjects generally had to come from some degree of Lutheran tradition and they had to be German-speaking. By 1900, as many German congregations became bilingual, the second criterion became less important. The growing acceptance of English was the result of generational changes and the arrival of Lutheran immigrants to Ontario from Scandinavia and the Baltics.

The foundation of the Canada Synod in 1861 and the Canada District in 1879 did not mark the end of the relationship between German-speaking Lutheran communities in Ontario and the United States. In 1866 and 1867, the Canada Synod was a founding member of the General Council along with the Pittsburgh Synod, the New York Ministerium, and the Pennsylvania Ministerium.[16] Even as the General Council grew, these four Lutheran bodies, including one in Canada, remained the four largest.[17] The General Council was one of four main Lutheran Church bodies in the United States, which would slowly develop into two Lutheran Churches.[18] At the turn of the twentieth century, the General Council contained both German- and English-language synods, including the Synod of New York and New England and the Synod of Central Canada. The German-language Canada Synod sent delegates to the annual meetings of the General Council. It cooperated with the council in charity work for Lutheran orphanages and an immigrant home in New York, in missionary activities among German immigrants in North America, and on missionary work in India. After 1910, the Canada Synod and other synods abandoned their individual publications and produced together a German-language Lutheran periodical in Philadelphia, the *Deutsche Lutheraner* (1910–22, succeeded by the *Lutherischer Herold*, 1922–43).[19] Furthermore, the Canada Synod cooperated with the General Council in pastor recruitment from a seminary in Germany and the training of German-speaking North Americans in Philadelphia.

, The cross-border ties between the Canada District and the Missouri Synod remained strong after 1879 as well. Most fundamentally, the district continued to be part of the institutional structure of the US-based synod. The Ontario congregations participated in the Missouri Synod's missionary work to German speakers in the United States and the Canadian Prairies, and the congregations supported social welfare organizations in the United States such as orphanages and immigrant homes. The pages of the *Lutherisches Volksblatt*, published by Canada District pastors in Ontario, referred regularly to the news and struggles of the Missouri Synod, described the flow of pastors between the synod's districts, and included many subscribers in the United States.

German-speaking Lutherans in Ontario drew from the cultural production of German America. The cities of Philadelphia, St Louis, New York, and Pittsburgh served as hubs for the production of many aspects of religious and secular German culture in the United States.[20] Much of this material found its way into Ontario. Some news stories from German-language American daily newspapers were reproduced into Ontario's German-language weeklies such as the secular *Berliner Journal* and *Deutsche Zeitung*, and the religious *Kirchen-Blatt* and *Lutherisches Volksblatt*. Many German textbooks written by German-American academics and published in these American cities found their way into Ontario's elementary schools. German-language bibles and songbooks used in Ontario came through the institutional framework created between the Lutheran congregations of the Canada Synod and Canada District and their overarching church bodies. While German Catholics would not have had a bible in the vernacular, they would have had prayer books and hymnals in German. By the 1880s, few if any of the German-language religious texts used in Ontario came from Germany, and thus it was the ties to German America that fostered the use of the German language north of the border.

The ties between Ontario and St Louis could be seen in other ways. The Ontario-based, bi-weekly *Lutherisches Volksblatt* regularly published the names of all readers who renewed their subscriptions, which revealed that the paper had a large circulation in the United States. In 1915, the paper had a circulation of 1,000, and the editors suggested that one in two households in the district received the paper.[21] The *Lutherisches Volksblatt* regularly carried out theological attacks on the teachings of the Canada Synod as well as those of the New York and Pennsylvania Ministeria.[22] The paper and the Canada District emphasized a version of Lutheranism that involved a specific interpretation of Martin Luther's ideas as well as the Augsburg Confession and the Book of Concord.[23]

In promoting its theology and its own version of what the Lutheran denomination should be, the paper and the district drew thousands of German speakers in Ontario into a North American debate. In advancing their theological views, pastors in Ontario specifically and repeatedly discussed other Lutherans in the United States. Moreover, in making this theological argument, the Canada District's pastors did more than emphasize the use of German in all institutional functions until the early twentieth century; their reference to Martin Luther, the Augsburg Confession, and the Book of Concord also bound their denomination to people, events, and texts from sixteenth-century Germany. In so doing, the Canada District blended followers' denominational identity with their ethnic heritage.

The Home Mission

Throughout this period, local congregations and the two Ontario-wide Lutheran bodies engaged in missionary work to integrate people with some loose affiliation to the Lutheran denomination into their local congregations. The lay and pastoral Lutherans involved in the home mission sought to improve church attendance, but they also sought to establish a web of Lutheran charities across North America. Charities were an essential component of this missionary work because social welfare services would represent Lutheran values and instill in recipients a range of religious mores. The Lutheran leadership of Ontario infused in its missionary work ideas of language and lineage, almost exclusively targeting German-speaking, non-practising Lutherans. This group consisted of German speakers with some connection to a Lutheran tradition, but to simply call them Lutherans would be to impose on them a homogenizing view of faith and ethno-religious identity. The ultimate goal of this missionary work was not to spread Lutheranism so much as to preserve it and to draw together a group defined by its heritage.

Bilingual Lutherans in Canada and the United States spoke of the *innere Mission* in German and the "home mission" in English. In Germany in this period, the term *innere Mission* described what many English North Americans called the home mission, namely proselytizing and social reform. As such, it was a clear translation of the concept. However, in Canada and the United States, the Lutheran *innere Mission* focused specifically on lapsed Lutherans and social welfare and reform aimed at German speakers, not people of other ethnic backgrounds. As a result, this home mission was decidedly different from the home missions of other North American Protestant denominations. The home mission existed in contrast to the "heathen mission" (*Heidenmission*) or "foreign mission" which will be examined shortly.

In the Canada Synod's records during the three decades before the First World War, the home mission in places such as Toronto, northern Ontario, and Manitoba was aimed at "fellow believers" (*Glaubensgenossen*). However, since these "believers" did not have any organized religion and had to be the target of the synod's missionary activities, the concept of *Glaubensgenossen* was more complex than making contact with believers. Pastors had a clear preference for the German language, and the missionary or itinerant pastors typically founded German-language congregations. Fellow believers' linguistic abilities and heritage are what motivated this missionary work, and these ethnic markers defined who should be Lutheran. Missionaries and those in southern Ontario who supported them believed that inaction risked "losing" German speakers unconnected to organized Lutheranism to another denomination.

The synod supported small congregations in Toronto and Hamilton as a way to target recent German immigrants, and the two cities attracted a significant portion of the synod's missionary activities. In 1892, E.M. Genzmer, a pastor from the main Toronto congregation, began missionary work in the Junction, an industrial area in the western part of the city. He reported to the synod at the annual meeting, however, that "the expected arrival of many German fellow believers [in this neighbourhood] has not taken place."[24] He decided to temporarily abandon the "West Toronto Mission," but he hoped that new German immigrants would join his downtown congregation.[25] In 1900, pastors J.F. Bruch and P.W. Müller began efforts to found English-language Lutheran congregations in larger Canadian cities as a way to engage with a new generation of Canadian-born Lutherans and to welcome new Lutheran immigrants who were not German speakers.[26] This led to the creation of the English-language St Paul's congregation in Toronto in 1906, led by P.W. Müller, alongside the continuation of the synod's German-language congregation.[27]

The leaders of the Canada District also hoped to expand in Toronto and Hamilton. In 1911, an article in the *Lutherisches Volksblatt* described Toronto as the new field of work for the district and spoke of the importance in succeeding in this project.[28] In 1911, W.C. Boese, the pastor of the Berlin congregation, happily reported in the *Volksblatt* that the Canada District would help the small congregation in Toronto to finance the construction of a church.[29] As a result, a small part of the contributions from every congregation in the province was funnelled to the church project for the sake of expanding the spatial network of German-language Lutheranism, making inroads in Toronto, and ensuring that German-speaking Lutheran immigrants stayed Lutheran and German. The Canada District's attempted expansion into Toronto and Hamilton faced off against the two congregations of the Canada Synod, which had been founded in 1851 and 1858 and which were noticeably larger.[30]

In 1903, W. Weinbach reported that the Canada District's missionary activities in Hamilton had not been particularly successful. He lamented that whereas in the past the pastor alternated weekly between English and German, in recent months people had requested that only English services be held.[31] By 1908, a full-fledged English-language congregation had been founded in Hamilton while work in German floundered.[32] The district's missionary work in Toronto began in 1902, but two different pastors struggled to gain a foothold. They ministered in both German and English to gain more members.[33] By 1910, the district had succeeded in founding a bilingual congregation, St John's Evangelical Lutheran.[34]

German immigration to northern Ontario encouraged the synod's leaders to spread the home mission to a larger spatial network. In 1910, the head itinerant pastor, M. Hamm, reported that immigration to northern Ontario was increasing rapidly and that the synod would need to found many congregations. The main reason for this, according to Hamm, was that it "is the holy duty of our synod to carry out the work of the Lord in New Ontario so that our brothers of stock and faith [*Stammes- und Glaubensgenossen*], our sons and daughters, do not fall into the hands of sects."[35] The use of the term *Stammesgenossen* (*Stamm* translates as tribe, stock, stem, or phylum) presents a certain racialized understanding of Germanness; it suggests that Lutheran leaders in Ontario saw a permanence to their ethnicity. Even when people involved in the home mission used English, the majority of the people that the pastors sought to bring into new congregations were of German heritage.

As an increasingly common destination for German-speaking immigrants between 1880 and 1914, Manitoba became an important site of the home mission for the Canada Synod and the Canada District. A spatial network extended from the missionary work in Muskoka northwards in Ontario, and then on to Manitoba. The Canada Synod began the Winnipeg Mission in 1890. The pastor there was one of the synod's seven missionary pastors, with one each in Auburn and Walkerton in western Ontario, one each in Denbigh and Elmwood in northern Ontario, one in Muskoka, and one in Thorne Centre in northwestern Quebec.[36] The average German Lutheran in southern Ontario was connected to the Winnipeg Mission and these other sites through small financial contributions that every congregation sent to the synod. The synod's official organ, the *Kirchen-Blatt*, also reported regularly on the progressive growth of organized German-language religion in Manitoba, and this bound Ontario to this larger German-language, discursive space.[37]

In 1891, however, the Canada Synod turned over the administration of the "northwest mission" to the General Council because of the high costs, which means that the US-based organization took the lead in missionary work in Canada west of Ontario.[38] The *Kirchen-Blatt* continued to report on the missionary work there, and the synod remained an important participant in that project. In 1899, the Winnipeg Mission developed into the autonomous Manitoba Synod, which then became a member of the General Council. The *Kirchen-Blatt* continued to report on the spread of Lutheranism and this home mission, thereby maintaining the connection between southern Ontario and Manitoba.[39] The Canada Synod and the German Home Mission Board of the General Council continued to support the new Manitoba Synod.[40] By 1902, it had thirteen pastors, sixty congregations, and 5,833 congregants.[41]

The Canada District of the Missouri Synod began missionary activities in Manitoba in the 1890s as well. The pages of the *Lutherisches Volksblatt* kept Lutherans in southern Ontario regularly informed about the missionary efforts they were supporting.[42] The periodical often contrasted these activities with the missionary work carried out in Alberta by an itinerant Missouri Synod pastor from Montana.[43] By 1915, while the spread of the home mission in Manitoba was still a prominent part of the news in the *Lutherisches Volksblatt*, the congregations there had come under the charge of the Minnesota District and out of the hands of the Canada District.[44] The multiple sites of cross-border connections further highlight the North American nature of these German-language institutions in Ontario and the Canadian Prairies.[45]

Charities were another aspect of the cross-border connections. Between 1880 and 1930, a web of Lutheran charities tied the congregations of the Canada Synod and Canada District to large cities in the United States. These Lutheran charities and social welfare services were organized at the synodical rather than congregational level. And many of these services were run and funded in conjunction with the Canada Synod's and the Canada District's parent organizations in the United States. This network was part of the home mission that targeted mainly working-class German speakers, often recent immigrants. Charities and welfare services received a noteworthy amount of attention in German-language congregations and the Lutheran press in Ontario. With small donations specifically for charitable causes, German speakers actively participated in a larger Lutheran world. A North American network of institutions provided social welfare along ethno-religious lines, and this vantage point offers a glimpse into an area of study that rarely considers the role of ethnic minorities as active promoters of social welfare – as opposed to recipients of paternalistic moral and social reform campaigns led by Canadian elites.[46]

Orphanages offer a particularly salient site to track the intersection of ideas about religion and language in the construction of German ethnicity in North America. In a variety of sources dealing with children, there appeared the idea that a child could be "lost" or somehow denied what should be a natural part of his or her cultural identity. Such a viewpoint asserts the primacy of lineage over actual linguistic abilities and assumes that ethnicity is a permanent rather than unstable category.[47] The creation of Lutheran orphanages ensured that a child of German parents would be given vital aspects of his or her cultural heritage. As early as 1880, the Canada Synod began making small contributions to a Lutheran orphanage in Buffalo.[48] This relationship remained constant until the First World War, but starting in 1911, the Canada Synod also began to fund its own orphanage.[49]

Both the General Council and the Missouri Synod both founded an immigrant home in New York City.[50] Russell Kazal has argued that the Pennsylvania Ministerium's home mission in Philadelphia took an interest in Americanizing a variety of immigrant groups as a way for middle-class Lutherans to assert their own "old-stock" American identities.[51] The two immigrant homes in New York appear, however, to have had a stronger ethnic focus. Throughout this period, the pages of the Canada Synod's *Kirchen-Blatt* and the Canada District's *Lutherisches Volksblatt* included advertisements for immigrant homes in New York City. Both papers informed German speakers about the homes' existence and the services they offered, and spread information well beyond the American metropolis that working-class German migrants could seek shelter in these German-speaking, Christian places.

The leaders of the General Council described its home as a site "for the protection and well-being of immigrants and emigrants."[52] The *Kirchen-Blatt* informed its readership in Ontario that the home "offers room and board to immigrants and emigrants at the lowest prices as well as free services necessary for world travel. The home arranges steamer tickets in the cheapest and most honest manner as well."[53] In the 1890s and after the turn of the century, advertisements for the "German Lutheran Immigrant Home" in New York were among a select group of advertisements in the *Kirchen-Blatt*.[54] Supporting this home financially, discursively, and symbolically seemed to be of prime importance for the leaders of the Canada Synod, and in so doing the pastors established an institutional network that went well beyond theological agreement within the General Council.

The immigrant home was part of the larger home mission run by the German Mission Committee of the General Council, a group that was separate from the English-language Mission Committee. Delegates from the Canada Synod to the General Council reported in 1882 that "one thing in particular that should be gratifying for every German Lutheran: in the General Council, a German spirit has begun to advance and it will care for the stream of German Lutheran immigrants so that they are not lost to our church."[55] A year later it was proposed that every congregation in the General Council have an annual collection to support the home mission in New York aimed at new immigrants.[56] The total amount sent by the Canada Synod was small compared to the amount it dedicated to either the Kropp seminary or missionary work in India.[57] Nevertheless, the flow of funds was one tangible marker of these connections between Ontario and larger hubs in the United States. Pastors from many synods often attended the annual meetings of the Canada Synod. On occasion, the pastor in charge of the immigrant home in New York also attended, thereby bringing the leaders of many German-language Lutheran communities in Ontario into contact with this aspect of the home mission.[58]

In 1912, the Canada Synod began to run its own immigrant home in Montreal. Emil Hoffmann complained to the synod in 1913 that efforts had been developing slowly.[59] The lack of immigration during the war further slowed the home's growth. Although immigrants could disembark in Quebec City, Saint John, and Halifax, the synod's leaders reasoned that German-speaking immigrants continued the journey westward by a train that would pass through Montreal.[60] By 1929, the Montreal home had become much more active. Dr Klaehn, the pastor in charge, reported that in the past two decades, approximately 95,000 Lutheran immigrants had landed in Canada, 15,445 of whom had come in that year.[61] Klaehn awaited the arrival of 304 ships and trains, and he made 438 visits to hospitals in Montreal in order to invite working-class, Lutheran migrants to use the services of the immigrant home rather than experiencing the morally problematic city or making use of social welfare services offered by other denominations in Montreal.

The Missouri Synod engaged in similar activities. It ran an "emigrant mission" and a "Lutheran Pilgrim House" in New York City which focused specifically on German immigrants, and the synod often discussed its interest in the ebb and flow of German migration through New York.[62] Although the home also took in Lutherans from other countries, its annual reports explicitly announced the goal of providing services mainly to Germans.[63] Like the *Kirchen-Blatt*, the *Volksblatt* included advertisements on a regular basis, thereby informing German speakers in Ontario about the services the home offered to immigrants and emigrants.[64] It also reminded its readers that the home in New York required the support of the Canada District.[65] The *Lutherisches Volksblatt* told readers that for the Pilgrim House to continue, every congregation in the whole Missouri Synod should have an annual collection.[66] This reveals something about the network behind one institution in New York City and the importance that the synod, the Canada District, and the *Lutherisches Volksblatt* gave to such social welfare activities.

The nature of the expansion of organized Lutheranism requires a spatial analysis. Missionaries from the nearby Pittsburgh Synod founded the Canada Synod and the Missouri Synod founded the Canada District in the mid-nineteenth century. As the new bodies stabilized in the 1880s and 1890s, they began their own missionary activities, spreading northwards and westwards; they founded another synod or district in Manitoba and supported the home mission in New York. Framing missionary work and social reform efforts in spatial terms reveals a rich web of connections that bound local communities to larger provincial, Canadian, and North American scales. Informed by ideas of religion, language, ethnicity, and morality, these two Lutheran bodies dedicated great attention to the home mission. In this way, leaders tied congregants in towns and cities across Ontario to a large spatial network. Linguistic and denominational bonds transcended the Canada-US border and gave rise to two Protestant Churches in Ontario.

Seminaries

Another important transnational influence on German-language religious life in Ontario was through the training and recruitment of pastors. Through the movement of these community leaders, the congregations and their congregants in Ontario were bound to a large North American Lutheran network, one that also had important ties to Germany. In addition to demonstrating how international networks sustained local communities, these connections also show a disconnect between leaders and parishioners. Those advancing certain language practices and producing documents were often newer arrivals than parishioners, especially by 1900.

Germany was the main source of pastors for the Canada Synod. A Lutheran seminary in Kropp, Schleswig existed between 1882 and 1931, and its main activity was training Lutheran pastors for service in North America.[67] John Schmieder, a pastor in Kitchener, estimated in 1927 that the Kropp seminary had trained more than 500 pastors.[68] In 1938, Wilhelm Hermann wrote that the seminar "has been the life-saver of the German-speaking element within our church."[69] Yet he estimated that only 200 pastors came from Kropp to the General Council over its fifty-year existence.[70] In 1883, the General Council's German Mission Committee – something the directors of the Canada Synod described as part of a larger "German spirit within the Council" – entered into an agreement with Kropp's director, Johannes Paulsen. After this point, the synod's directors commonly described the Kropp seminary as "our institution."[71] In 1886, the Canada Synod's *Kirchen-Blatt* reported that although the General Council had colleges and seminaries in the northeastern United States, "these are either completely English or almost completely. In the future, only a few German pastors can and will develop from them and serve our German congregations. And even if it were 2 or 3 – how would that help? It is necessary that we have a German seminary in Kropp."[72] According to J.J. Kündig, in 1886 all of the pastors in the Canada Synod had come from Germany.[73] The way these pastors came to Canada, however, was through the institutional connections that the Pittsburgh Synod and the Pennsylvania Ministerium had with Germany.

Figure 4.1 shows five students at the Kropp seminary before departing for North America. Among them is Max Voelker (1872–1945). Ordained in Germany before departing in 1898, he worked in New Jersey and Pennsylvania until 1910 when he moved to Ontario. He served several churches in Ontario and became president of the Canada Synod for two years starting in 1918. Voelker moved to New York City in 1925.[74] His trajectory – training in Germany and spending his career with the Canada Synod and US counterparts such as the New York Ministerium – mirrored that of many other Lutheran leaders in Ontario.

4.1 Future pastors for the General Council in Kropp, Schleswig, 1897.

The Canada Synod had a strong interest in supporting the German language, and its leaders were concerned about the growing use of English by younger, Canadian-born Lutherans. The continued use of German in many Lutheran congregations into the 1920s – despite clear indications of a language shift to English in many other public domains in Ontario, such as education, newspapers, and business – was linked to the ongoing process that bound Lutheran churches to a larger German-language network. As part III will show, many adult Lutherans in Ontario were active promoters of the German language, while others, particularly children and youth, increasingly preferred English.

In 1886, the General Council gave the seminary in Kropp $9,000 for the construction of a new building.[75] An editor of the Ontario *Kirchen-Blatt* praised this substantial amount of funding and argued that "should German missionary work, German morals, German worship, and true Lutheranism not be crippled, then we need a German seminary."[76] It added that too few young men from the congregations in the Great Lakes region were available to be trained as "German pastors."[77] J.J. Kündig added that all seventy students at the Kropp seminary in 1886 were German (rather than bilingual Americans or Canadians), that they would all become German Lutheran pastors, and that for this reason congregations throughout the General Council needed to raise money.[78] He concluded, "We need capable workers from Germany, who not only can speak German in a jam but who have a German heart and who are enthusiastic about German missionary work."[79] He feared that Canadian-born German speakers were linguistically capable when necessary but that they did not actively seek to carry out German-language missionary work and promote linguistic interests alongside religious ones.

In 1885, the seminary sent eight pastors to North America: one to Ontario, two to the Pennsylvania Ministerium, three to the New York Ministerium, one to the Pittsburgh Synod, and one to Texas. In 1886, the Kropp seminary sent three more pastors to North America, one of whom was Emil Hoffmann, the young pastor who opened this chapter.[80] In 1886, Kropp had fifty-three students and twenty new students were to join later that year. The arrival of new pastors from Kropp continued over the next four decades, as did the relationship between the Canada Synod and the seminary in Philadelphia.[81] The Canada Synod also sent and supported young German-speaking men from Ontario to a Lutheran theological seminary in Philadelphia for their training.[82] In the 1880s and 1890s, the synod gave small scholarships to young men, often the sons of pastors in Ontario who had immigrated from Germany, who upon completing their studies returned to Ontario to be ordained by the Canada Synod and to begin working as pastors.[83]

In 1909, the *Kirchen-Blatt* wrote that "our Canada Synod has relied almost exclusively on Kropp over the past 20 years in order to fill vacancies. In the future the Synod will continue to look to Kropp."[84] In June 1914, Emil Hoffmann wrote in his annual synodical report that "Kropp owes a good part of its existence to our synod,"[85] thereby emphasizing the importance of the Canada Synod within the larger German-language activities of the General Council.

By 1908, five bodies within the General Council were concerned about the changing linguistic character of their congregations. At the "First General Conference of German Pastors of the General Council," pastors from the Canada Synod, the Manitoba Synod, the New York Ministerium, the Pennsylvania Ministerium, and the Pittsburgh Synod met to discuss the creation of a German-language seminary in North America. Attendees resolved that it would be better to train pastors from the United States and Canada, and this was a notable change from Kündig's views in 1886 about the value of pastors trained in Germany. However, the men who attended this conference also decided that the lack of capable young men in North America, according to the criteria of the church leadership, required the synods to draw more from the seminary in Kropp.[86] This was most likely a reference to the linguistic abilities of young men in either North America or Germany.

In 1909, the General Council strengthened its relationship with Kropp and a new agreement was made to govern the latter. Emil Hoffmann represented the Canada Synod in these negotiations with American and German representatives.[87] The pastors who published the *Kirchen-Blatt* described the Canada Synod as "one of the most German in the Council," and they wrote that the synod was, therefore, particularly interested in the relationship with Kropp.[88] The General Council was given the power to approve or reject all instructors working at the Kropp seminary, and the seminary agreed to teach the doctrinal principles of the General Council (the Ministerial Acts). Finally, the pastors established a concrete rule that required all candidates in Kropp to spend an additional year studying at the theological seminary in Philadelphia. In return, the council pledged to support the seminary with $4,000 annually.[89] Throughout this period, the money sent to Kropp came from the constituent bodies of the General Council such as the Canada Synod.[90]

During and after the First World War, the relationship that the Canada Synod had with Kropp via the General Council was weakened but did not end. In 1911 and 1912, the synod sent $800 to Kropp, and in 1914 before the outbreak of war it sent $400. In June 1917, even after the United States had entered the war, the Canada Synod again sent $400 to Kropp.[91] In 1918, the synod was unable to transfer money to Germany, but it earmarked just over $700 for the German seminary.[92] In the same year, the synod spent $3,900 on Waterloo Lutheran College.[93] As late as 1925, the synod sent $350 to Kropp, while its contribution to the growing Waterloo Lutheran College rose to over $13,000.[94] In 1926, after the merger with the Synod of Central Canada, the now officially bilingual Canada Synod sent only $25 to Kropp.[95]

In 1930, the Canada Synod stopped sending money; nevertheless, three new pastoral candidates from Kropp came to Ontario that year.[96] The Canada Synod's delegates to the General German Conference reported that the new pastoral candidates from Kropp should improve their English skills before they take over a congregation, and this requirement attests to the changing nature of the relationship.[97] The connections between the Canada Synod, the General Council, and Kropp brought on average one or two pastors trained in Germany to Ontario each year, and some of these men would later migrate on to congregations in other parts of North America. The Kropp seminary closed in 1931, as the result of its shrinking relationship with church bodies in North America. The seminary could have reoriented its focus to train pastors for careers in Germany or sought to establish new relationships with synods in Latin America or eastern Europe.

After the synods of the General Council joined two other church bodies to form the United Lutheran Church in America in 1918, the new Church did not place German at the forefront the way the General Council had before the war.[98] The German-language synods within the new Lutheran Church by no means instantly or completely removed their linguistic focus as the result of the war or the institutional merger. By joining with other religious bodies and many more synods, the Canada Synod took a significant step away from the autonomy that it previously enjoyed as a German-language organization connected to another German-language organization. A great deal of power remained at the synodical level, but there was no longer a General Council through which several German-language synods could work to maintain a network that advanced the dual goal of linguistic and denominational maintenance.

In the face of the growing need for bilingual pastors to serve both older and younger congregants, the Canada Synod created its own seminary, even as it continued its relationship with Kropp and Philadelphia. The foundation of Waterloo Lutheran Seminary in 1911 marked a pivotal transition in a long process that had kept the many Lutheran congregations of Ontario in close contact with a larger Lutheran world. In 1910, the Canada Synod and the newly founded English-language Synod of Central Canada agreed to work together to found Waterloo Lutheran Seminary. The official decision was delayed a year until 1911 so that the General Council could give its approval. Emil Hoffmann, the president of the Canada Synod, noted that the directors of the General Council felt that the addition of a seminary to the collective group should receive the approval of the other member synods.[99] Other synods could, after all, use this seminary, and a seminary in Ontario would change the relationship between Philadelphia, the Canada Synod, and the Synod of Central Canada. When Waterloo Lutheran Seminary was founded, the two governing synods decided that four men should first approve its charter and constitution: the president of the Canada Synod, the president of the Synod of Central Canada, the president of the German Home Mission Board, and the president of the General Council. This procedural fact reflects the intimate ties between Ontario and the United States and the importance of North American structures in shaping institutions at the local level.[100]

The training and recruitment of pastors played a particularly important role in making and sustaining German-language Lutheran churches in Ontario. Pastors became a tangible marker of the international connections linking the province to both the United States and Germany, but they also gave religious communities in Ontario a steady supply of leaders with an interest in the German language and maintaining connections along linguistic lines.

Missionary Work in India

Congregations in Ontario were not only tied to the United States and Germany but also involved in missionary work in India. Pastors usually described their work amongst German immigrants in Canada as the home mission (*innere Mission*), and it was presented in contrast to the "heathen mission" (*Heidenmission*). Yet unlike other denominations in Canada, the only proselytization done by the Canada Synod and the Canada District to people not of Lutheran heritage took place in a space far removed from the home mission in Ontario, Manitoba, and New York. The spatial separation of these two Lutheran bodies' missions delineated the boundaries of ethnic and non-ethnic activities.[101] In many ways, contrasting the home and "heathen" missions further demonstrates the ethnic focus of these two German-language Lutheran bodies and the ways that the General Council and the Missouri Synod integrated their denomination into North American Protestantism at the same time.

Other Protestant denominations viewed missionary work among Indigenous North Americans and among the peoples of Asia and Africa as part of the same project. For example, the pages of *The New Era*, the periodical of the Missionary Society of the Church of England in Canada, regularly told Canadian supporters about progress and projects in all of the mission's foreign fields (primarily, Japan, China, and India) and in the same issue discussed proselytizing efforts among Indigenous peoples in the Yukon or northern Ontario.[102] By focusing on India but overlooking Japan and China, Lutherans had a reduced global footprint compared to other Canadian denominations.[103] The Missouri Synod in fact did have small missions in the United States, such as the "Indian Mission" in Wisconsin and the "Negro Mission" in Kentucky, but the Canada Synod and the Canada District did not undertake similar projects in Canada. They instead focused only on the German home mission or foreign missionary work in India. Lutheran retention and converting others were spatially separated.

Through the pages of the *Kirchen-Blatt* and the *Lutherisches Volksblatt* and in special financial collections in congregations across Ontario, German speakers were active participants in missionary efforts in India. Both Lutheran publications discussed the importance of the "heathen" mission as a major concern of their churches. Nevertheless, as the *Lutherisches Volksblatt* put it, the home mission was the "main mission of the synod."[104] The dual interest in the home mission and the heathen mission reveals a way that both ethnicity and race informed ideas of religion. As Joshua Paddison has argued about the United States in the nineteenth century, notions of religion and race often overlapped. The label "heathen" was infused with both racial and religious perspectives on American citizenship; both demarcated the boundaries of who could belong.[105]

4.2 Young Women's Missionary Society, St Peter's Evangelical Lutheran Church, Preston, Ontario, ca. 1926–34.

Support of missionary activities required the broader mobilization of local congregants. Young women, such as those depicted in figure 4.2, raised money and spread information about the cause. These young women from St Peter's Evangelical Lutheran in Preston, Ontario and many others fostered community at the local level while connecting themselves to people and ideas thousands of kilometres away.

The editors of the *Kirchen-Blatt* often warned readers that two-thirds of the world's people were either heathens or Mohammedans (*Muhammedaner*), and the subtext of such information was that this should be changed.[106] The *Lutherisches Volksblatt* also worried that there were "still one billion heathens on earth."[107] Conversely, the paper reported happily in 1894 that there were 65,000 native-born Lutherans in British India.[108] Much of the paper's discussion of missionary work in India, however, drew from English-language sources and informed German speakers in Ontario of broader Protestant activities in India. Translating an English-language speech made in London, UK, the

Volksblatt informed readers about the "crisis of the heathens and the duty of Christians." It quoted and translated into German the ideas of an advocate of missionary work, Mrs Bishop, who said that "one billion fellow humans wander in gloom and are in the shadow of death, without God in the world. The natural increase of heathen populations surpasses all of our efforts."[109]

Starting in 1900, the Canada Synod sponsored its own missionary pastor to travel to India where he began missionary work with the Telugu people in the area around Hyderabad. The young pastor, Ernst Neudörffer – who was born in Brazil and came to Canada when he was five years old – published weekly reports about his activities that German speakers in Ontario were funding.[110] His running article "From My Diary" spoke about his cultural encounters and religious work among South Asians.[111] Neudörffer was listed as a full member of the synod like any other pastor in Ontario, and he was noted simply as absent in the annual synodical meetings. Lutheran international missionary work was considerably smaller than that of other Canadian denominations. The Anglican Church, for example, had a separate missionary society, and its missionaries were not members of a specific diocese.[112] Before the Canada Synod sent Neudörffer, it contributed a small annual sum to the larger missionary efforts of the General Council in India, and it continued to do so after it sponsored its own missionary.[113] When the Canada Synod sent Neudörffer in 1900, he was one of twenty missionary pastors in India taking part in the General Council's Telugu Mission. In total, all congregations within the General Council contributed between $40,000 and $50,000 towards this mission each year between 1900 and 1911.[114] In this period, the congregations of the Canada Synod provided approximately $1,000 of this North American total every year, and this surpassed the financial contributions that the synod made to the Kropp seminary.[115]

The Missouri Synod also carried out missionary work in India. The Canada District did not sponsor its own missionary, but congregations in Ontario were connected to this missionary work through the information provided in the *Lutherisches Volksblatt* and through the missionary work coordinated through St Louis. The district's main organ informed readers about the importance of this mission. It disparaged the fact that "in India, for example, millions of people fall before millions of idols and pray to them. Sun and moon, good and evil spirits, and apes and snakes are among this collection of gods."[116]

The Missouri Synod cooperated with a Leipzig-based missionary society on its activities in India.[117] The Leipzig *Tamulen-Mission* (Tamil mission) in southern India began in 1840, seven years before the Missouri Synod was founded in the United States. By the 1880s, the Leipzig missionary efforts in India operated 156 schools. The *Volksblatt* told readers in 1889 that 4,000 children attended, 1,800 of whom were "heathens."[118] In 1894 the Missouri Synod began to organize its own mission in India, and it hoped to rely on the Lutheran Church in Saxony for support when it began.[119]

These connections between congregations in Ontario and people in South Asia and the collaborative efforts between the synods of the General Council or between the Missouri Synod and the Leipzig missionary society reveal another layer of the transnational world that shaped Lutheranism in the United States and Canada. In this case, ethno-religious connections between Ontario and the United States or North America and Germany led to missionary work in India using English and South Asian languages, and it likely fostered or relied on Protestant ecumenicalism once in India. It is through this involvement in missionary work that German-speaking Lutherans integrated their denomination into North American Protestantism.

Conclusion

The institutional network that bound Lutheran congregations into the Canada Synod and the Canada District and then further connected these two bodies to otherwise US institutions influenced local German-language communities. The networks that extended to Pittsburgh, St Louis, Philadelphia, and New York integrated German-language Lutheran communities into an institutional structure otherwise based solely in the United States. German ethnicity was tied to a single but evolving German North America, and German-language institutions in Ontario were intricately bound to the linguistic behaviour of people functioning in another national context.

The similarities between the Lutheran Church and other denominations in Canada – Ontario as a hub for westward expansion, a significant portion of the clergy trained in Europe, the growth of religious social welfare institutions, and foreign missionary work – shows how immigrants participated in key aspects of the religious culture of Canadian society. Yet the ethnic interests that accompanied the spread of Lutheranism suggest that religion and ideas of national belonging in Canada could intersect in a variety of ways not fully recognized by the historiographic focus on English-language denominations. For many people, religious participation and denominational identity created the meaning and boundaries of ethnicity. There was no single German community in Ontario or in any single city or town, and the very existence of German-language Lutheran congregations meant that mutually exclusive communities organized around denomination rather than ethnic heritage emerged.

THREE / Ethnic Practice

What did it mean to be German in Ontario? How did that differ in 1880 and 1930? There are several answers to this question. *Being German* could coexist with being Canadian in the minds of people of German birth or heritage, so being German was not an exclusive category. Perhaps a better question would be: how did people who *were* German, in the many meanings that they and others ascribed to being German, do things that were German? The two chapters in part III focus on ethnic *practice*. In particular, they offer a linguistic history of German speakers, with the aim of contributing a broader theoretical and analytical approach to the study of ethnicity, community, and children in North America.

These chapters focus on the *practice* of German ethnicity rather than the *fate* of German-speaking communities. The chapters are interested first and foremost in how people used the German language, organized along ethnic lines, and viewed the relationship between language, religion, and children. Over time, English became increasingly present in the daily lives of German speakers in Ontario, but between 1880 and 1930, there were many continuities. The processes of integration, acculturation, and assimilation have been mainstays in the historiography on immigration and ethnicity in the Americas. As Adam McKeown notes, "The glory days of assimilation as a central issue in the social sciences are long past. But issues of acceptance and integration still dominate most migration studies."[1] At this point, we can accept that cultural change over generations took place, but that it did not recast newcomers, their children, and their grandchildren into a uniform mould.

Processes of change and adaptation do not mean that cultural pluralism ceases to exist.[2] Here, I seek to analyze how people talked regularly about ethnicity, built institutions, and interacted with the state and participated in a dialogue about ideas of citizenship and national belonging. These were important activities in and of themselves. Rather than framing generational differences as a question of assimilation, it can be helpful to query how children's interest in ethnicity differed from adults' views. Ethnicity mattered for these young actors, but in asserting a new balance between language, denomination, and national belonging, they constructed new meanings for ethnicity. The linguistic transformations shown in chapters 5 and 6 had little to do with the war years in which an anti-German sentiment took hold in Canada. To suppose that the First World War could radically change that is to ascribe far too much importance to a single external pressure from English-speaking society.

Historians of immigration have often used the term *language loss* in their analyses of assimilation and acculturation. However, language acquisition is a process that begins in the home and carries on in schools and society. If a child does not continue to acquire German at school and instead adds a growing vocabulary and literacy in English to his or her limited German, he or she has not necessarily *lost* a language. If a three-, five-, or fifteen-year-old never expresses various concepts in the language of her parents, she has not lost a language but rather missed an opportunity to acquire a language. Any assumption that a "German" child born in North America necessarily speaks German, or that she has lost it if she does not, is informed by turn-of-the-twentieth-century ideas that asserted that genetics defined ethnicity and that ethnic heritage defined one's linguistic abilities. Nationalist community leaders, their contemporary census takers, and education bureaucrats may have held racialized or biological ideas about children's ethnicity and language, but these observations deserve to be analyzed rather than quoted as evidence of linguistic persistence or decline.

The focus on bilingualism and children's linguistic behaviour – that is to say, two forms of ethnic practice – reconceptualize notions of "language loss" and cultural change. Rather than "losing," people who grew up or grew old in Ontario acquired varying degrees of proficiency in German and English. Into the late 1920s, adults continued to speak German while children, particularly those born after 1900, began their lives with another form of bilingualism where English occupied a dominant position.

In this period, many people used the term "mother tongue" to describe genetic inheritance or biology rather than one's dominant language.[3] In so doing, they suggested that one's lineage defined one's linguistic abilities. Those assumptions continue to influence scholarly discussions and interpretations of language and ethnicity. Yet people's behaviour contradicted and undermined the concept of mother tongue on numerous occasions, and particularly by the time the children of immigrants reached adulthood. As Yasemin Yildiz notes, the concept of the mother tongue in nineteenth-century Europe suggested that people and social groups were "organically linked to an exclusive, clearly demarcated ethnicity, culture, and nation."[4] The mother "stands in for the allegedly organic nature of this structure by supplying it with notions of maternal origin, affective and corporeal intimacy, and natural kinship."[5] Yildiz contends that the focus on the "mother" as a predetermined transmitter of language presents this biological figure – rather than social surroundings – as "the single locus of affect and attachment."[6] The fusing of the concept of mother tongue with linguistic behaviour and ability oversimplifies human relations in culturally plural societies.

The belief in German as the mother tongue and the idea that churches offered another point of contact with the German language in addition to the household put women at centre stage in debates about language and denomination. Despite German speakers' use of the terms *Muttersprache* or "mother tongue" in Ontario, German was sometimes not the language of some mothers because of exogamous marriage patterns. Nevertheless, that did not necessarily remove a child from a bilingual speech community. In their actions, children themselves – despite the protestations of adults – also rejected the idea that a biological or first language had to be their dominant language or the language of emotional meaning. Chapter 5 focuses on how both German and English were used in church activities, whether devotional or social, and on the discourse about religion as a cornerstone of

German ethnicity. Chapter 6 tracks the growing formalization of bilingualism in religious organizations. Both chapters analyze the role of children and youth in these transformations and the efforts of adults to strike a balance between the competing interests of various members of German speech communities.

5. THE LANGUAGE OF RELIGION
Children and Denominational Identity

Can one complain if we want our children to retain the splendid heritage of the mother tongue and with it all of the exquisite treasures that our church calls its own such as its prayers, songs, and liturgy? Certainly not.

Kirchen-Blatt, 14 January 1909, 7.

In the winter of 1891–92, Toronto's city council debated prohibiting streetcar service on Sundays. The ensuing discussion revealed much about ideas of labour, sociability, morality, and religiosity. Yet at least one of the city's many ethnic minorities perceived this proposal in an entirely different light. A special correspondent in the *Deutsche Zeitung*, one of Ontario's German-language weeklies, implored readers to take an interest in the matter. The author worried that 6,000 German "souls" were scattered across the city and "since very few of them have the luxury to pay for a coach, the use of streetcars on Sundays is a comfort that many do not treasure enough."[1] The author suggested that the proposed bylaw would have a particularly negative impact on the city's "German church" – meaning the local Lutheran congregation – because of the distances that many people had to travel to attend weekly services. He worried that "particularly the children of Germans would be harmed because they would be unable to attend German Sunday school; they would visit the English church schools nearer to their homes and as a result they would be lost to Germandom."[2]

Many German speakers in Ontario drew strong connections between language and their religious institutions. Whether Lutheran or Catholic, they stressed that language supported their denomination, the nature of their communities, and the meaning of German ethnicity. Ideas about language and religion, in turn, fostered the lasting presence of German ethnicity in the province. These ideas were particularly salient when children were involved. Children's linguistic abilities in German were influenced in part by the pervasive presence of English in their lives and in ways that adult immigrants' linguistic abilities were not. For practising Lutherans and Catholics, children of German heritage needed to acquire an advanced proficiency in German. Yet children often had different ideas. For many, denominational identity and linguistic ability were not as related as adults asserted. Over time, German and English became the language of religion for congregations and communities labelled by themselves and others as "German."

This chapter argues that both children's autonomy and adults' strategies shaped the nature of German-English bilingualism in Ontario. It explores the language of religion for practising Lutherans and Catholics of German birth and heritage in Ontario between 1880 and 1930. There were notable differences between Lutherans and Catholics in their language use in weekly worship and in the ways religious leaders imparted religious education. Through Lutheran Sunday schools, Catholic and Lutheran youth groups, and state-controlled Catholic elementary schools (discussed in chapter 1), language and denomination interacted in varying ways.

Even in the early decades of this period, the interlocutors who identified with the German language, a German community, and German-language religion were bilingual, and they had differing opinions and uses of German and English. Over time, children of German heritage increasingly chose English over German, but this was not a linear progression. Both denominational differences and the institutional support offered by Lutheran and Catholic churches breathed life into German speech communities in ways that complicate narratives of a group-level language shift.[3] Although religious institutions supported German-English bilingualism in Ontario well into the twentieth century, they often gave priority to their denomination rather than to the German language; for them, language was a tool to foster religiosity.

The bilingual children and youth in this chapter left little written documentation. Pastors and priests – often educated in German-speaking Europe – had a disproportionate amount of power in documenting the language of religion. Working-class parents typically remained outside of the lay leadership of their congregations and therefore were often absent in written records as well. In church records, however, people discussed and worried about the linguistic behaviour and attitudes of children, and these documents described the linguistic composition of the ethnic spaces in which thousands of people habitually participated. Although filtered by adults, the sources do reveal children's linguistic attitudes and ideas about bilingualism. Children had the power to have conversations with adults in either German or English, and in particular to respond in English. As they grew up and interacted with others their age, children could advance their own ideas about the language of religion and the importance of German for their denominational identity.

The nature of extant sources makes it difficult to uncover all children's opinions about language, denomination, and ethnicity. Other historians of childhood have faced similar problems. Neil Sutherland and Mona Gleason have had fruitful results using oral interviews decades after their subjects were children.[4] Cynthia Comacchio has focused both on sources produced by youth, such as diaries, and extensive adult discussion of adolescents' behaviour.[5] Yet as both Sarah Maza and Gleason caution, children's voices (quoted by historians from text or memory) are not necessarily the best or only source we should draw on when documenting young lives.[6] Indeed, much of the discussion that German-speaking adults had about children's linguistic practices focused on children not doing what adults wanted, and in many cases reveals adult complaints about the growing presence of English in children's lives.

Children have agency.[7] Yet as Kristine Alexander cautions, the prevalence of agency in current studies of childhood and youth "needs to be rethought and used far more critically."[8] Steven Mintz contends that "children are clearly social actors ... To be sure, children's agency exists along a spectrum or continuum, and their ability to make choices and decisions and exert influence varies widely depending on a child's age and social and cultural context."[9] And as Maza adds, "the uncanny power of the child has pervaded adults' understandings of their own identity and destiny, offering a plethora of strategies and justifications for the building of national, social, racial, and cultural hierarchies."[10] An imbalance in economic, social, and political power between the German and English languages was a structural factor that influenced the actions of bilingual children and youth. However, that alone does not mean that young, Canadian-born bilinguals did not shape the language of religion for their own reasons.

If children have agency, even if constrained, what could a focus on children tell us about histories of immigration and cultural pluralism? What do children's linguistic practices and abilities tell us about language policies in schools or language practices in institutions such as churches? And what role do little bilinguals play in the history of bilingual institutions? This chapter answers those questions particularly in regard to Lutheran and Catholic churches in Ontario between 1880 and 1930, thereby indirectly offering insights into the changing enrolments and languages of instruction at publicly funded "German schools" in Ontario that appeared in chapter 1 and the bilingual religious colleges that were the focus of chapter 3. It also serves as a case study that could cast light on other histories of immigration and ethnic communities in North America in this period. In addition to generational change, which has long been a topic of social historical inquiry, children themselves made and remade the boundaries of ethnicity.

Sunday Schools

A central feature of Lutheran churches in Ontario between 1880 and 1930 were German-language Sunday schools. In promoting Protestant mores, values, and piety, German-speaking pastors, church leaders, and female and male teachers engaged in a common North American religious activity. Bringing children into Lutheran Sunday schools was also important for the retention of adult members. Brian Clarke notes that at Methodist churches in Canada in the early 1900s, 60 per cent of members were recruited through Sunday schools.[11] If Lutheran churches did not do the same, potential future Lutherans would have joined other denominations. According to Steven Mintz, Sunday schools emerged alongside public schools in the mid-nineteenth century and were part of a growing trend to classify children based on age.[12] Yet these Lutheran Sunday schools also advanced a distinctly ethnic project. Throughout this period and even into the 1920s, Sunday schools became a means for adults to promote German proficiency to a new generation. Through these classes, adults aimed to give young "scholars" the language skills that adults felt met their ethno-religious interests. This German-language, religious education reveals adults' attitudes about language as well as children's agreement with or rejection of these ideas.

German-language Sunday schools were heterogeneous and changing spaces. Because German immigration to most parts of Ontario slowed by the 1880s, the children who attended by the turn of the twentieth century were the offspring of both European- and North American-born German speakers. Particularly in this period's later years, it is likely that for many children and at many of these schools, congregations created a space that promoted a receptive exposure to German (through reading and aural comprehension) more than a space that promoted written and oral production of the language. The linguistic abilities of these young Canadians varied greatly, and a group analysis cannot fully explain children's use of German. At all schools there was also an influx of children of recent immigrants throughout this period, and it is difficult to distinguish between subgroups.

Sunday schools were a fundamental part of Lutheran congregations, and the schools were one of the defining aspects of young churchgoers' experience. They began in the mid-nineteenth century in the early stages of organized Lutheranism in the province. In 1909, in addition to the 11,072 teenagers and adults taking communion or the 4,191 voting members of the various congregations of the Canada Synod (adults), there were 3,986 children and 590 teachers at the congregations' Sunday schools and another 1,237 children and thirty-two teachers at Saturday schools.[13]

Nancy Christie and Michael Gauvreau have argued that "the Sunday school [at Presbyterian, Methodist, and Anglican churches] was explicitly designed to circumvent the family, which was no longer seen to be the crucible for Christian nurture and conversion."[14] They add that "the impact of the rise in importance of the Sunday school within the church apparatus was to reduce the independent control of the family in how they religiously socialized their children and to dramatically enhance the power of the clergy in shaping the religious values of the rising generation."[15] In the case of Lutheran Sunday schools – and as may be the case at any church in Ontario organized around a language other than English – it seems that other factors were in play. Unlike their English counterparts, German-language Sunday Schools also had a clear ethnic and linguistic component. Parents and children had a great deal of power when they decided to participate in Lutheran Sunday schools, and it seems that pastors and the lay committees that ran the Sunday schools were eager to encourage participation. This education could also help parental authority by supporting children's linguistic development in their weaker language, but the one that parents preferred to speak.

In the 1880s, the Canada Synod's *Kirchen-Blatt* made several references to the importance of Lutheran Sunday schools in ensuring that children become proficient in German. In an article copied from an American Lutheran periodical, the *Kirchen-Blatt* worried that parents were sending their children to English-language Sunday schools run by other denominations. Stressing both the linguistic and theological value of Lutheran Sunday schools, its editors told readers, "The German Sunday schools of the Lutheran congregation to which the parents belong and in which the children are baptized has a completely different and more modest and simple environment than other sects, particularly the English ones. [We regret that] many foolish parents support their children in their absurd addiction to become 'English' as quickly as possible."[16]

Such concerns reveal the differing ideas that some adults and children had about language and denomination. The adult leadership of these Sunday schools stressed the need to teach children German, and some parents agreed. These adults tried to find a balance between religious education and their children's desire to speak English. However, other parents supported children in their wishes to reject German. All of these perspectives were legitimate expressions of German speakers' understanding of language, denomination, and ethnicity, and the tension between these opinions reveals how different groups such as children, parents, and religious leaders constructed ethnicity. As the tendency to embrace English in churches at the expense of German grew in the early decades of the twentieth century, congregations began to create

5.1 First Sunday school at Zion English Lutheran Church, Sault Ste. Marie, Ontario, 1924.

English-language Sunday schools in order to balance the interests of parents, religious leaders, and children.

German-language Sunday schools were linked to the larger educational experience taking place at the elementary schools of Ontario in this period. While parents could lobby a local school board to offer German, this was a difficult battle to win for a group if it was not a clear majority in a local area, and even more so because generational differences meant that some people of German heritage had stronger or weaker relationships with the language. The *Lutherisches Volksblatt* worried about the declining place of German in schools and how that would affect religion, noting in 1894 that "since Lutheran children receive Christian teaching in the German language, parents should not miss the opportunity to promote the teaching of German alongside English" at public schools.[17]

Lutheran Sunday schools, such as the one in figure 5.1 in Sault Ste. Marie, dotted the landscape of Ontario in this period. As they shifted to English and shed their interest in German, they also resembled more closely the goals of other denominations in the province.

Around 1910, noting lower-than-hoped-for participation in Sunday schools, officially German-language congregations began to introduce English-language Sunday schools. In 1912, the Lutheran congregation in the town of Waterloo had 350 children and fifty teachers.[18] In that year, it began an English Sunday school with forty children and seven teachers.[19] Emil Bockelmann, the congregation's pastor, noted that "there have been a number of unfortunate changes as a result of limited immigration to our region and now many do not speak enough German to receive a blessed sermon of the Word and the holy sacraments. All instruction in the Public School takes place in English while children are only offered half an hour of German language instruction, and there are marriages with purely English people."[20] Over the next decade and despite Bockelmann's laments, the congregation moved away from German. In 1919, the separate German and English schools were merged into one with two streams, and in 1923 the German stream was fully disbanded.[21]

In 1930, C.S. Roberts, the new pastor at the same church, noted that many parishioners had begun requesting that the German Sunday school return. When he approached several German-speaking families who had immigrated to Waterloo in the 1920s, "it was discovered, however, that most parents were sending their children to our English Sunday School and showed no inclination to make a change because they wanted their children to learn the English language as quickly as possible."[22] Despite some parents' lack of interest in the generational transmission of language, in 1930 Roberts continued to offer one of his three Sunday services in German to adults.[23] The changing linguistic constitution of this congregation between 1912 and 1930 demonstrates a generational division. First the congregation's leadership abandoned its goal of ensuring that all children receive German-language education in Sunday schools; by the end of this period, German-language services appeared to be offered only to an older generation and recent immigrants, while Sunday school and two-thirds of the sermons had become an English-language activity.

In the same period, the St Matthäus congregation in nearby Berlin followed a different path. From its foundation in 1904 until 1918, it operated only a German Sunday school. While the congregation grew steadily, participation in the Sunday school remained relatively constant until 1918, with enrolment fluctuating between 300 and 350 children.[24] Starting in early 1919, however, the congregation began a second, English-language stream, which John Schmieder, the pastor, described as teaching "the religion of our fathers in the language of our country."[25] By 1922, fifty-two women and thirty men taught over 500 children in the two streams.[26] The combined school then swiftly grew to 802 children and eighty-six teachers in 1925.[27] The German stream had approximately 250 children, and Schmieder reported that it was the "largest Sunday school in the Dominion of Canada using the German language exclusively."[28] By 1927, however, Schmieder began to worry about the "the rapid expansion of the English Sunday school."[29] While the English stream added 110 new children in that year, the German stream gained only twenty-three. In the same year, twenty-two teachers taught 133 children in German while fifty-eight teachers taught 448 children in English.[30]

St Paul's Church, a congregation in the same city but a member of the Canada District of the Missouri Synod, began an English stream parallel to the German Sunday school in 1917. Church leaders reasoned that "a great number of children could understand little, if any, German."[31] Both streams remained strong throughout the 1920s.[32] During the 1920s, children's personal preferences and abilities significantly altered the relationship between religion and language, but the decade still witnessed the persistence of the previous balance for some people.

The goals of the German stream in the 1920s reveal many of the changing ideas about the relationship between language, denomination, and children. In 1922, Schmieder reasoned that "to reach the child's heart you must speak to it, not in the language of the schools and universities of the country but in the language of the child's mother." Blending ideas of denomination and mother tongue, he also argued that "happy are the children that may learn the hymns and prayers that mother used to sing and pray in the language that was nearest to mother's own heart."[33] In 1925, Schmieder proudly announced – in German – that "it is worth noting that St Matthäus is the only church in our city that still has a purely German Sunday school and confirmation classes and that with beautiful success it works in the mother tongue of the Reformation. At the same time, the rapidly growing English section of the Sunday school carefully carries out its work and raises the children in faith."[34]

In 1927, he told congregants – now in English – that "parents looking for a Sunday school which not only carries on its instruction in German, but where all the hymns and prayers are also German, and which has its German Christmas celebration and its German confirmation class must turn to St. Matthews [sic]."[35] In 1930, William Weicker, the superintendent of the German Sunday school, noted, "we are the only congregation in Kitchener that still has a purely German Sunday school. We therefore have a special responsibility to our newly immigrated brothers of faith [*Glaubensbrüder*] and their children. It is our duty to invite them to attend our Sunday school. We request all members of our congregation to help us and when possible to bring these children for their first time to our Sunday school."[36]

Because enrolment at the St Matthäus congregation stagnated before the introduction of an English stream, it seems that children's pressure on their parents and the church leadership influenced the relationship between language and religion. Adults strove to reconcile their own ideas about the transmission of language to their children and the language of their religion, but children could also push back. Adults made decisions to open Sunday schools up to English, but the role of some children in calling for an English stream or by demonstrating their uninterest in a German stream should not be overlooked.

The creation of an English stream at the St Matthäus Church came just months after the end of the First World War, but to attribute this change solely to the war would overlook important factors, including the agency of children and decades of language contact. The congregation offered religious services in German throughout the war and continued to promote the German language to a significant portion of children during the 1920s. It seems that the St Matthäus congregation added an English stream because many children convinced their parents and church leaders that they did not want to attend Lutheran Sunday school if they could not do so in English. When Schmieder wrote in 1922 that the two streams did not "hinder the work of teaching the Religion of our blessed Saviour" and that operating two Sunday schools meant that "we can do so most effectively and efficiently in a manner exactly suited to our people,"[37] among his people were clearly children, teenagers, and young adults who had their own views on the language of religion. These changes came from within this congregation while it remained a largely German-language institution. It is important to emphasize the power of children, parents, and their congregations to determine their own linguistic behaviour rather than attributing it solely to pressure from anglophone society.

Practising German-speaking Lutherans placed great weight on language as a key component of their religiosity. However, blending religion and language allowed a large group of German speakers in the province to reconcile their desire for the generational reproduction of ethnicity with the pervasive presence of the English language in other spaces. The insistence on German in religious practices did not isolate these German speakers from the larger society but rather helped some people balance diverse interests and participate in their surrounding society.

Youth Groups

Pastors, lay leaders, and clergy encouraged the creation of youth groups as a strategy to ensure that the ever-evolving group that comprised youth would remain proficient in German. Like the youth groups of other denominations, Lutheran and Catholic ones promoted a set of social, moral, and religious ideas in an attempt to contribute to a larger social reform movement in early twentieth-century Ontario. Yet these youth groups, as would likely be the case for any other church not operating in English, focused strongly on fostering bilingualism. While Sunday schools were a common experience for children whose families attended Lutheran congregations across Ontario, bilingual adolescents participated in Lutheran and Catholic youth groups on their own accord. Youth groups were smaller and less widespread than the Sunday schools. In 1917, for example, only twenty-three of the more than eighty congregations of the Canada Synod had a youth group, and these groups had a total of 1,152 members.[38]

The youth group in the Toronto Trinitatis Congregation was one of the oldest in Ontario, founded in 1889 with both male and female members. It elected a large board of directors with both young men and women.[39] The group frequently gave concerts in the halls of Toronto's German singing societies at the Germania Hall and in the Victoria Hall.[40] In an article in the secular *Deutsche Zeitung*, E.M. Genzmer, the pastor in Toronto, wrote in 1891 that "the Youth Association took on the task of caring for Christian convictions, but it also took on the task of promoting the language of our ancestors and helping youth speak it natively."[41] In its first two years, the group grew from twenty to sixty members, and Genzmer noted that while he used to address the group only in English, "German now has the upper hand!"[42] Appealing to parents to enrol their children, Genzmer announced that the group offered a "helping hand" to teach children German.[43] For Genzmer the reasons were numerous, noting that "in addition to its [the German language's] beauty, parents should not overlook that German emigrants to Canada are ever increasing in numbers, and as a result, for purely material concerns, parents should impress German upon children so that they may use it in business and commerce."[44]

In 1909, a moment when many young Lutherans had begun to take less interest in German in their local congregations, the Canada Synod founded an Ontario-wide *Jugendbund* (Youth Federation). It brought local activities and linguistic attitudes into a regional framework, and this represents a tangible example of the spatial networks that linked Lutherans to a larger world, in this case at the provincial rather than North American level. Led by Heinrich Rembe, a pastor in Hamilton, the federation advanced the dual goal of strengthening youth's religiosity and their German abilities. Rembe composed the federation's song (the *Bundeslied*), which followed the melody of the German national anthem. Yet the lyrics both spoke of Luther's teaching and included the line "But I also want to love you, mother tongue and mother sound!"[45]

In the 1920s, as the Canada Synod began preparations to merge with the smaller English-language Synod of Central Canada and become an officially bilingual synod, its youth federation began to take a new direction. In 1925, the federation's bulletin in the otherwise German-language annual report of the Canada Synod was in English.[46] The next year it merged with the English-language Luther League.[47] In the 1920s, as a new group of young people took control of Lutheran youth groups, they largely abandoned the goal of using their associations to promote both Lutheran religiosity and the German language. However, most of their

5.2 Luther League, St Peter's Evangelical Lutheran Church, Preston, Ontario, 1914.

churches remained as interested as ever in offering German-language services to older parishioners. An evolving group of youth started a different negotiation between German and English in the 1920s.

The English-language Luther League, like German-language youth groups, infused social activities and the very nature of community with a religious zeal. It brought together youth from individual congregations, as was the case of the group in Preston depicted in figure 5.2, and the league fostered bonds between towns and cities in Ontario.

While adults' involvement in promoting Lutheran youth groups reflected a relatively successful attempt to use the space afforded by organized religion to foster the generational reproduction of ethnicity, at other times these adults were confronted with youth who took little interest in German or in participating in this aspect of church life. Particularly in the synod's missionary activities to German speakers (the home mission), pastors were concerned about youth. In 1881, J. Brezing, the leader of the synod's home mission, worried about small German-speaking settlements on the southeastern shores of Lake Huron. He complained that not only did few families attend the missionary pastor's services, "the youth do not want to have anything to do with German."[48] Decades later, in northern Ontario, where the synod undertook missionary work to prevent German-speaking Lutherans from "falling into the hands of sects," youth posed a particular challenge.[49] C.F. Christiansen, the missionary pastor in Denbigh, told his fellow pastors in 1917 that the future of the congregation "depends on preaching the gospel in the language of the country since English ways and customs have become dominant amongst the youth. Members of the congregation have even married English people. Children from such marriages are taught and confirmed in English."[50]

Parents, lay leaders, and pastors adopted other strategies to encourage their children to make use of the German-language spaces that they had carved into Ontario society. Emil Hoffmann reported in 1914 that twelve congregations had a German library with a total of approximately 1,200 books. Yet Hoffmann complained that "these books appear to be read only infrequently. Should nothing be done? These days young people certainly read a lot, but what?!"[51] Hoffmann and likely others who supported these libraries with their labour and donations probably hoped that through organized institutions and by focusing on youth, they could ensure German's longevity in Ontario society.

Largely as the result of new German-speaking immigrants to Toronto, particularly from Yugoslavia, German-speaking Catholics founded a new parish in the city in 1929.[52] Sharing the building with an English-language congregation, this new German parish in St Patrick's Church brought with it a vibrant community life that pursued the dual goal of promoting religiosity and the German language, a duality that it has retained to this day, much like the city's nearby Lutheran church. The activities of its many lay associations reveal an important aspect of the changing presence of German ethnicity in Ontario and the ways that German-speaking Catholics spoke about the significance of language for their denomination. From 1929 onwards, the parish ran an evening school for adults to teach them English, and starting in 1935 the parish offered a German

Saturday school for children to improve their reading and writing skills. Between 1935 and 1939, 240 children enrolled in this program.[53]

The activities of this German parish in Toronto were in part a result of a broader set of ideas that had been circulating in the Catholic world for several decades.[54] As Pierre Savard and Roberto Perin have both argued, an anxiety emerged in late nineteenth-century Europe and North America that the religiosity of immigrants to the United States – particularly from Germany, Quebec, and Italy – would decline due to the lack of linguistic diversity in the Catholic Church in that country. Led by the German Peter Paul Cahensly (the founder of the St Raphael Society, a member of the Prussian parliament, and a member of the Reichstag), a group of prominent European Catholics lobbied the Vatican to permit separate parishes, schools, and when possible bishops for each linguistic group in the United States.[55] Reminiscing about his visit to many German Catholic regions in the United States, Cahensly wrote, "I became convinced that the only immigrants who, along with their children, remain loyal followers of the Catholic Church are those who preserve the German mother tongue."[56] He added, "I also became convinced that a great number of European Catholic immigrants had only lost their faith because on arrival they found no priests who could pronounce the word of God in their language and none who could teach their children the catechism in their language."[57]

Catholic youth groups gave concerts, often for charitable fundraisers. In the 1930s, largely under the leadership the German-language St Patrick's parish in Toronto, the Ontario-wide *Deutschkatholischer Jugendverband* (German Catholic Youth Federation) began a youth choir. In 1939, F. Kaelble told fellow parishioners in Toronto that "where German songs ring out, Germandom lives and blossoms in its purest form. In folksongs, we find the soul of the *Volk*, and the poet sees and glorifies this."[58] Particularly if there were any rehearsals, a choir created a habitual space that promoted and was defined by proficiency in German. If one chose to participate in such a choir, furthermore, he or she engaged in a performative act that affirmed linguistic abilities and identities. Although choirs often sing in foreign languages that participants have phonetically memorized, music played a different role in these German-language congregations.

The *Jugendverband* at St Patrick's brought together teenagers and young adults, and it had 110 members by 1939.[59] It was mainly a sports association and members participated in gymnastics, wrestling, boxing, and baseball. In 1934, the federation was divided into men's and women's associations and a sport club.[60] In the mid-1930s, the Toronto youth group began meeting with other German Catholic youth groups in Ontario, and in 1939 F. Kaelble wrote that "it is in fact the goal of these meetings to incorporate these German cells into a large association of Ontario's German Catholics."[61] These meetings integrated young people into a spatial network defined by and created to strengthen ethnicity. At St Patrick's parish, priests created a German theatre group that they described as "a tool that undeniably helps with the retention of the mother tongue."[62] When describing the group's performance of the Passion of Christ, F. Kaelble reasoned that "German and Catholic is an inseparable term."[63] In 1935, twenty-four women of the congregation founded the *Rosenkranzverein* (Rosary Association), and by 1939 it had grown to ninety-five participants. It officially pursued the religious objectives "of deepening religious life in the family, of strictly complying with the personal duties of Catholic faith, and of serving as role models in their neighbourhood."[64] That these women did such things in German meant that their association promoted a form of social organization based on both denomination and language.

Lay and ordained leaders of different Lutheran and Catholic congregations in Ontario regularly spoke about the German abilities of youth, and much of their discussion revolved around the need to strike a balance between the adult generation's needs and the younger generation's behaviour. In supporting German youth groups or offering English-language services in addition to German, adults tried to incorporate young, practising Lutherans and Catholics into a denominational community where language played an important but changing role.

Conclusion

Understanding how bilingualism functioned challenges the idea of language loss. A more detailed analysis of language use and the process through which young people attained or did not attain a balanced bilingualism shows the heterogeneity of so-called groups and of the very boundaries of ethnicity. When adults spoke about children, they often announced their fears of children losing their mother tongue, but people's everyday behaviour and openness to English contradicted the negative and nostalgic nature of this fear on a regular basis. Many people spoke about the interdependence of language and denomination. Lutherans created a number of lay associations explicitly organized around language. The case of Catholics in Toronto shows a vibrant presence of Catholic youth activities, linked closely with the rising immigration of German-speaking Catholics to the growing metropolis. Half of all German nationals in Canada by 1931 had come in the past decade, with Ontario one of the main destinations.[65]

German-language Lutheran Sunday schools add an important component to our overall understanding of bilingual education in Ontario between 1880 and 1930. State-controlled elementary schools in Ontario were not particularly fertile sites to promote a balanced proficiency in German and English, and this was surely a factor in the embrace of Sunday schools, a widespread phenomenon in North American Protestantism. German-speaking Catholics did not create Sunday schools, but their slightly greater ability to promote German in the state-controlled Catholic separate schools across Ontario meant that one denomination found a different balance between its places of worship and the education of its children.

Lutheran and Catholic churches in Ontario were sites where adults actively tried to instill in children key aspects of ethnicity. Denominations created ethnic boundaries, but the loosely defined communities organized around churches were far from linguistically homogeneous spaces. Between the 1880s and the 1920s, many people actively struggled to ensure that churches, particularly Lutheran ones, remained German-language spaces in terms of worship, adult lay associations, youth groups, and Sunday schools. Some children and youth disagreed wholly with these goals while others pushed for another understanding of bilingualism, one that required neither a complete shift to English nor a strict focus on German so as to not be "lost to Germandom," as some adults described it. For both denominations, churches served as spaces where German was the language of communication, song, and spirituality. As the next chapter will show, Lutherans and Catholics of German heritage in Ontario had a dynamic relationship with German and English in the first three decades of the twentieth century. Their institutions moved away from German monolingualism, but they remained bilingual into the 1920s.

6. THE RISE OF BILINGUALISM

At turn of the twentieth century, many German Lutheran and German Catholic churches in Ontario were becoming bilingual. Driven by the preferences and abilities of parishioners and often slowed by the leadership of German-born pastors and priests, German congregations across the province became bilingual in practice. All of these changes occurred long before they formally became English-language congregations. By the turn of the twentieth century, both German and English became the language of religion for German speakers in Ontario. Lutheran and Catholic churches supported the German language, but linguistic boundaries became porous, and people lived with two (or more) languages.

Every German speaker in Ontario was to some extent also an English speaker. The varying levels of language proficiency that immigrants and their children had, and that others worried about, are important but little researched in the history of migration. Language was a central issue that people regularly discussed and acted upon. The bilingualism of "German" congregations and of a group of people defined by one language (German) underscores some of the complexities in the ways that immigrants and their children constructed their ethnicity in Ontario society.

In this chapter, I argue that the changing relationship between German and English resulted from the competing ideas and abilities of adults, youth, and children. I outline the ways that linguistic adaptation took place in some of the longest-lasting German-language institutions in Ontario, namely places of worship. This linguistic history of generational differences and religious activities proposes that people's ideas and activities about language, religion, and ethnicity at any given moment between 1880 and 1930 are interesting questions in and of themselves.

It emphasizes ethnic *practice*. Language mattered to many practising Lutherans and Catholics of German birth or heritage in Ontario. Understanding how German speakers navigated between German and English highlights a problem with the category of "German speakers." Like the terms "Germans" or "German community," the label "German speakers" simplifies bilingualism.

Bilingualism refers to the habitual use of two or more languages in a person's everyday life.[1] An interlocutor does not have to be equally proficient in both languages, and indeed a completely balanced bilingualism rarely exists. Even in bilingual societies, a person rarely feels equally comfortable in the written or spoken versions of two languages. German speakers in Ontario had many forms of bilingualism. The textual documents left behind mask multiple relationships with the standard forms of these two languages. In particular, the presence of German dialects in Ontario as well as illiteracy in either English or German complicate assumptions about or definitions of bilingualism.[2] Moreover, people educated in a German-speaking society who immigrated to North America made use of German and English differently from those who had been educated in Ontario and became literate in German through bilingual German-English education in schools and religious institutions. Children raised in Ontario after the 1890s – when the German language had become increasingly marginalized from the public educational system – likely considered English their dominant language. However, through their contact with and participation in ethnic spaces such as churches, many Ontario children of German heritage habitually used both the English and German languages. Children grew up in the broader linguistic environment created by anglophones and by German-speaking parents, educators, and religious leaders.

It is important to stress the occurrence of exogamous marriage. German-language congregations in Ontario did not provide data on the ethnicity, nationality, and denomination of the marriages performed in their churches. Nonetheless, towns and cities such as Toronto, Berlin, and Waterloo were ethnically heterogeneous. We can speculate that the presence of English in weekly worship and children's increasing preference for English Sunday schools was partially the result of adults marrying people who spoke another language or who belonged to another denomination. If churches, Sunday schools, and youth groups promoted the generational reproduction of ethnicity, it is important to highlight that the ethnicity of mothers and fathers was not always the same. The support of German-language activities through organized religion was sometimes an effort to reproduce only a father's or only a mother's ethnicity and to transmit the ethnicity of men or women to children of mixed ethnic heritage. The fact that both Catholic and Lutheran churches sometimes turned to the English language to foster religious participation was likely related to a negotiation that took place within the household and the congregation.

Lutheran Bilingualism

In the early decades of the twentieth century, Lutheran churches across Ontario kept German as the main language of their congregation while also allowing a growing space for English. They added weekly services in English. Yet lay associations generally held their meetings in German, and music in German could be found in even English-language Lutheran spaces. Pulled between the changing linguistic practices and abilities of some parishioners and the weight of their German-language institution, which was supported by German-trained pastors, printed materials, and an identity as a German denomination, Lutheran congregations struggled to find a balance between the two languages.

After the turn of the twentieth century, English began to stand beside German on special occasions at many churches that remained largely German-language institutions. The pervasive presence of English in many aspects of people's everyday lives, mixed marriages, and a public education system fixated on the English language surely provoked this reconstitution of the relationship between German and English. In 1912, the St Johannis congregation in Waterloo celebrated its seventy-fifth anniversary. At the anniversary event, M. Arendt, a visiting pastor from Grey County, and Emil Hoffmann, president of the Canada Synod, led anniversary services in German over two days while J. Ch. Hoffman, a visiting pastor from Philadelphia, gave an English sermon. The leaders of three different lay associations gave speeches in German as well.[3]

When the St Matthäus congregation inaugurated its new church building in Berlin in 1915, German and English shared the space.[4] The inaugural service, including all of the hymns, was in German, and Emil Hoffmann, a former pastor of the congregation, presided over it. In the evening of the same Sunday, there was an English service with English hymns that included the singing of the Canadian/British anthem. The following day, another English service took place, and the local members of Parliament, Provincial Legislature, and the mayor of the city of Berlin attended. This was followed the next day, however, by a fourth and final inaugural service, with both the sermon and choir songs in German. Several speeches were made in German on topics such as the work of the Ladies' Aid Society and missionary activities, as well as one in English on the efforts of the Young People's Society.[5] These bilingual practices in 1912 and 1915 continued in the 1920s. Of the six services that the St Matthäus congregation offered in the week between Palm Sunday and Easter Sunday in 1924, four were in German and two in English; in 1925, four were in German and three in English.[6]

In the 1920s at one of Kitchener's largest congregations, German and English existed in a relational form.[7] Both had clear functions and both retained an important place within this bilingual space. In 1923, John Schmieder, the pastor of the St Matthäus congregation invited new people to join his church. He wrote – in German – that "we invite German Lutherans, with the greatest confidence, to join us. They will feel comfortable with us. Not only do we hold a German service every Sunday but we also have a large, purely German Sunday school, a purely German confirmation class and the related German liturgies [Festfeier]."[8] Schmieder noted that this was the only church in Kitchener where this was the case.[9] He continued in German, "With the same confidence we invite all English Lutherans to join us so long as they do not belong to any other church in Kitchener. They will also feel at home with us and with the many young and old people who attend our English services … We have a large, purely English Sunday school where we use the best and newest materials, and in the English confirmation class we have a considerable number of boys and girls, as was the case in previous years."[10] Organized primarily around denomination, leaders of congregations like St Matthäus wanted to incorporate people into Lutheran congregations in the language they preferred. This decision applied to adults, youth, and children, and appeals such as this reveal the linguistic negotiation and accommodation that maintained Lutheran churches as ethnic spaces as well as sites of bilingualism.

In the previous two citations, Schmieder used the German word "purely" (*rein*) to describe the German-language Sunday school and confirmation classes as well as the English-language Sunday school. Such a framing reveals a clear interest in establishing linguistic boundaries, but it also highlights concerns about people crossing those boundaries. In two citations in the previous chapter, *rein* was used to describe "purely English people"[11] and the blossoming of Germandom "in its purest form."[12] In the two quotations above, Schmieder was discussing children and the transmission of linguistic and denominational identities. He used the concept of purity to describe the children who did not come from exogamous marriages and those who participated in a German-language space.

The oldest German-language Lutheran congregation in Toronto arrived at its bilingualism – something it has retained to this day – in a different manner. Between 1927 and 1930, the larger German-language Lutheran congregation in the city merged with a smaller English-language one. Despite its larger size, the German congregation was undergoing an internal process of change as well. As a result, the union of the two congregations and speech communities caused some concern for the elected lay leaders of the German-language church. In addition to outlining the financial holdings and debts of the two congregations, the amalgamation committee dedicated special attention to language. It resolved to hold separate morning services in both German and English, and stipulated that "this provision regarding the German Services can only be changed by a two-thirds majority in a special congregational meeting on the language question."[13] Both languages were placed on equal footing for all members of the congregation. The time of morning services were not set to serve different age groups or to attract people from other denominations, as was commonly the case in Kitchener and Waterloo.

Between 1910 and 1930, many Lutheran congregations began to complement their main German-language Sunday service with an evening service in English.[14] This suggests that the primary language of worship of these congregations was German, but it also shows that a unified congregation with one board of directors and a single pastor was open to change. The transformation of an ethnic space defined by language into a bilingual one defined by denomination resulted from several factors. First, falling into a more widespread phenomenon in Ontario and North America, these English-language evening services were likely part of an effort to reach out beyond the congregation to attract new parishioners from other denominations and non-practising people with some interest in joining a church. Second, these churches were likely trying to cater to the linguistic needs of families composed of one German-speaking and one English-speaking parent as well as their children with varying degrees of proficiency in these two languages. Third, the decision was likely an attempt on the part of the congregation's leadership to offer an attractive option to young people. The evening service could have been perceived as a rupture with tradition, and services in English could have appealed to adolescents' preferred language.

Between 1910 and 1930, lay and ordained Lutheran leaders began adding English-language sections to the publications they sent to parishioners and the congregation's private records. Authors did not mix the two languages, and the documentary evidence suggests that different groups with differing linguistic interests came together under the umbrella of a single congregation. The language used in the annual reports and commemorative publications of all of these Lutheran congregations required an explicit choice. Between 1910 and 1920, the sections of financial reports and youth groups tended to be in English, while the pastor's annual address, reports from the Ladies' Aid Society and reports on missionary work, and the various histories of the congregations that often prefaced the annual reports remained in German.[15] These publications provide evidence of a bilingual institution, and the people that congregated around Lutheranism were members of a bilingual speech community. Younger members had a different relationship with this bilingualism, to be sure, but it seems that the vast majority of practising Lutherans who were registered members of these congregations and who received such publications were functionally proficient in both German and English.

At St Paul's in Berlin/Kitchener, the annual report was published in German until 1918 when it switched to English, and it remained this way throughout the 1920s.[16] Yet despite the complete language shift in its publications, Albert Orzen, the congregation's pastor, offered weekly church services in both German and English. Even in 1935, during the weekend celebration of the congregation's one-hundredth anniversary, the congregation retained this duality.[17] Moreover, the congregation's Ladies' Aid Society kept its minutes entirely in German until 1924. For the next seven years they were kept in both English and German. In 1927, the female members "expressed the wish that the meetings be as heretofore in the German and English language."[18] During the 1928 meetings, it appears that the minutes were taken entirely in German and that they were translated afterwards.[19] It is likely that minutes reflected the spoken language of the meeting. It is unlikely that the minute-taker engaged in simultaneous translation into German, a language that she used infrequently in other social spaces such as schooling, daily newspapers, business, and consumption practices. Only in 1931 did these female, adult German speakers switch their minute keeping to English.[20]

Affiliation with a Lutheran congregation created a series of German-language spaces for adult women and men. At the monthly meetings of the Ladies' Aid Societies or church boards of directors, and in the fundraisers and church social gatherings that these groups organized, people actively maintained their German abilities. In addition, as younger Lutherans joined these female and male organizations, their differing proficiency in German was likely elevated. While the Sunday schools and youth groups of the previous chapter demonstrate a decreasing interest in German over time, Ladies' Aid Societies in particular show that the German language was alive and well in the 1920s in many bilingual Lutheran congregations.

The role of music in these congregations reveals other important facets of the linguistic negotiation that took place in the first third of the twentieth century. The average attendee's passive listening to a German sermon was complemented by the need to actively sing German hymns. Singing complemented many people's use of German in other spaces such as the home, their weekly worship, the meetings of Ladies' Aid Societies, Sunday schools, and youth groups. In 1924, the St Johannis congregation in Waterloo bought new German-language hymnals and the following year bought new English-language *Common Service Books*, which had both recently been published in Philadelphia.²¹ With these purchases, church leaders and congregants actively strengthened the place of German while they also embraced the English language and strengthened English-language worship in other ways. That these texts came from Philadelphia further highlights the argument of chapter 4; the use of German in this ethno-religious space depended on connections to major German-speaking centres in the United States.

In a 1905 celebration of Kaiser Wilhelm's birthday at the Concordia Club in Berlin, John Rittinger lamented the language choices of youth. The *Berliner Journal* described his attitude: "what would be regrettable ... is that some young Germans do not take enough interest in their mother tongue. For example, when at church, [Rittinger] always sees that not only parents but also children sing hymns from German hymnals. But when he later runs into these young people on the street and attempt to get them to subscribe to the newspaper, he also always gets the same answer, 'I can't read the German language' [in a marked dialect: '*ich kann die deitsch Sproch net lese*']."²²

In discussing the merger in 1904 of two German-language newspapers, the *Berliner Journal* and the *Ontario Glocke*, the editors noted that "one of our main goals will remain the preservation of the German language in Canada. As Canadian born we know that the language of the country is English, and everyone who strives for success in business must learn it. What we do not believe, however, is that one can be a loyal Canadian citizen if he only speaks one language when he is capable of speaking two."²³ In 1913, the paper similarly told parents who speak foreign languages that "you have the opportunity to easily teach your child a language. Do not miss it and do not rob the children of this chance. The ability to read, speak, and understand a second language means that a whole world of thoughts and feelings are revealed to them, which remain hidden to others."²⁴ This claim that teaching a child a second language was a service to Canadian citizenship was common to immigrants throughout the Americas.²⁵ Jeffrey Lesser and Raanan Rein contend that leaders consistently asserted that "their groups represent the best citizens because they combine national and foreign traits."²⁶ Community leaders asserted that citizens whose parents were immigrants should embrace their duality and be better Canadians by embracing their ethnic difference.

Between 1880 and 1925, the Canada Synod remained officially a German-language institution. Within it, however, many of its constituent congregations began to become bilingual spaces. The synod accommodated the changing linguistic practices of congregations. Another reason why the Canada Synod remained officially a German-language institution was that starting in 1901, the congregations that completely adopted the English language and stopped using German left the synod. According to the Canada Synod's leadership in 1911, this separation took place "merely for the sake of language."[27] After temporarily affiliating with the Synod of New York and New England, fourteen Ontario congregations with ten pastors and 1,425 members formed the Synod of Central Canada in 1910.[28] The two synods in Ontario maintained good relations, and they immediately began working together to found the bilingual Waterloo Lutheran Seminary.

In 1917, the two synods began working towards a merger, something they achieved in 1925.[29] The new synod retained the name of the larger Canada Synod. The enlarged Canada Synod continued to publish its annual reports in German as well as an English-language version. The leaders printed 2,500 copies of the new synodical constitution in both German and English, suggesting a degree of equality between the two languages.[30] John Schmieder wrote that unlike the creation of the United Church of Canada in the same year, "For us it is a union of two Lutheran church bodies that are one in faith and teaching. We unite on the basis of an agreement that stipulates that both languages, German and English, have equal rights at synodical meetings, a point in the constitution that can only be modified with a three-quarter majority."[31] There was clear concern over the linguistic implications of this merger and the changing linguistic character of many Lutheran churches in Ontario.

Those who emphasized the significance of German often spoke of their success in conserving a linguistic space for the sake of future immigrants, something that coexisted with efforts to promote the German language among Canadian-born Lutherans. The editors of the *Kirchen-Blatt* wrote in 1909 that:

the English language is the language of the country, and if immigration were to completely stop, it would only be a matter of time before the English language gradually pushed out all others and finally reigned alone. Yet things are not yet so, and this will also not likely occur in the foreseeable future. Our country is large and still has space for many. As soon as the economic situation improves, the influx of immigration will again return. We will again receive people not only from the Catholic south but also from the Protestant north and from the motherland of the Reformation [Germany]. In such circumstances it would be more than foolish if we were to search for salvation in our Lutheran church only using the English language. We are much more German and we want to stay German, as long as it pleases God. This is not only for our own sake but for the sake of those who come after us.[32]

The interest in the future and in maintaining the status quo was a recurring goal in the discourse and actions of many Lutheran leaders.

Temporality and the future should be important foci in the study of migration and ethnicity in the Americas.[33] As David Engerman notes, how historical subjects envisioned their future reveals much about those subjects and the period in which they lived.[34] Reinhart Koselleck stresses the value of studying not only historical subjects' experience but also their "horizons of expectation." According to Koselleck, *experience* – a key focus of social and cultural historians – can only truly be understood by also analyzing *expectation*.[35] The two are interdependent; "no expectation without experience, no experience without expectation."[36] Revolutionaries do not spring into action, workers do not spend long days in factories, and young people do not rise in protest without having given some thought to the future. As the authors of the *Kirchen-Blatt* quotation above reveal, part of the project of maintaining a German-language church was "for the sake of those who come after us." More broadly, when German speakers in Ontario spoke about "preserving" or "maintaining" their language and culture, about the "next generation," and about children "losing" language or culture, they were expressing an interest in keeping Ontario a culturally plural society long into the future.[37]

Catholic Bilingualism

German-speaking Catholics in Ontario navigated a different path between English and German. At times, priests and lay leaders promoted German, but there was a smaller interest in pushing for a widespread use of the language. If religious institutions played a key role in constructing and supporting ethnicity, a denominational comparison demonstrates that people talked about and carried out activities regarding language differently. Many German-speaking Catholics had different ethnic practices.

A major cause of this variation between Lutherans and Catholics was structural. German-speaking Catholics joined a well-established church while German-speaking Lutherans started from scratch. German-speaking Catholics shared an institution with French and English speakers and two groups that had their own power struggle over the structure and form of their church.[38] German-speaking Catholics heeded local ecclesiastical structures in a way that did not apply to the Lutheran members of the autonomous Canada Synod. In Ontario, particularly under the leadership of the bishop of London, Michael Francis Fallon, starting in 1910, there was a push for English in Ontario's Catholic institutions.[39]

Beginning in the 1850s and 1860s with the missionary work of the brothers Eugen and Ludwig Funcken, priests from the Congregation of the Resurrection were charged with the task of serving German speakers in the Diocese of Hamilton, which included Waterloo, Bruce, Grey, and Brant Counties. They were joined by a German Catholic parish in Toronto.[40] According to the papers of both Eugen Funcken and his successor, William Kloepfer, St Mary's Church in Berlin offered sermons in German from its foundation in 1857 and until 1910. This practice resumed again in the 1920s in response to new German-speaking immigration.[41] With the exception of German sermons, by the 1890s, St Mary's parish appeared to function almost entirely in English, and this is quite telling in light of the emphatic interest in German at the nearby Lutheran churches in the same decade. The lay and ordained leaders of St Mary's used less German in the 1890s than their counterparts at many Lutheran churches in the 1920s. In the parish's records in 1892, for example, the minutes from monthly meetings were taken solely in English, suggesting that the conversation also took place in that language.

Between 1895 and 1898, John Motz, a recent graduate of St Jerome's College and son of the editor of the *Berliner Journal*, was the chairman of the parish's building fund collection. Although proficient in German, as evidenced by his later editorship of his father's newspaper, Motz organized the fundraiser in English.[42]

By 1910, St Mary's lay church groups such as the Young Men's Sodality and the Christian Mothers Association conducted their meetings and organized their activities in English as well.[43] In the early twentieth century, the parish had a thriving group of lay associations aimed at promoting Catholic values and mores in society. In 1916, the parish had seven such associations including the Childhood of Jesus, the Sodality of the Blessed Virgin, the St Boniface Sick Benefit Society, and the League of the Sacred Heart. Each association had over one hundred members, and two had "nearly the whole parish as members."[44] In comparison to the German-language activities of Lutherans, Catholics in the same town and also of German heritage struck a different balance between English and German.

Sermons reveal the linguistic behaviour of these priests, and to some extent they also reflect the desires of a larger group who attended church. Priests such as Anton Weiler and Theobald Spetz were capable of working in German. Their transition to English was, therefore, likely a response to parishioners' wishes. Not tied to a larger North American institutional network defined by the German language (as were the pastors of the Lutheran Canada Synod and the Canada District), communities organized around Catholicism and language did not have the same external factors that reinforced the place of German over time.

The papers of the priests of the Congregation of the Resurrection cast light on the languages used more broadly in Catholic parishes in the region. Anton Weiler, born in New Germany (now Maryhill), Ontario, in 1855, was the priest in Preston from 1886 to 1897 and then in New Hamburg from 1898 to 1902 before spending more than two decades in Rome.[45] His sermons from 1885 to 1904 were mainly in German, and evidence of the occasional sermon in English further strengthens the point that the parish he ran functioned predominantly in German. In 1886–87, twenty-one of his sermons were in German and none were in English. In 1891, twelve of his fourteen sermons were in German. Nevertheless, by the turn of the twentieth century things began to change. In 1898, four of Weiler's sermons were in German and four were in English.[46] His colleague Theobald Spetz, who was the pastor in Waterloo and then Berlin between 1890 and 1915 (in addition to his leadership role at St Jerome's College), gave a large majority of his sermons in English.[47] By the 1920s, moreover, the pastor of St Mary's in Kitchener, Albert Zinger, gave sermons exclusively in English, while a curate offered German-language worship to recent Catholic immigrants.[48]

The Catholic case adds an important counterexample to Lutherans. It shows how language and ethnicity could be reconstituted over time. For both groups – as exemplified not only by clergy but also by members of lay associations – language was seen as an important tool to support the denomination. Yet people of both denominations were also aware of the place of English in their secular and spiritual lives, and local congregations changed over time. A new influx of German-speaking immigration to the province in the 1920s rekindled waning debates, and Catholicism remained a denomination that supported the German language alongside English. Yet because of denomination, people with comparable origins in Europe and comparable migratory timelines had different linguistic practices in their own ethnic spaces. Not tied to a German-language institution that was embedded in a larger North American framework, Catholics followed a different path.

Conclusion

In the early decades of the twentieth century, "German" religious institutions became bilingual in *practice*. Church leaders tried to engage young people with German, but they were also were willing to accept English. As a result of the competing interests of children, adults, lay leaders, and pastors, English became prevalent in the German Lutheran and German Catholic churches of Ontario. Although churches resisted a language shift more than most other institutions and social spaces such as schools, newspapers, and business, they too became bilingual over time.

Lutheran and Catholic churches created a boundary that defined ethnic space. Yet from the 1880s onwards, these increasingly became bilingual spaces. Between 1900 and 1920, individual Lutheran congregations added services in English at another time of day to complement the ongoing German-language services, English Sunday schools were opened parallel to the older and larger German ones, and publications increasingly came to have English sections. Catholic parishes increasingly used English alongside German in the meetings of lay associations and for devotions such as the recitation of the rosary, novenas, the Stations of the Cross, processions, and special missions. At the same time, however, German maintained a privileged position in what retained the title "German congregations." It was the preferred language of pastors, elected lay leaders, and the female and male members of different church groups such as aid societies and social committees. German also stood at the forefront in music and religious holidays.

While churches – perhaps obviously – chose promoting faith over language as their main goal, they walked a complex line. German was the language of religion when Lutheran and some Catholic institutions were founded in Ontario, and competing ideas about the relationship between denomination and language transformed "German" religious institutions over time. Into the 1920s, that uneasy balance continued. Yet rather than pinpointing the moment of group-level language shift, this chapter has shown how bilingualism defined ethnic institutions for decades.

CITIZENSHIP, ETHNICITY, AND PLURALISM

Cultural pluralism is a negotiation. It is something actively maintained by various groups of people, and it cannot be wiped out simply by the desires of cultural nationalists. The removal of markers of cultural and linguistic difference in some domains – business, education, and so on – does not mean the end of cultural pluralism. A deeper examination shows persistence and transformation in other places. As this book has shown, the competing interests of children, educators, politicians, and religious leaders shaped German ethnicity in Ontario. In an era transformed by mass migration, these actors – alongside hundreds of thousands of other immigrants and Canadians of different backgrounds – created a system in which ethnic difference and civic belonging could coexist.

Ideas about citizenship and a belief in belonging marked the efforts of thousands of people to carve out a place for German ethnicity in Ontario in the late nineteenth and early twentieth centuries. Citizenship and belonging motivated parents to enrol children in schools and youth groups and remain involved with a larger group of German speakers across the province and across the Canada-US border. As debates over the language of instruction in Ontario showed, anglophones and francophones both believed they had more rights to education in their "mother tongue" than other groups, even more than the one group (German speakers) that did historically have the same privilege.

According to Anna Lundberg, citizenship describes "the relationship between individuals and a controlling authority in which rights and obligations are regulated."[1] At the same time, however, through this very relationship "women, minority groups, and the poor become outsiders or second-class citizens."[2] Various social groups have a vested interest in limiting or expanding the boundaries of inclusion and in acquiring rights or denying them to others.[3] By negotiating the meaning of citizenship, various groups – in political, social, cultural, and economic spheres – define it in terms of rights and duties that every resident of a society has to one another and to the overarching system. Sonya Rose has proposed that it can be helpful to think of citizenship "as a discursive framework, as a malleable language referring to the relationship between individuals and a political community."[4]

No matter what the nationality and language of parents, the rise of compulsory schooling in the final third of the nineteenth century in Ontario brought a set of civic values, ideas about work and capitalism, and language politics into spaces that had previously been reserved for families and religious communities. Education expanded the meaning of citizenship. It was part of a concept of social citizenship that went beyond the previous rights afforded by citizenship (e.g., to inhabit a territory, to vote, and to receive guarantees of civil rights) to also include rights to opportunity, health, and family life.[5] This expansion in North America fundamentally transformed how ethnic groups and parents could foster cultural pluralism. After an early era in which other languages could be used as alternate languages of instruction in public schools, provincial and state governments created regulations, policies, and laws that ensured that all young citizens would attain a reasonable proficiency in English.

Citizenship and the state depend on one another.[6] Rogers Brubaker contends that "every modern state identifies a particular set of persons as its citizens and defines all others as noncitizens" and that citizenship is an instrument of social closure.[7] Even the broadest definition of citizenship (extending beyond questions of nationality and voting rights) revolves entirely around the relationship between the state and a group of people who inhabit the territory that the state controls. That is not to suggest a top-down imposition of bureaucratic or elite desire. However, even if a social group succeeds in setting the terms of civic inclusion and forces public officials to change their policies of inclusion, the primary locus of their engagement is the state. As Kathleen Canning and Sonya Rose note, "Invocations of citizenship can serve at times to buttress the integrative practices of states, while in other instances they might enunciate visions or claims of those formally excluded from citizenship."[8] If the nation is a cultural definition of groupness and the state a political one, citizenship – with its flexible usages – is the analytical category that brings the two together and that can either shrink or expand the boundaries of the nation or the authority of the state.

As the First World War showed, the definition of cultural and political belonging could narrow. Wartime paranoia limited the rights of immigrants, naturalized British subjects mainly from Germany and Austria-Hungary, and ultimately Canadian-born German speakers. In early orders-in-council, citizenship was the point of departure. Immigrants who were still citizens of their country of origin were targeted because of suspected disloyalty. Yet as the war progressed, the boundaries of belonging narrowed, and German and other languages were targeted in a publication ban that made some languages used by people in Canada – whether immigrants or Canadian-born – illegal in written communication.

As this book shows, however, the war was only one of many factors that shaped the public and private expression and generational transmission of German ethnicity. Schools that the province called "German" turned a language of instruction into a subject of instruction in the 1890s. Some church congregations formally became English-language institutions in the first decade of the twentieth century, while others went to great lengths to hold Protestant services or give Catholic sermons in German both during the First World War and in the 1920s. Lutheran congregations also actively fostered the bilingualism of young Canadians through Sunday schools at a time when the federal government passed a number of orders-in-council and laws that blurred the boundaries between foreign citizenship and German ethnicity. The rise of bilingualism before 1914 and the persistence of it for the next two decades challenge any monocausal explanation of cultural change and any assumption about the power of anglophone nationalism to wipe out the culture and language of hundreds of thousands of bilingual Canadians.

Many groups of people espoused conflicting definitions of German ethnicity. The schools that education bureaucrats described as German were bilingual institutions where German was one of two languages of instruction. With this description, state bureaucrats excluded Canadian children from the national body, even though the same education authorities were adamant about promoting civic education in these schools. The Canadian census lumped every Canadian who could trace his or her lineage through the paternal line to a German-speaking immigrant from anywhere in the world as being of German heritage. Clerical and lay leaders of Catholic and Lutheran communities promoted an inclusive understanding of German ethnicity to a wide group of people with a variety of linguistic abilities and national origins, but they excluded German speakers of other denominations from the linguistic-religious communities they were trying to forge. Canadian children reconciled their ethnicity with their citizenship, linguistic abilities, and religious denomination very differently than any of the aforementioned groups.

Many German speakers saw language and denomination as two interrelated cornerstones of German ethnicity, and families and communities worked to maintain both. Nonetheless, even the most adamant supporters of German language and culture were very aware of their place in Ontario society, and organized German-language religion in Ontario integrated all those involved into their surrounding society. Being Catholic or a member of a theologically mainstream Protestant denomination (Lutheranism) meant that German-speaking immigrants and their bilingual children would come to share many of the ideas of their surrounding society about religion, morality, and family.

The role of Catholic parishes and Lutheran religious bodies in creating social welfare institutions and in running or supporting elementary schools meant that they integrated German speakers into the broader society in other ways as well. These religious structures filled a gap left open by the liberal state, and they asserted a place for their denomination in Canadian society. Adults' interest in ensuring that children participated in key rites of passage and that they received a certain amount of religious education determined the support that many German speakers gave to organized religion. Adult concerns about children also gave organized religion the specific task of promoting the German language.

The bilingualism of Germans in Ontario underscores a fundamental aspect of ethnicity often overlooked in the historiography. Studies of ethnic groups in the Americas tend to speak of Italians, Ukrainians, Swedes, and so forth while repeating external – but often conflicting – definitions of ethnicity. Nationality, oral and/or written language proficiency, denomination, or biological heritage can all define the human subjects that historians study, and there seems to be a lack of critical analysis of who belongs, should belong, or wants to belong to our groupings. People's interest in language, the role of denomination in shaping this interest, and children's differing opinions about language and bilingualism demonstrate the centrality and relational nature of language in the construction of ethnicity in North America. This book's attention to bilingualism, language policy and practices in schools, and the intersection of ideas about language and denomination in the construction of ethnicity all cast light on how people envision ethnicity and cultural pluralism in the Americas.

A great number of German speakers in Ontario spoke about and participated in community. There was no single German community in the province nor in specific places such as Toronto, Berlin, or Waterloo. The communities that people talked about or engaged with were not defined by the numbers presented in censuses or in the assertions of self-proclaimed community leaders. Nonetheless, in going to church, funding a college, or running an orphanage, people were involved with communities. Concerned parents, Catholic or Lutheran clergy and laypeople, German-speaking newspaper editors, and small clubs of cultural nationalists defined community in different ways, placing different emphases on language, denomination, and citizenship. Denomination drove community formation, encouraged people to make ethnic spaces, and fuelled the desire to reproduce ethnicity. Religious institutions served as spaces and provided autonomous control to many people who sought to use foreign languages in their new societies or who wanted to equip their children with a balanced proficiency in two languages.

The number of mutually exclusive German communities in towns, cities, or the province of Ontario that people created reveals much about the divergent meanings of being German in North America. The collective understanding of German ethnicity in Ontario was not linked to a concrete community but rather to spaces. Some English speakers described vast swaths of Ontario as "German settlements." People of other backgrounds who found themselves within these German spaces clearly contradicted this definition, as did the preference of many "German" children to speak English. Surely the various German-language churches that dotted the Ontario landscape well beyond Waterloo County led the residents of those cities, towns, and villages to have a broader perspective on where Germans dwelled as well.

In societies across the Americas and now also in Europe, debates about bilingual education continue. In English Canada, a consensus has been reached about the value of educating children in French immersion programs that foster bilingualism, and the need to offer government support to English- or French-language schooling in areas where either language is in a minority situation. Another consensus, however, has also emerged, and it is one that traces its origins to debates about language and national belonging in provinces such as Ontario in the 1880s and 1890s. Politicians and bureaucrats slowly removed foreign languages from Ontario schools and made clear that the role of public education would not only be to eradicate illiteracy but to impose a written and spoken proficiency in official languages. The supplemental German classes that the province began to offer and the learning materials that were insensitive to the unique abilities of heritage speakers set the tone for the language of schooling in Ontario for almost the entirety of the following century. Official support of foreign-language education may have returned in after-school programs and Saturday schools, but this is a far cry from using any language other than English or French as a habitual language of instruction.

Debates about language and nation in the Americas today stand upon the foundations that children, parents, educators, religious leaders, bureaucrats, and politicians built in the early twentieth century. Across national borders, there is a strong belief that young citizens must learn to speak and write a single language – be it English, Spanish, Portuguese, or French – and perhaps, if the dominant speech community so desires, other languages can be taught in supplemental hours. New fields for bilingual education have opened up in many countries in Europe, and the perspectives on multilingualism, integration, and citizenship surely feed off debates that have circulated in the Americas for the past century.

The cultural pluralism of Ontario society in the early twentieth century was the precursor to the multicultural society that emerged in the second half of the twentieth century. By paying attention to how people spoke about language, ethnicity, and national belonging between 1880 and 1930, we can trace the continuity of the ideas about cultural pluralism and the national body that one finds in the subsequent decades. In struggles over the language of education – in which German occupied a charmed space not far from English and French in late nineteenth-century Ontario – French emerged as the natural "other language" in Canada. While that might have been clear in 1867, the sustained immigration of approximately 4.5 million people to the country in the next four and half decades by no means made that a guaranteed outcome.[9] The bilingual education that slowly disappeared in Ontario in the late nineteenth century has not returned under the framework of official multiculturalism that began in the 1970s.[10] It is indeed revealing that Canadian multiculturalism stresses ambiguous and unstable categories of culture and ethnic identity while taking little interest in fostering multilingualism in any meaningful or lasting way.

The debates about language and citizenship throughout the twentieth century can trace their origins to the inception of universal education and the rise of cultural pluralism between 1880 and 1930. The agency of migrants and bilingual people born in Canada and the United States played an important role in setting the tone for decades to come. How government officials in places like Ontario interacted with those interests also shows how the state attempted to manage diversity. Bureaucrats and politicians pushed first for a broad use of English in elementary schools and then the removal of other languages of instruction. Yet they also left religious institutions – churches, Sunday schools, religious colleges, and to some extent even Catholic separate schools – free to foster bilingualism and denominational diversity in a society transformed by migration.

Notes

Introduction

1 I first discussed the ideas in this paragraph in Bryce, *To Belong in Buenos Aires*, 6–7. See also Sollors, ed., *The Invention of Ethnicity*; Conzen, Gerber, Morawska, Pozzetta, and Vecoli, "The Invention of Ethnicity"; Lesser, *Negotiating National Identity*; Lesser, *Immigration, Ethnicity, and National Identity*; and Goldstein and Thacker, eds., *Complicating Constructions*.

2 Brinkmann, "The Dialectics of Ethnic Identity," 68. See also Brinkmann, *Von der Gemeinde zur ,Community'*, 12–14.

3 Pavlenko, *Emotions and Multilingualism*, 6.

4 Mintz, "Why the History of Childhood Matters," 21.

5 Loewen, *Family, Church, and Market*; Epp, *Women without Men*.

6 According to the 1911 census, there were 12,828 Mennonites in Ontario and 31,797 in all of Canada. There were a total of 192,320 people of German origin in Ontario and 393,320 in all of Canada (*Fifth Census of Canada 1911, Volume II* (Ottawa: Printed by CH Parmlee, 1913), 2–3, 162, 204).

7 Ibid.

8 Zahra, *Kidnapped Souls*, 13.

9 Otero, *Historia de los franceses en la Argentina*, 20–1.

10 Ibid.

11 Raska, *Czech Refugees in Cold War Canada*, 17.

12 Lesser and Rein, "Challenging Particularity," 251, 256.

13 Brinkmann, *Von der Gemeinde zur ,Community'*, 23.

14 Brubaker and Cooper, "Beyond 'Identity'," 2.

15 Ibid., 34.

16 Ibid., 14.

17 Ibid., 27.

18 This is the case in McLaughlin, *The Germans in Canada*, in his sections on Ontario in this early period. See also Bausenhart, *German Immigration and Assimilation in Ontario*; McKegney, *The Kaiser's Bust*; Frisse, *Berlin Ontario*; Löchte, *Das Berliner Journal*; Coschi, "From Wilhelm to Hans." Both Barbara

Lorenzkowski and Elliot Worsfold put Waterloo County in a productive, comparative dialogue with either Buffalo, NY, or St Louis, MO: Lorenzkowski, *Sounds of Ethnicity*; Worsfold, "Welcoming Strangers."

19 This was 36,597 of the 192,320 people counted as being of German origin (*Fifth Census of Canada 1911, Volume II* [Ottawa: Printed by CH Parmlee, 1913], 348–57).

20 Bausenhart, *German Immigration and Assimilation*; McKegney, *The Kaiser's Bust*; Frisse, *Berlin Ontario*; Löchte, *Das Berliner Journal*.

21 Lorenzkowski, *Sounds of Ethnicity*; Conolly-Smith, *Translating America*; Kazal, *Becoming Old Stock*.

22 Conolly-Smith, *Translating America*, 13–14.

23 McLaughlin, *The Germans in Canada*, 12.

24 "1569 gegen 1488," *Berliner Journal*, 24 May 1916, 1.

25 Kalbfleisch, *The History of the Pioneer German Language Press*, 105.

26 Das Komitee, "Sind Sie dafür, daß der Name dieser Stadt geändert wird? Nein!" *Berliner Journal*, 17 May 1916, 7.

27 Löchte, *Das Berliner Journal*, 184.

28 Kelley and Trebilcock, *The Making of the Mosaic*, 200.

29 *Fifth Census of Canada 1911, Volume II* (Ottawa: Printed by CH Parmlee, 1913), 334.

30 *Sixth Census of Canada, 1921. Volume I. Population* (Ottawa: F.A. Acland, Printer to the King's Most Excellent Majesty, 1924), 354–5.

31 *Seventh Census of Canada 1931. Volume II. Population by Areas* (Ottawa: J.O. Patenaude, I.S.O., Printer to the King's Most Excellent Majesty, 1933), 294–5.

32 Bertram, *The Viking Immigrants*, 14.

33 Roediger, *How Race Survived U.S. History*, 141.

34 McLaughlin, *The Germans in Canada*.

35 Bausenhart, *German Immigration and Assimilation*, 19–20.

36 Ibid., 36.

37 Ibid., 42–3.

38 Ibid., 44.

39 Ibid., 71.

40 McCalla, *Planting the Province*, 13–14; Bausenhart, *German Immigration and Assimilation*, 46.

41 For more on this topic, see Bertram, "'Eskimo' Immigrants and Colonial Soldiers," 63–97; Azuma, *In Search of Our Frontier*.

42 McCalla, *Planting the Province*, 85.

43 Miller, *Compact, Contract, Covenant*, 95.

44 Bausenhart, *German Immigration and Assimilation*, 62.

45 Ibid., 70.

46 Ibid., 64.

47 Ibid., 68.

48 Ibid., 58.

49 "Sir Adam Beck," Dictionary of Canadian Biography, http://www. biographi.ca/en/bio/beck_adam_15E.html, accessed 5 April 2021.

50 Parr, *The Gender of Breadwinners*, 126–9.

51 Ibid., 133.

52 Bausenhart, *German Immigration and Assimilation*, 79.

53 Ibid., 80.

54 Avery, *"Dangerous Foreigners,"* 14, 20; Avery, *Reluctant Host*, 17, 107, 234; Whitaker, *Canadian Immigration Policy since Confederation*, 7–8; Palmer, *Ethnicity and Politics in Canada*, 5.

55 G. Shimono, president, "Memorandum Presented to the Fisheries Commission of the Dominion Government of Canada," Vancouver, BC: September 1922, Box 123-3, "Reference Files Maps and Other Documents 1922–1931," p. 3, Chung Collection, UBC Rare Books and Special Collection.

56 Grams, *German Emigration to Canada*, 231.

57 *Census of Canada, 1880–1881. Volume I* (Ottawa: Printed by Maclean, Roger and Co., Wellington St. 1882), 395.

58 *Fifth Census of Canada 1911, Volume II* (Ottawa: Printed by CH Parmlee, 1913), 334, 442.

59 *Seventh Census of Canada 1931. Volume I. Summary* (Ottawa: J.O. Patenaude, I.S.O., Printer to the King's Most Excellent Majesty, 1936), 528–9.

60 See for example the scholarly works of C.B. Sissons, *Bilingual Schools in Canada*; C.B. Sissons, "The Language Issue in the Schools of Canada"; or Lionel Groulx's *L'appel de la Race* (1922).

61 Jacobson, *Whiteness of a Different Color*, 6.

62 Ibid.

63 *Fourth Census of Canada 1901. Volume I. Population* (Ottawa: Printed by S.E. Dawson, Printer to the King's Most Excellent Majesty, 1902), xx.

64 *Seventh Census of Canada 1931. Volume I. Summary* (Ottawa: J.O. Patenaude, I.S.O., Printer to the King's Most Excellent Majesty, 1936), 249.

65 *The Canadian Newspaper Directory*, 2.

66 Ibid.

67 *Verhandlungen der Jahresversammlung der Evangelisch-Lutherischen Synode von Canada, 1900* (No bibliographic information), 41; Malinsky, *Grace and Blessing*, 30.

68 Curtis, *The Politics of Population*.

69 In the instructions given to census enumerators, it was noted that "a person whose father is English, but whose mother is Scotch, Irish, French, or any other race, will be ranked as English, and so with any others – the line of descent being traced through the father in the white races." However, although a father's lineage normally determined the ethnicity of a child (termed "racial origin" in the census), male lineage lost its power to transmit ethnicity for the purposes of the Canadian census when miscegenation with Indigenous peoples was

involved (*Fourth Census of Canada 1901. Volume I. Population* [Ottawa: Printed by S.E. Dawson, Printer to the King's Most Excellent Majesty, 1902], xviii).

70 Perin, *The Many Rooms of This House*, 6, 84.

Part One

1 Kelley and Trebilcock, *The Making of the Mosaic*, 100–1, 128–9; Avery, *Reluctant Host*; Avery, *"Dangerous Foreigners."*

2 Yildiz, *Beyond the Mother Tongue*, 2.

3 Anderson, *Imagined Communities*, 67.

4 Hobsbawm, *Nations and Nationalism since 1780*, 20.

5 Ibid., 102.

6 Brubaker, "Migration, Membership, and the Modern Nation-State," 63.

7 Scott, *Seeing Like a State*, 81–2.

Chapter One

1 Studies of French-language schooling have ignored this dual focus of the state, and Irish Catholics are the sole deviation from a narrative of two founding peoples. Prang, "Clerics, Politicians, and the Bilingual Schools"; Oliver, "The Resolution of the Ontario Bilingual School Crisis"; Choquette, *Language and Religion*; Choquette, *L'Ontario francais*; Simon, *Le Règlement XVII*; Jaenen, ed., *Les Franco-Ontariens*.

2 Miller, *Shingwauk's Vision*, 199, 200.

3 Winks, *The Blacks in Canada*, 365–76.

4 Buckner, ed., *Canada and the British Empire*; Buckner, ed., *Canada and the End of Empire*; Buckner and Francis, eds., *Canada and the British World*; Buckner and Francis, eds., *Rediscovering the British World*; Pickles, *Female Imperialism and National Identity*; Chilton, *Agents of Empire*.

5 Bryce, "Citizens of Empire," 607–29.

6 Martel, *French Canada*, 9; Bock, *A Nation beyond Borders*.

7 Bourassa was a member of federal Parliament, 1896–1907 and 1925–35, and member of the Legislative Assembly of Quebec, 1908–12.

8 Martel, *French Canada*, 1–4, 24–8.

9 Martel and Pâquet, *Langue et politique au Canada et au Québec*, 14.

10 Ibid., 59.

11 Blanton, *The Strange Career of Bilingual Education in Texas*, 42–3, 53.

12 Ramsey, "In the Region of Babel," 290.

13 Luebke, "Legal Restrictions on Foreign Languages in the Great Plains States," 2.

14 *Education Department High School Entrance Examination, 1900* (No bibliographic information).

15 Curtis, *Building the Educational State*.

16   For more on religious separate schools, see Fraser, *"Honorary Protestants,"* 10.

17   *Regulations and Correspondence Relating to French and German Schools*, 3; C.B. Sissons, *Bilingual Schools in Canada*, 22–3.

18   George Hodgins, *The Legislation and History of Separate Schools in Upper Canada*, 190–1, 192.

19   "Hodgins, John George," *Dictionary of Canadian Biography*, accessed 6 July 2017 http://www.biographi.ca/en/bio/hodgins_john_george_14E.html; Hodgins, *The Legislation and History of Separate Schools in Upper Canada*, 193.

20   *Regulations and Correspondence Relating to French and German Schools*, 12.

21   Belcourt, *Regulation 17 ultra vires*, 7.

22   *Regulations and Correspondence Relating to French and German Schools*, 49.

23   George Ross, *The Separate School Question and the French Language*, 12.

24   George Ross, "The French Language in Our Public Schools," 2.

25   George Ross, "Report of a Speech Delivered by the Minister of Education at the Reform Demonstration, Toronto, June 29th, 1889," in Ross, *The Separate School Question and the French Language*, 5.

26   *Report of the Minister of Education. Province of Ontario, Canada, 1890* (Toronto: Warwick and Sons, 1891), 59. See also *Acts Relating to the Education Department. Public and High Schools and Truancy. Ontario 1896* (Toronto: Warwick Bros and Rutter, 1896), 95.

27   *Report of the Minister of Education. Province of Ontario, Canada, 1890* (Toronto: Warwick and Sons, 1891), 59.

28   Ibid. See also *Report of the Minister of Education, 1897* (Toronto: Warwick Brothers and Rutter, 1898), 86.

29   Goldberg, "'I Thought the People Wanted to Get Rid of the Teacher:'"; Milewski, "'I Paid No Attention To It.'"

30   George Ross, "The French Language in Our Public Schools," 3.

31   *Regulations and Correspondence Relating to French and German Schools*, 105.

32   *Report of Commissioners on Public Schools in Ontario in which the French Language is Taught* (Toronto: Warwick and Sons, 1889), 5.

33   Ibid., 16–19.

34   *Report of the Minister of Education (Ontario), 1893. With the Statistics of 1892* (Toronto: Warwick Bros and Rutter Printers, 1894), xlii.

35   *Regulations and Correspondence relating to French and German Schools*, 111.

36   Ibid., 112.

37   Ibid.

38   Ibid.

39   Education Department, *A Brief History of the Public and High School Text-Books Authorized for the Province of Ontario, 1846–1889* (Toronto: Warwick and Sons, 1890), 53. This new regulation was also stated in the annual *Report of the Minister of Education. Province of Ontario, Canada, 1890* (Toronto: Warwick and Sons, 1891), 59.

40   *Regulations and Correspondence Relating to French and German Schools*, 108.

41 John Millar, *The Educational System of the Province of Ontario, Canada* (Toronto: Warwick and Sons, 1893), 83.

42 *Departmental Text-Book Regulations and Text-books Authorized for Use in Public, High and Continuation Schools and Collegiate Institutes, 1917,* 10.

43 John Millar, *The Educational System of the Province of Ontario, Canada,* 57–62.

44 Simon, *Le Règlement XVII;* Welch, "Early Franco-Ontarian Schooling."

45 *Report of the Minister of Education. Province of Ontario, Canada, 1890* (Toronto: Warwick and Sons, 1891), 65.

46 P. Henn, *Ahn's First German Book.*

47 P. Henn, *Ahn's Fourth German Book.*

48 Ibid.

49 *Departmental Text-Book Regulations and Text-books Authorized for Use in Public, High and Continuation Schools and Collegiate Institutes. 1898.*

50 Otto Klotz, *Leitfaden zur deutschen Sprache,* cover page.

51 Curtis, *Building the Educational State,* 288–90.

52 Klotz, *Leitfaden zur deutschen Sprache,* iii.

53 Ibid.

54 Ibid., iv.

55 Ibid.

56 *Regulations and Correspondence Relating to French and German Schools,* 34.

57 Ibid., 37.

58 Figuier, *Les grandes inventions modernes dans les sciences, l'industrie et les arts.*

59 *Regulations and Correspondence Relating to French and German Schools,* 111.

60 Lorenzkowski, *Sounds of Ethnicity,* 61.

61 *Regulations and Correspondence Relating to French and German Schools,* 112.

62 Ibid.

63 Gaffield, *Language, Schooling, and Cultural Conflict.*

64 *Regulations and Correspondence Relating to French and German Schools,* 94–103.

65 Ibid., 114.

66 Ibid., 111.

67 Ibid., 114.

68 *Regulations and Correspondence Relating to French and German Schools,* 99. The term *form* or *class* was used rather than the contemporary term *grade.* In 1888, there were five forms, and many of them were divided into two separate years.

69 Ibid., 99.

70 Ibid., 119.

71 Ibid., 121.

72 Ibid.

73 Spetz, *Catholic Church in Waterloo County,* 43.

74 Ibid., 125

75 McKegney, *The Kaiser's Bust,* 125–8; Löchte, *Berliner Journal,* 167; Lorenzkowski, *Sounds of Ethnicity,* 73.

76 Coschi, "'Be British or Be D–d'"; Lorenzkowski, *Sounds of Ethnicity*, 44–76; Löchte, *Das Berliner Journal*, 93–104.

77 "Kitchener Public School Board Minutes. 1915–1920," 19, Archive of the Waterloo Region District School Board.

78 Lorenzkowski, *Sounds of Ethnicity*, 66–7.

79 The trustees on the Catholic school board in 1897 were Rev. Wm. Kloepfer, Rev. Theo Spetz, Rev. Jos. Schweitzer, Rev. Francis Breitkopf, and the Very Rev. Louis Elena (*Busy Berlin, Jubilee Souvenir*, "Educational Matters" [Berlin, ON: Berlin News Record, 1897]).

80 Chas. Boeher, Rev. Wm Kloepfer, Jos Fehrenbach, Philip Ringle, Andrew Englert, Hy. A Dietrich, and Joseph Winterhalt ("Minutes. Berlin Catholic School Board. 1902–1910." SB/A/Minutes: 3, Archive of the Waterloo Catholic District School Board).

81 Jacob Gies, Hartman Krug, J.A. Fuhrman, J.E. Haller, F. Schmuck, P. Ringle, A. Englert, *Issued in Commemoration of its Celebration of Cityhood. July 17, 1912* (Berlin: German Printing and Publishing Company Limited, 1912).

82 *Report of the Minister of Education, Province of Ontario, for the Year 1910* (Toronto: L.K. Cameron, 1911), 7–9. 3,559 children studied English literature, 3,555 studied composition, 1,657 children in certain grades studied English grammar, and ninety-seven children studied German.

83 Ibid., 14–17.
While 473 children studied English literature and composition, thirty-five studied German.

84 *Report of the Minister of Education, Province of Ontario, for the Year 1916*, 147.

85 "Erfreuliche Fortschritte," *Berliner Journal*, 4 January 1905, 6.

86 L. Breithaupt, 16 May 1902, "German and French languages – Instruction," RG 2-42-0-3518, Archives of Ontario.

87 Deputy Minister, 19 May 1902, "German and French languages – Instruction," RG 2-42-0-3518, Archives of Ontario.

88 Ibid.

89 Thomas Pearce, "Inspector's Reports. Public School Board," 14 November 1904, 3–4, Archive of the Waterloo Region District School Board.

90 Ibid., 1.

91 *Berlin Collegiate – Calendar of Pupils, 1855–1904* (No bibliographic information).

92 Thomas Pearce, "Inspector's Reports. Public School Board," Archive of the Waterloo Region District School Board. The inspector for other parts of Waterloo County was F.W. Sheppard in the decade before the First World War.

93 *Report of the Minister of Education, Province of Ontario, for the Year 1910* (Toronto: L.K. Cameron, 1911), 46–9. 693 children studied English composition, 647 English literature, and 342 German.

94 Ibid. 384 pupils studied English literature and composition, and 327 German.

95 Ibid., 50–3.

96 Ibid., 54–7.

97 Ibid., 21.

98 *Report of the Minister of Education, Province of Ontario, for the Year 1918* (Toronto: A.T. Wilgress, 1919), 211.

99 Ibid., 209–11.

100 Ibid.

101 For more on the flexible boundaries between separate and public schools in the late nineteenth century, albeit twenty years before the evidence discussed here, see Gaffield, *Language, Schooling, and Cultural Conflict*, 130.

102 I have not found any clear document announcing the discontinuation of German. However, according to the *Report of the Minister of Education, Province of Ontario (Canada), 1919* (Toronto: A.T. Wilgress), 102–19, German was no longer listed as a possible subject in the broad overview of courses offered. In addition, in *Departmental Text-Book Regulations and Text-books Authorized for Use in Public, High and Continuation Schools and Collegiate Institutes, 1919*, the Education Department ceased to list approved textbooks for German instruction at the elementary school level. Because the use of unauthorized textbooks could be punished with the retention of the provincial grant, this can be viewed essentially as the prohibition of German at elementary schools.

103 In 1921, a total of fifty-five children studied German in the Catholic schools, and only eighty-three in 1922 (*Report of the Minister of Education, Province of Ontario (Canada), 1923* [Toronto: Clarkson W. James, Printer to the King's Most Excellent Majesty, 1924], 162–3).

104 Belcourt, *Regulation 17 ultra vires*, 1; Cecillon, *Prayers, Petitions, and Protests*, 3.

105 This was Regulation 18 (1913). See Cecillon, *Prayers, Petitions, and Protests*, 90.

106 Ibid., 7.

107 Belcourt, *Regulation 17 ultra vires*, 17.

108 Ibid., 9.

109 Ibid., 11.

110 C. de la Légalité, *The Juridical and Pedagogical Position of English-French Schools in Ontario* (Ottawa: Imprimerie du "Droit," 1915), 28.

111 Tremblay, *Le français en Ontario*, 6.

112 Ibid., 33.

113 Belcourt, *Regulation 17 ultra vires*, 15.

114 Ibid.

115 Association canadienne-française d'éducation d'Ontario, *Bi-lingualism in Ontario*, 4.

116 Ibid., 5.

Chapter Two

1 Loewen, *Family, Church, and Market*, 237.

2 *Fifth Census of Canada 1911: Religions, Origins, Birthplace, Citizenship, Literacy and Infirmities, by Provinces, Districts and Sub-Districts, Volume II* (Ottawa: Printed by C. H. Parmelee, Printer to the King's Most Excellent Majesty, 1913), 440.

3 Zahra, *The Great Departure*, 4–5; Schober, "Austrian Immigration to Canada in the Imperial Period," 47–8.

4 Burpee et al., *Canada in the Great World War*, 146.

5 Order-in-Council 1914-2085, "German officers and reservists in Canada – Message Secretary of State of Colonies," Approved 7 August 1914, Series A-1-d, Volume 2811, RG2, Privy Council Office.

6 Otter, *Internment Operations, 1914–1920*, 3.

7 "PC Order-in-Council 2721 (Respecting Enemy Aliens, 28 October 1914)," in *Canadian State Trials, Volume IV*, edited by Barry Wright, Eric Tucker, and Susan Binnie, 480.

8 Order-in-Council 1914-2150, "War with Germany and with Austria Hungary – Authority to Police and Militia to arrest and intern all German and Austrian subjects suspecting of joining armed forces of the enemy or intending to give aid to release under certain conditions those who sign engagement not to serve," Approved 15 August 1914, Series A-1-a, RG2, Privy Council Office.

9 "Proclamation Respecting Immigrants of German or Austro-Hungarian Nationality," in *Canadian State Trials, Volume IV*, edited by Barry Wright, Eric Tucker, and Susan Binnie, 477.

10 Ibid., 478.

11 Kordan, "First World War Internment in Canada," 12.

12 "Aufruf an die Deutschen in Ontario," *Berliner Journal*, 12 August 1914, 2.

13 Bryce, "Germans in Ontario and Buenos Aires."

14 Kordan, "'They Will Be Dangerous,'" 42, 56.

15 Otter, *Internment Operations*, 9.

16 Kordan, "First World War Internment in Canada," 18.

17 Kordan, "'They Will Be Dangerous,'" 63.

18 Otter, *Internment Operations*, 12.

19 Ibid., 13.

20 "Order-in-Council," *Berliner Journal*, 2 December 1914, 4.

21 "Die deutschen und österreichischen internirten Reservisten in Toronto," *Berliner Journal*, 2 December 1914, 11.

22 Female rates of naturalization were similar to men's. Until the Canadian Citizenship Act in 1946, married women's citizenship was "dependent" on husbands'. For all married immigrant women, they attained or lost British subjecthood through marriage, and if a husband naturalized, so too would his wife (Bredbenner, *A Nationality of Her Own*; Iacovetta, "'In the Case of a Woman' or 'The Headache'").

23 Otter, *Internment Operations*, 6–7.

24 Ibid., 6.

25 *Fifth Census of Canada 1911: Religions, Origins, Birthplace, Citizenship, Literacy and Infirmities, by Provinces, Districts and Sub-Districts, Volume II* (Ottawa: Printed by C. H. Parmelee, Printer to the King's Most Excellent Majesty, 1913), 440.

26 Kordan, "First World War Internment in Canada," 2.

27 Ibid., 5–9, 22–3.

28 Peter McDermott, "Enemy Aliens in the First World War: Legal and Constitutional Issues," in *Canadian State Trials, Volume IV*, edited by Barry Wright, Eric Tucker, and Susan Binnie, 72.

29 Order-in-Council 1914-2085, "German officers and reservists in Canada – Message Secretary of State of Colonies," Approved 7 August 1914, Series A-1-d, Volume 2811, RG2, Privy Council Office.

30 Stefan Manz and Panikos Panayi, "The Internment of Civilian 'Enemy Aliens' in the British Empire," in *Internment during the First World War*, edited by Stefan Manz, Panikos Panayi, and Matthew Stibbe, 32.

31 Order-in-Council 1915-2039, "German Civilian Prisoners in Canada – Note Verbal of German Govt [Government] that prisoners Kapuskasing, Ont. [Ontario] and forced to work answered that only those willing work and are paid – S. S. External Affairs [Secretary of State External Affairs] 1915/08," Approved 28 August 1915, Series A-1-d, Volume 2811, RG2, Privy Council Office; Kordan, "Internment in Canada," 174.

32 Although naturalization in another country often caused German citizens to lose their citizenship, article 25 of the 1913 German Imperial and State Citizenship Law stated, "Citizenship is not lost by one who before acquiring foreign citizenship has secured on application the written consent of the competent authorities of his home State to retain his citizenship" ("German Imperial and State Citizenship Law. July 22, 1913," 225).

33 Otter, *Internment Operations*, 6.

34 Ibid.

35 Among the 1,964 people deported, there were sixty women and children. Their nationality was undefined, but 84 per cent of all deportees were Germans. Women and children were not counted in the total count of internees (8,579) but they were included in the data on deportation (Otter, *Internment Operations*, 14).

36 Ibid., 13.

37 Ibid., 14.

38 Ibid., 6.

39 Kordan, *Enemy Aliens, Prisoners of War*, 36.

40 Hinther and Mochoruk, "Introduction," in *Civilian Internment in Canada*, edited by Rhonda Hinther and Jim Mochoruk, 2.

41 Kealey, "State Repression of Labour and the Left in Canada," 293.

42 Keshen, "All the News That Was Fit to Print," 328.

43 Thompson, *Ethnic Minorities during Two World Wars*, 5.

44 Brown, *A Biography of No Place*, 39.

45 Otter, *Internment Operations*, 6.

46 *Fifth Census of Canada 1911: Religions, Origins, Birthplace, Citizenship, Literacy and Infirmities, by Provinces, Districts and Sub-Districts*, Volume II (Ottawa: Printed by C. H. Parmelee, Printer to the King's Most Excellent Majesty, 1913), 440.

47 Order-in-Council 1914-2283, "Ammunition etc not to be in the possession of any persons of Austro-Hungarian and German nationality," Approved 3 September 1914, Series A-1-d, Volume 2810, RG2, Privy Council Office.

48 Keshen, "All the News That Was Fit to Print," 318.

49 Bohdan Kordan, "Internment in Canada during the Great War: Rights, Responsibilities and Diplomacy," in *Internment during the First World War*, edited by Stefan Manz, Panikos Panayi, and Matthew Stibbe, 164.

50 Ibid., 165.

51 Kordan, "'They Will Be Dangerous,'" 45.

52 "Die deutschen und österreichischen internirten Reservisten in Toronto," *Berliner Journal*, 2 December 1914, 11.

53 Kordan, "Internment in Canada during the Great War," 165.

54 Otter, *Internment Operations*, 6.

55 Ibid., 8.

56 Order-in-Council 1915-1501, "Aliens of Enemy Nationality who are found competing for employment with aliens of our allies or whose presence in company with friendly aliens on public works," Approved 26 June 1915, Series A-1-a, Volume 2811, RG2, Privy Council Office.

57 Kordan, "'They Will Be Dangerous,'" 49.

58 Ibid.

59 Ibid.

60 Thompson, *Ethnic Minorities during Two World Wars*, 6.

61 Kordan, "'They Will Be Dangerous,'" 47.

62 Peter Melnycky, "The Internment of Ukrainians in Canada," in *Loyalties in Conflict*, edited by Frances Swyripa and John Herd Thompson, 4.

63 Order-in-Council 1915-0858, "German and Austrian labourers in Vancouver permitted to go to the United States to obtain employment if they promise not to take part in the war," Approved 24 April 1915, Series A-1-d, Volume 2811, RG2, Privy Council Office; Order-in-Council 1915-2699, "Exeats for Aliens of Enemy Nationality to leave the Country to be issued by officers in Victoria, B.C. and Toronto," Approved 20 November 1915, 1915, Series A-1-d, Volume 2811, RG2, Privy Council Office.

64 "The war-time elections act," *Acts of the Parliament of the Dominion of Canada*. Passed in the session held in the seventh and eighth years of the reign of His Majesty King George V. Vol. 1. Public general acts (Ottawa: J. de L. Taché, 1917), 370–1.

65 English, "Wartime Elections Act."

66 The act did make brief reference to Christian Syrians and Armenians, who were exempted from·this disenfranchisement.

67 "The War-Time Elections Act," *Acts of the Parliament of the Dominion of Canada*. Passed in the session held in the seventh and eighth years of the reign of His Majesty King George V. Vol. 1. Public general acts (Ottawa: J. de L. Taché, 1917), 371.

68 Yildiz, *Beyond the Mother Tongue*, 4; Tara Zahra, *Kidnapped Souls*, 6.

69 Frank Carvell, Robert Borden, and Arthur Meighen, *Official Report of the Debates of the House of Commons of the Dominion of Canda, Seventh Session-Twelfth Parliament*, 7–8 George V, 1917 (Ottawa: J. de Labroquerie Taché, 1918), 5699.

70 In addition to the East Cantons, which were annexed from Germany in 1920, Belgium has historical communities that spoke Germanic dialects that, on a spectrum, had much in common with dialect speakers in the German Empire.

71 Arthur Meighen, *Official Report of the Debates of the House of Commons of the Dominion of Canada, Seventh Session-Twelfth Parliament*, 7–8 George V, 1917 (Ottawa: J. de Labroquerie Taché, 1918), 5700.

72 This act was the Canadian implementation of the British Nationality and Status of Aliens Act from the same year, which sought to standardize the question of citizenship in light of rising Dominion autonomy.

73 "An Act Respecting British Nationality, Naturalization and Aliens," 12 June 1914, in *Acts of the Parliament of Canada* (12th Parliament, 3rd Session) (Ottawa: Brown Chamberlin, Law Printer to the Queen's Most Excellent Majesty, 1914), 290.

74 "Ansichten der Presse," *Ontario Journal*, 26 September 1917, 2.

75 Ibid.

76 "Stimmen der Presse," *Ontario Journal*, 12 September 1917, 2.

77 Arthur Meighen, *Official Report of the Debates of the House of Commons of the Dominion of Canda, Seventh Session-Twelfth Parliament*, 7–8 George V, 1917 (Ottawa: J. de Labroquerie Taché, 1918), 5417.

78 Ibid.

79 Charles Murphy, *Official Report of the Debates of the House of Commons of the Dominion of Canda, Seventh Session-Twelfth Parliament*, 7–8 George V, 1917 (Ottawa: J. de Labroquerie Taché, 1918), 5619.

80 Georges Henri Boivin, *Official Report of the Debates of the House of Commons of the Dominion of Canda, Seventh Session-Twelfth Parliament*, 7–8 George V, 1917 (Ottawa: J. de Labroquerie Taché, 1918), 5627.

81 Price, "Naturalising Subjects, Creating Citizens," 3.

82 Ibid., 12.

83 Ibid., 3.

84 Rodolphe Lemieux, *Official Report of the Debates of the House of Commons of the Dominion of Canda, Seventh Session-Twelfth Parliament*, 7–8 George V, 1917 (Ottawa: J. de Labroquerie Taché, 1918), 5634.

85 Otte, "A 'German Paperchase.'"

86 Wilfrid Laurier, *Official Report of the Debates of the House of Commons of the Dominion of Canda, Seventh Session-Twelfth Parliament*, 7–8 George V, 1917 (Ottawa: J. de Labroquerie Taché, 1918), 5576.

87 Ibid., 5575–6.

88 Order-in-Council 1914-2150, "War with Germany and with Austria Hungary," Approved 15 August 1914, Series A-1-a, RG2, Privy Council Office.

89 Order-in-Council 1918-2381, "Order Respecting Enemy Publications," *The Canada Gazette* 52, no. 14 (5 October 1918): 1277.

90 Ruthenian, listed separately from languages such as Ukrainian, probably refers to what could also be called Ruthene, the language spoken in the southwestern part of present-day Ukraine and in the border region of Slovakia and Poland.

91 Bausenhart, "The Ontario German Language Press and Its Suppression," 45.

92 Kalbfleisch, *The History of the Pioneer German Language Press*, 111.

93 "Shrapnel," *Ontario Journal*, 4 December 1918, 1.

94 Keshen, "All the News That Was Fit to Print," 322.

95 Ernest Chambers to Scammel, 25 February 1916, in Keshen, "All the News That Was Fit to Print," 326.

96 Kealey, "State Repression of Labour," 288.

97 Grenke, *The German Community of Winnipeg*, 161.

98 Keshen, "All the News That Was Fit to Print," 322.

99 Ibid., 341.

100 "Past and Future," *Ontario Journal*, 25 December 1918, 1.

101 "The Local German Weekly and the Order-in-Council," *Ontario Journal*, 2 October 1918, 3.

102 "The Reason Why," *Ontario Journal*, 9 October 1918, 1.

103 Conolly-Smith, *Translating America*, 2, 250.

104 Ibid., 2, 251.

105 Luebke, "Legal Restrictions on Foreign Languages," 1, 10.

106 Ibid., 11.

107 Ibid.

108 Kinbacher, "Life in the Russian Bottoms," 45.

109 In 1921, a total of fifty-five children studied German in the Catholic schools of the province, and only eighty-three in 1922 (*Report of the Minister of Education, Province of Ontario [Canada], 1923* [Toronto: Clarkson W. James, Printer to the King's Most Excellent Majesty, 1924], 162–3). In 1919, the number of pupils studying German at all high schools and collegiate institutes in the province increased to 1,638 (*Report of the Minister of Education, Province of Ontario [Canada], 1919* [Toronto: A.T. Wilgress, Printer to the King's Most Excellent Majesty, 1920], 212, 224; see also the annual *Report of the Minister of Education, Province of Ontario [Canada]*, 1919–30).

110 "Berlin und der patriotische Fond," *Berliner Journal*, 30 September 1914, 6.

111 Ibid.

112 "Der Name unserer Stadt," *Berliner Journal*, 1 March 1916, 1.

113 Keshen, "All the News That Was Fit to Print," 326.

114 Ibid., 328.

115 Ibid.

116 Luebke, *Bonds of Loyalty*, 116.

117 Ibid., 158.

118 Ernest Chambers to John Motz, 23 August 1915, quoted in Keshen, "All the News That Was Fit to Print," 329–30.

119 Regulations (Unlawful Associations, Promoting Change by Unlawful Means) under the War Measures Act, 1914, 15 September 1918 (PC 2384, Proclamations and Orders-in-Council), in *Canadian State Trials, Volume IV*, edited by Barry Wright, Eric Tucker, and Susan Binnie, 487–90.

120 Beginning in January 1919, *Das Ontario Journal* joined with the *Daily Record* of Kitchener, which William Motz already owned, and discontinued its separate office. Arndt and Olson, *The German Language Press of the Americas*, 240–53.

Part Two

1 Christie and Gauvreau, *Christian Churches and Their Peoples*, 3.

2 Orsi, *The Madonna of 115th Street*, 12–13.

3 Lorenzkowski, *Sounds of Ethnicity*, 66; Parr, *The Gender of Breadwinners*, 139; English and McLaughlin, *Kitchener*; McLaughlin, *The Germans in Canada*; McKegney, *The Kaiser's Bust*; Conolly-Smith, *Translating America*; Kazal, *Becoming Old Stock*. Two exceptions to this are: Conzen, "Immigrant Religion and the Public Sphere"; Worsfold, "Welcoming Strangers."

4 Bryce, *To Belong in Buenos Aires*, 125–9.

Chapter Three

1 The first female entered the high school stream at Waterloo Lutheran College in 1929 (Lyon, *The First 60 Years*).

2 *St. Jerome's College, 1905–1906* (No bibliographic information), 7; *St. Jerome's College, 1915–1916* (Berlin, ON: No publisher information), 17.

3 *St. Jerome's College, 1915–1916* (Berlin, ON: No publisher information), 17.

4 Perin, "French-Speaking Canada from 1840," 205.

5 Ibid., 219.

6 Conzen, "Immigrant Religion and the Public Sphere," 74.

7 Perin, *Rome in Canada*, 162

8 Bryce, *To Belong in Buenos Aires*, 110–11, 125–7.

9 Axelrod, *Scholars and Dollars*, 77.

10 Gidney and Millar, *Inventing Secondary Education*, 254, 263, 273.

11 Ibid., 7.

12 Ibid., 243.

13 Ibid., 278–9.

14 Chad Gaffield, Lynne Marks, and Susan Laskin, "Student Populations and Graduate Careers: Queen's University, 1895–1900," in *Youth, University and Canadian Society*, edited by Paul Axelrod and John Reid, 12.

15 Gauvreau, *The Evangelical Century*, 9.

16 *St. Jerome's College, 1891–1892* (Berlin, ON: Rittinger and Motz Printers, 1892), 3.

17 *St. Jerome's College, 1901–1902* (Berlin, ON: Rittinger and Motz, 1902), 6–7.

18 "Modern" was used in opposition to the classical languages of Latin and Greek.

19 *St. Jerome's College, 1901–1902* (Berlin, ON: Rittinger and Motz, 1902), 9–13.

20 "St. Jerome's College, Documents and Correspondence, 1838-59," 15 August 1866, Multicultural History Society of Ontario Collection, Microfilm 4 of 15, Archives of Ontario.

21 Ibid.

22 "Affiliation Papers, 7 May 1927," CR 1-2-3 B51, Folder: CR Province Office, Subject Files: Pre-1948 Affiliations, Archive of the Congregation of the Resurrection, St. Jerome's University.

23 Ibid.

24 Axelrod, *Scholars and Dollars*, 59–60.

25 *St. Jerome's College, 1889–1890* (Berlin, ON: Rittinger and Motz Printers), 18.

26 William J. Motz, "Toast to the College and the Alumni," *The Schoolman. Golden Jubilee Number. St. Jerome's College, Berlin, Ontario* (No bibliographic information), 230.

27 Theobald Spetz, "History of St. Jerome's College," *The Schoolman. Golden Jubilee Number. St. Jerome's College, Berlin, Ontario* (No bibliographic information), 172; *St. Jerome's College, 1913–1914* (Berlin, ON: No bibliographic information), 21.

28 Wahl, "Father Louis Funcken's Contribution to German Catholicism," 522.

29 Ibid.

30 Fr Louis Funcken, "A Brief History of the Congregation of the Resurrection," *The Schoolman. Golden Jubilee Number. St. Jerome's College, Berlin, Ontario* (No bibliographic information): 177–93; Iwicki and Wahl, *Resurrectionist Charism*.

31 Fr Louis Funcken, "A Brief History of the Congregation of the Resurrection," *The Schoolman. Golden Jubilee Number. St. Jerome's College, Berlin, Ontario* (No bibliographic information): 177–93.

32 "Ludwig Funcken," 12 October 1886, Funcken Papers, CR 1-1-4 C13, Archive of the Congregation of the Resurrection, St. Jerome's University.

33 Theobald Spetz, "History of St. Jerome's College," *The Schoolman. Golden Jubilee Number. St. Jerome's College, Berlin, Ontario* (No bibliographic information): 154–77. See also the annual catalogue of St. Jerome's College.

34 Iwicki and Wahl, *Resurrectionist Charism*, 59–61, 113.

35 Bryce, *To Belong in Buenos Aires*, 56, 115.

36 See annual catalogue of St Jerome's College.

37　"Funcken Papers," CR 1-1-4 C13; "Spetz Papers," CR 1-1-3 B37; "Schweitzer and Kloepfer Papers," Box and folder unnamed, Archive of the Congregation of the Resurrection, St. Jerome's University.

38　*Annual Catalogue, The Evangelical Lutheran Theological Seminary of Canada and Waterloo College at Waterloo, Ont. 1918–1919* (No bibliographic information), 10.

39　*Jubiläums-Büchlein*, 16.

40　According to the 1911 census, there were 66,798 Lutherans in Ontario (*Fifth Census of Canada 1911, Volume II*, 2).

41　Lyon, *The First 60 Years*.

42　*The Evangelical Lutheran Theological Seminary at Waterloo Ontario, 1913–1914* (No bibliographic information), 5.

43　*Annual Catalogue, The Evangelical Lutheran Theological Seminary of Canada and Waterloo College at Waterloo, Ont. 1918–1919* (No bibliographic information), 10.

44　*Announcement 1926–1927, Waterloo College* (No bibliographic information), 42.

45　*St. Jerome's College, 1894–1895* (Berlin, ON: Rittinger and Motz Printers, 1895), 18–19.

46　*St. Jerome's 1907–1908* (Berlin, ON: Rittinger and Motz, 1908), 52–6.

47　*St. Jerome's 1916-1917* (Kitchener, ON: No bibliographic information), 59–63.

48　*Catalogue of St. Jerome's College, 1929–1930* (No bibliographic information), 45–9.

49　*Verhandlungen der einundzwanzigsten Jahres-Versammlung der Evangelisch-Lutherischen Synode von Canada, 1881* (Neu-Hamburg: Gedruckt von Preßprich and Ritz, Volkblatt Office, 1881), 18.

50　Ibid., 19.

51　*Verhandlungen der 51sten Jahres-Versammlung der Evangelisch-Lutherischen Synode von Canada, 1912* (Pembroke, ON: Druckerei der Deutschen Post, 1912), 31; *Verhandlungen der 54sten Jahres-Versammlung der Evangelisch-Lutherischen Synode von Canada, 1915* (No bibliographic information), 40; *Verhandlungen der 56sten Jahres-Versammlung der Evangelisch-Lutherischen Synode von Canada, 1918* (No bibliographic information), 38; *Verhandlungen der 63sten Jahresversammlungen der Evangelisch-Lutherischen Synode von Canada, 1925* (No bibliographic information), 28–9.

52　*Verhandlungen der 63sten Jahresversammlungen der Evangelisch-Lutherischen Synode von Canada, 1925* (No bibliographic information), 28–9.

53　*Verhandlungen der 52sten Jahres-Versammlung der Evangelisch-Lutherischen Synode von Canada, 1913* (No bibliographic information), 35.

54　*Announcement 1925–6, The Evangelical Lutheran Seminary of Canada at Waterloo, Ontario* (No bibliographic information), 12.

55　*Announcement 1926–1927, Waterloo College* (No bibliographic information), 10.

56　Axelrod, *Scholars and Dollars*, 59–60.

57 *St. Jerome's College, 1891–1892* (Berlin, ON: Rittinger and Motz Printers, 1892), 5.

58 *St. Jerome's College, Scholastic Year 1887–1888* (Berlin, ON: No publisher information), 5. See also *St. Jerome's College, 1889–1890*, 5; *St. Jerome's College, 1891–1892*, 5; *St. Jerome's College, 1893–1894*, 6; *St. Jerome's College, 1897–1898*, 15.

59 *St. Jerome's College, 1901–1902* (Berlin, ON: Rittinger and Motz, 1902), 5–6.

60 *St. Jerome's College, 1908–1909* (No bibliographic information), 14.

61 Perin, "French-Speaking Canada from 1840," 244.

62 *St. Jerome's College, 1887–1888* (Berlin, ON: No publisher information), 10; *St. Jerome's College, 1889–1890* (Berlin, ON: Rittinger and Motz Printers), 11.

63 *St. Jerome's College, 1896–1897* (Berlin, ON: Rittinger and Motz, 1897), 22.

64 *St. Jerome's College, 1899–1900* (Berlin, ON: Rittinger and Motz, 1900), 21.

65 *St. Jerome's College. 1901–1902* (Berlin, ON: Rittinger and Motz, 1902), 29.

66 Lorenzkowski, *Sounds of Ethnicity*, 103.

67 St. Jerome's College, Berlin, Ontario, Canada. Scholastic Year 1887–1888 (No bibliographic information), 3–4.

68 Ibid.

69 *St. Jerome's College. 1901–1902* (Berlin, ON: Rittinger and Motz, 1902), 13.

70 *St. Jerome's College, Berlin, Ontario, Canada. Scholastic Year 1887–1888* (No bibliographic information), 5.

71 Worman, *Elementary Grammar of the German Language*.

72 *St. Jerome's College, Scholastic Year, 1893–1894* (Berlin, ON: Rittinger and Motz Printers, 1894), 7.

73 Ibid., 8–10.

74 *St. Jerome's College, 1907–1908* (Berlin, ON: Rittinger and Motz, 1908), 20–1.

75 *St. Jerome's College, 1913–1914* (Berlin, ON: No publisher or year), 32–5.

76 *St. Jerome's, 1907–1908* (Berlin, ON: Rittinger and Motz, 1908), 65–71.

77 *Catalogue of St. Jerome's College, 1911–1912* (Berlin, ON: No publication information), 63–70.

78 See annual catalogues of St. Jerome's College.

79 *St. Jerome's College, 1894–1895* (Berlin, ON: Rittinger and Motz Printers, 1895), 13–15.

80 For more on this, see the annual reports of the Berlin and Waterloo Hospital Trust or newspaper articles in the *Berliner Journal* and the *Deutsche Zeitung*.

81 *St. Jerome's College, 1905–1906* (Berlin, ON: Rittinger and Motz, 1906), 4; *St. Jerome's 1910–1911* (Berlin, ON: No publisher information, 1911), 64–6; Lorenzkowski, *Sounds of Ethnicity*, 164–7.

82 See annual *Catalogue of the Evangelical Luthzeran Seminary*.

83 *Verhandlungen der 54sten Jahres-Versammlung der Evangelisch-Lutherischen Synode von Canada, 1915* (No bibliographic information), 40.

84 *Catalogue of the Evangelical Lutheran Seminary for the Second Year, 1912–1913* (Hamilton, ON: H.A. Martin), 5.

85 *The Evangelical Lutheran Theological Seminary at Waterloo Ontario, 1913–1914* (No bibliographic information), 7.

86 *Annual Catalogue, 1921–1922 of the Evangelical Lutheran Theological Seminary of Canada and Waterloo College at Waterloo* (No bibliographic information), 13; *Annual Catalogue, 1923–1924 of the Evangelical Lutheran Theological Seminary of Canada and Waterloo College at Waterloo, Ontario* (No bibliographic information), 5.

87 *Catalogue of the Evangelical Lutheran Seminary for the Second Year, 1912–1913* (Hamilton, ON: H.A. Martin), 8.

88 *The Evangelical Lutheran Theological Seminary at Waterloo Ontario, 1913–1914* (No bibliographic information), 16–17.

89 *The Evangelical Lutheran Theological Seminary at Waterloo, Ontario, 1914–1915* (No bibliographic information), 16.

90 *The Lutheran Theological Seminary of Canada at Waterloo, Ontario, 1915* (No bibliographic information), 25.

91 Ibid., 26.

92 Ibid., 25.

93 Ibid., 26.

94 *Announcement 1926–1927, Waterloo College*, (No bibliographic information), 33.

95 Ibid., 22.

Chapter Four

1 *Verhandlungen der 42sten Jahres-Versammlung der Evangelisch-Lutherischen Synode von Canada, 1902* (Walkerton: Ontario Glocke Office, 1902), 2; *Verhandlungen der 64sten Jahresversammlung der Evangelisch-Lutherischen Synode von Canada, 1926* (No bibliographic information), 44.

2 "Emil Hoffmann, 5.0.6 Lutheran Synod," Wilfrid Laurier Rare Books Collection; *Verhandlungen der 64sten Jahresversammlung der Evangelisch-Lutherischen Synode von Canada, 1926* (No bibliographic information), 43–4.

3 Emil Hoffmann, "My Life," in "Emil Hoffmann, 5.0.6 Lutheran Synod," Wilfrid Laurier University Rare Books Collection.

4 "Emil Hoffmann, 5.0.6 Lutheran Synod," Wilfrid Laurier University Rare Books Collection.

5 Ibid.

6 For more on this, see Westfall, *Two Worlds*; Marks, *Revivals and Roller Rinks*; Christie and Gauvreau, *Christian Churches and Their Peoples*.

7 Christie and Gauvreau, *Christian Churches and Their Peoples*, 73.

8 *Jubiläums-Büchlein: Festschrift zur Feier des 50-jährigen Jubiläums der evang.-luther. Synode von Canada* (No bibliographic information, 1911), 44–54.

9 *Verhandlungen der zwanzigsten Jahres-Versammlung der Evangelisch-Lutherischen Synode von Canada, 1880* (Berlin: Gedruckt bei Rittinger und Motz, "Berliner Journal" Office, 1880), 3.

10 *Verhandlungen der zweiundzwanzigsten Jahres-Versammlung der Evangelisch-Lutherischen Synode von Canada* (Listowel, ON: Dr. Al. Sommer's Privat-Office, 1882), 8.

11 In 1910, the Synod of Central Canada had fourteen congregations and ten pastors (*Jubiläums-Büchlein*, 8–16).

12 Malinsky, *Grace and Blessing*, 17–23.

13 Ibid., 19–23. Ernst founded the *Lutherisches Volksblatt* in 1871 (Malinsky, *Grace and Blessing*, 17).

14 Malinsky, *Grace and Blessing*, 23.

15 "Unsere Synode," *Lutherisches Volksblatt*, 19 November 1914, 4.

16 *Jubiläums-Büchlein*, 44–5.

17 Wilhelm Herrmann, "The Kropp Lutheran Seminary 'Eben-Ezer' Germany, and Its Relation to the United Lutheran Church in America" (Master of Sacred Theology Thesis, Lutheran Theological Seminary at Philadelphia, 1938), 61.

18 The four church bodies were the General Council, the General Synod, the General Synod of the South, and the Missouri Synod.

19 *Deutsche Lutheraner* was published between 1910 and 1922 and then was replaced by the *Lutherischer Herold*, published between 1922 and 1943.

20 See Peterson, *Popular Narratives and Ethnic Identity*; Conolly-Smith, *Translating America*; Kazal, *Becoming Old Stock*.

21 "Das lutherische Volksblatt," *Lutherisches Volksblatt*, 18 February 1915, 4.

22 For more on this, see for example "Erwiderung auf Pastor Hoffmanns Artikel: Lutherisch oder nicht?" *Lutherisches Volksblatt*, 1 March 1889 and 1 May 1889; "Aus Hamburg," *Lutherisches Volksblatt*, 19 July 1894; "Erklärung," *Lutherisches Volksblatt*, 21 January 1897.

23 "Unser doppeltes Jubiläum am 23. Juni 1880," *Lutherisches Volksblatt*, 1 June 1880, 2.

24 *Verhandlungen der 32ten Jahres-Versammlung der Evangelisch-Lutherischen Synode von Canada, 1892* (Walkerton: Ontario Glocke Office, 1892), 15.

25 Ibid., 15.

26 *Verhandlungen der 40sten Jahres Versammlung der Evanglisch-Lutherischen Synode von Canada* (1900), 19.

27 *Verhandlungen der 64sten Jahresversammlung der Evangelisch-Lutherischen Synode von Canada* (1926), 39.

28 "Toronto, das Arbeitsfeld unseres Distrikts," *Lutherisches Volksblatt*, 15 November 1911, 3–4.

29 Pastor Boese, "Toronto Kirchenbau," *Lutherisches Volksblatt*, 15 August 1911, 5. See also: "Notschrei aus Toronto," *Lutherisches Volksblatt*, 15 July 1911, 2.

30 *Jubiläums-Büchlein*, 46, 54.

31 *Synodal-Bericht: Verhandlungen der deutschen evang.-luth. Synode von Missouri, Ohio und anderen Staaten. Canada-District, 1903* (St Louis, MO: Concordia Publishing House, 1903), 61.

32 "Gemeinde-Nachrichten," *Lutherisches Volksblatt*, March 1908, 6–7.

33 *Ernest Hahn: His Life, Work and Place among Us* (No bibliographic information, 1951).

34 *Toronto Evening Telegram,* 16 April 1910, 20.

35 *Verhandlungen der 49sten Jahres-Versammlung der Evangelisch-Lutherischen Synode von Canada, 1910* (Pembroke, ON: Deutsche Post, 1910), 15.

36 *Verhandlungen der 30. Jahresversammlung der Evangelisch-Lutherischen Synode von Canada, 1890* (Walkerton: J.A. Rittinger, Die Ontario Glocke Office, 1890), 20.

37 See for example "Winnipeg," *Kirchen-Blatt,* 15 February 1890, 182; "Kirche und Mission, *Kirchen-Blatt,* 11 August 1898, 191.

38 *Verhandlungen der 31. Jahres-Versammlung der Evangelisch-Lutherischen Synode von Canada, 1891* (Walkerton: Ontario Glocke Office, 1891), 8.

39 "Kirchliche Nachrichten," *Kirchen-Blatt,* 25 February 1904, 398.

40 *Verhandlungen der 42sten Jahres-Versammlung der Evangelisch-Lutherischen Synode von Canada, 1902* (Walkerton: Ontario Glocke Office, 1902), 20.

41 Ibid.

42 "Nachrichten aus dem Missionsgebiet im canadischen Nordwesten," *Lutherisches Volksblatt,* 21 January 1897, 15; "Nachrichten aus dem Missionsgebiet im canadischen Nordwesten," *Lutherisches Volksblatt,* 4 February 1897, 21; "Nachrichten aus dem Missionsgebiet im canadischen Nordwesten," *Lutherisches Volksblatt,* 4 March 1897, 37.

43 "Nachrichten aus dem Missionsgebiet im canadischen Nordwesten," *Lutherisches Volksblatt,* 4 March 1897, 37.

44 "Aus Zeit und Kirche," *Lutherisches Volksblatt,* 15 April 1915, 6.

45 In 1922, congregations of western Canada formed their own district and in that year the Canada District was renamed the Ontario District (Malinsky, *Grace and Blessing,* 23).

46 See for example, Valverde, *The Age of Light, Soap, and Water.*

47 For more on the instability of ethnicity, see Sollors, ed., *The Invention of Ethnicity.*

48 *Verhandlungen der zwanzigsten Jahres-Versammlung der Evangelisch-Lutherischen Synode von Canada, 1880* (Berlin: Gedruckt bei Rittinger und Motz, "Berliner Journal" Office, 1880), 28.

49 *Verhandlungen der 54sten Jahres-Versammlung der Evangelisch-Lutherischen Synode von Canada, 1915* (No bibliographic information), 30; *Verhandlungen der 50sten Jahres-Versammlung der Evangelisch-Lutherischen Synode von Canada, 1911* (No bibliographic information), 25.

50 Both were called *Emigrantenhaus.*

51 Kazal, *Becoming Old Stock,* 243.

52 Advertisement, "Deutsches Emigrantenhaus in New York," *Kirchen-Blatt,* 1 May 1880, 8.

53 Advertisement, "Deutsches Emigrantenhaus in New York," *Kirchen-Blatt,* 15 March 1883, 8.

54   Advertisement, "Deutsches Emigrantenhaus in New York," *Kirchen-Blatt*, 27 September 1894, 8; Advertisement, "Deutsches Lutherisches Emigrantenhaus in New York," *Kirchen-Blatt*, 4 March 1897, 8; Advertisement, "Deutsches Lutherisches Emigrantenhaus in New York," *Kirchen-Blatt*, 13 July 1899, 160; Advertisement, "Deutsches Luth. Emigrantenhaus in New York," *Kirchen-Blatt*, 1 January 1903, 360.

55   *Verhandlungen der zweiundzwanzigsten Jahres-Versammlung der Evangelisch-Lutherischen Synode von Canada, 1882* (Listowel, ON: Dr. Al. Sommer's Privat-Office, 1882), 17–18.

56   *Verhandlungen der dreiundzwanzigsten Jahres-Versammlung der Evangelisch-Lutherischen Synode von Canada, 1883* (Neu-Hamburg: Otto Preußpich, Volksblatt Office, 1883), 16.

57   In 1911, for example, the Canada Synod sent $83 to New York for missionary work amongst immigrants and sailors while it sent $1,344 to the General Council's fund for missionary work in India and $808 for the Kropp seminary (*Verhandlungen der 50sten Jahres-Versammlung der Evangelisch-Lutherischen Synode von Canada, 1911* [No bibliographic information], 25).

58   *Verhandlungen der 52sten Jahres-Versammlung der Evangelisch-Lutherischen Synode von Canada, 1913* (No bibliographic information), 4.

59   Ibid., 13.

60   *Verhandlungen der 64sten Jahresversammlung der Evangelisch-Lutherischen Synode von Canada, 1926* (No bibliographic information), 33.

61   *Verhandlungen der 68sten Jahresversammlung der Evangelisch Lutherischen Synode von Canada, 1930* (No bibliographic information), 56.

62   "Unsere Emigrantenmission und das 'Lutherische Pilgerhaus' im Jahre 1888," *Lutherisches Volksblatt*, 15 March 1889, 44.

63   "Das Lutherische Pilgerhaus und seine Mission im Jahre 1896," *Lutherisches Volksblatt*, 18 March 1897, 44.

64   See, for example, Advertisement, "Lutherisches Pilgerhaus for Ein- und Auswanderer," *Lutherisches Volksblatt*, 7 January 1897, 8; Advertisement, "Lutherisches Pilgerhaus," *Lutherisches Volksblatt*, 27 December 1900, 208.

65   See, for example, "Aus Zeit und Kirche," *Lutherisches Volksblatt*, Augst 20, 1914, 5.

66   "Das Lutherische Pilgerhaus und seine Mission im Jahre 1896," *Lutherisches Volksblatt*, 18 March 1897, 44.

67   "Deutsche Einheimische Mission," *Kirchen-Blatt*, 15 March 1886, 4; Herrmann, "The Kropp Lutheran Seminary," 12, 56.

68   *Annual Report 1927. St Matthews Evangelical Lutheran, Kitchener, Ontario* (No bibliographic information), 7.

69   Herrmann, "The Kropp Lutheran Seminary," 1.

70   Ibid., 61.

71 *Verhandlungen der dreiundzwanzigsten Jahres-Versammlung der Evange-lisch-Lutherischen Synode von Canada, 1883* (Neu-Hamburg: Otto Preußpich, Volksblatt Office, 1883), 16.

72 "Deutsche Einheimische Mission," *Kirchen-Blatt*, 15 March 1886, 4.

73 J.J. Kündig, "Deutsches Predigerseminar," *Kirchen-Blatt*, 1 May 1886, 6.

74 "Kropp Seminary students, 1897," Wilfrid Laurier University Archives and Special Collections, http://images.ourontario.ca/Laurier/3082265/data?n=1, accessed 22 August 2020.

75 Amicus, "Woher nehmen wir unsere Pastoren," *Kirchen-Blatt*, 15 March 1886, 6.

76 A.R.S., "Anmerkung," *Kirchen-Blatt*, 15 March 1886, 6.

77 "Der Beachtung werth," *Kirchen-Blatt*, 15 April 1886, 4.

78 J.J. Kündig, "Deutsches Predigerseminar," *Kirchen-Blatt*, 1 May 1886, 6.

79 Ibid.

80 J.J. Kündig, "Deutsches Predigerseminar," Kirchen-Blatt, 1 May 1886, 6; *Verhandlungen der 64sten Jahresversammlung der Evangelisch-Lutherischen Synode von Canada, 1926* (No bibliographic information, 1926), 43.

81 For example, a pastor came from Kropp to Normandy, Ontario in 1901 ("Kirchliche Nachrichten," *Kirchen-Blatt*, 5 September 1901, 221).

82 See the annual reports of the Canada Synod (*Verhandlungen der Jahres-Versammlung der Evangelisch-Lutherischen Synode von Canada*).

83 In 1880, the synod supported three men (*Verhandlungen der zwanzigsten Jahres-Versammlung der Evangelisch-Lutherischen Synode von Canada, 1880* [Berlin: Gedruckt bei Rittinger und Motz, Berliner Journal Office, 1880], 27–8); in 1891, the two sons of the pastor in Genzmer in Toronto both completed their training in Philadelphia and returned to Ontario (*Verhandlungen der 31. Jahres-Versammlung der Evangelisch-Lutherischen Synode von Canada, 1891* [Walkerton: Ontario Glocke Office, 1891], 6).

84 "Unsere neue Verbindung mit Kropp," *Kirchen-Blatt*, 16 December 1909, 6.

85 *Verhandlungen der 53sten Jahres-Versammlung der Evangelisch-Lutherischen Synode von Canada, 1914* (No bibliographic information), 11.

86 *Verhandlungen der 49sten Jahres-Versammlung der Evangelisch-Lutherischen Synode von Canada, 1909* (Pembroke, ON: Druckerei der Deutschen Post, 1909), 16–17.

87 "Unsere neue Verbindung mit Kropp," *Kirchen-Blatt*, 16 December 1909, 5.

88 Ibid., 4.

89 Ibid., 5.

90 See the "Jahresbericht des Schatzmeisters" in the annual reports of the synodical meetings (*Verhandlungen der Jahres-Versammlung der Evangelisch-Lutherischen Synode von Canada*).

91 See the "Jahresbericht des Schatzmeister" in the annual reports of the synodical meetings (*Verhandlungen der Jahres-Versammlung der Evangelisch-Lutherischen Synode von Canada*), particularly for the years mentioned.

92 *Verhandlungen der 56sten Jahres-Versammlung der Evangelisch-Lutherischen Synode von Canada, 1918* (No bibliographic information, 1918), 29.

93 Ibid., 48.

94 *Verhandlungen der 63sten Jahresversammlungen der Evangelisch-Lutherischen Synode von Canada, 1925* (No bibliographic information, 1925), 28–31.

95 *Verhandlungen der 64sten Jahresversammlung der Evangelisch-Lutherischen Synode von Canada, 1926* (No bibliographic information, 1926), 55.

96 *Verhandlungen der 68sten Jahresversammlung der Evangelisch-Lutherischen Synode von Canada, 1930* (No bibliographic information), 12, 31–2.

97 Ibid., 74–5.

98 Until this year, the highest bodies that organized congregations and synods were called the General Council, the General Synod, or the General Synod of the South. See Herrmann, "The Kropp Lutheran Seminary," 50.

99 *Verhandlungen der 50sten Jahres-Versammlung der Evangelisch-Lutherischen Synode von Canada, 1911* (No bibliographic information), 14.

100 *The Evangelical Lutheran Theological Seminary at Waterloo Ontario, 1913–1914* (No bibliographic information), 8.

101 See, for example, "Missions-Tisch," *Lutherisches Volksblatt*, June 1908, 3.

102 See, for example, *The New Era: A Monthly Missionary Review*, 1910–14.

103 Prang, *A Heart at Leisure from Itself*; Ion, *The Cross and the Rising Sun*; Hollinger, *Protestants Abroad*.

104 "Aus Zeit und Kirche," *Lutherisches Volksblatt*, 15 April 1915, 6.

105 Paddison, *American Heathens*, 1, 5.

106 "Auch ein Missionsfest," *Kirchen-Blatt*, 15 March 1886, 6; "Bilder aus der Mission unter den Muhammedanern," *Kirchen-Blatt*, 21 February 1895, 407.

107 "Kirchliche Nachrichten aus anderen Weltteilen," *Lutherisches Volksblatt*, 7 January 1897, 6.

108 "Kirchliche Nachrichten," *Kirchen-Blatt*, 1 March 1894, 415.

109 "Noth der Heiden und Pflicht der Christen," *Kirchen-Blatt*, 18 October 1894, 258.

110 *Jubiläums-Büchlein*, 60.

111 See, for example, any article of the *Kirchen-Blatt* in 1904 entitled "Aus meinem Tagebuch," the "Kirchliche Nachrichten" in 1906, or "Aus unserer Telugmission" in 1909.

112 Bryce, "Seeing Japan."

113 In 1881, the Canada Synod contributed $180 for the Telugoo-Mission (*Verhandlungen der einundzwanzigsten Jahres-Versammlung der Evangelisch-Lutherischen Synode von Canada, 1881* [Neu-Hamburg: Gedruckt von Preßprich and Ritz, Volkblatt Office, 1881], 22). By 1901, the contribution to the General Council's "heathen" mission had risen to $801 (*Verhandlungen der 41sten Jahres-Versammlung der Evanglisch-Lutherischen Synode von Canada, 1901* [Walkerton: Ontario Glocke Office, 1901], 23). In 1911, the annual sum rose to $1,344 (*Verhandlungen der 50sten Jahres-Versammlung der Evangelisch-*

Lutherischen Synode von Canada, 1911 [No bibliographic information, 1911], 25. In 1915, the Canada Synod still gave the Council $1,139 for the heathen mission in India (*Verhandlungen der 54sten Jahres-Versammlung der Evangelisch-Lutherischen Synode von Canada, 1915* [No bliographic information, 1915], 30).

114　*Jubiläums-Büchlein*, 23–4.

115　See annual reports of the Canada Synod (*Jahres-Versammlung der Evanglisch-Lutherischen Synode von Canada*).

116　"Mission," *Lutherisches Volksblatt*, 15 May 1871, 38.

117　"Leipziger Mission," *Lutherisches Volksblatt*, 15 July 1880, 4.

118　*Lutherisches Volksblatt*, 15 February 1889, 29.

119　"Ueber unsere geplannte Heidenmission," *Lutherisches Volksblatt*, 7 June 1894, 93.

Part Three

1　McKeown, *Chinese Migrant Networks and Cultural Change*, 10.

2　Loewen, *Family, Church, and Market*; McGowan, *The Waning of the Green*; Kazal, *Becoming Old Stock*; Conolly-Smith, *Translating America*; Lorenzkowski, *Sounds of Ethnicity*; Kazal, "Revisiting Assimilation."

3　I first discussed the ideas in this paragraph in Bryce, *To Belong in Buenos Aires*, 140, 7.

4　Yildiz, *Beyond the Mother Tongue*, 2.

5　Ibid., 10.

6　Ibid., 13.

Chapter Five

1　"Spezial-Correspondenzen. Aus Torontos deutschen Kreisen," *Deutsche Zeitung*, 29 December 1891, 4; "Spezial-Correspondenzen. Aus Torontos deutschen Kreisen," *Deutsche Zeitung*, 12 January 1892, 4.

2　"Spezial-Correspondenzen. Aus Torontos deutschen Kreisen," *Deutsche Zeitung*, 12 January 1892, 4.

3　Grosjean, *Life with Two Languages*, 39; Gal, *Language Shift*.

4　Sutherland, *Growing Up*; Gleason, *Small Matters*.

5　Comacchio, *Dominion of Youth*.

6　Maza, "The Kids Aren't All Right," 1264; Gleason, "Avoiding the Agency Trap," 446.

7　Gleason, "Avoiding the Agency Trap."

8　Alexander, "Agency and Emotion Work," 120.

9　Mintz, "Children's History Matters," 1291.

10　Maza, "The Kids Aren't All Right," 1285.

11　Clarke, "English-Speaking Canada from 1854," 309.

12　Mintz, "Why the History of Childhood Matters," 20.

13 *Verhandlungen der 49sten Jahres-Versammlung der Evangelisch-Lutherischen Synode von Canada, 1909* (Pembroke, ON: Druckerei der Deutschen Post, 1909), 34.

14 Christie and Gauvreau, *Christian Churches and Their Peoples*, 82.

15 Ibid.

16 "Können lutherische Eltern ihren Kindern den Besuch fremder Sonntagsschulen gestattet?" *Kirchen-Blatt*, 15 March 1886, 4–5.

17 "Aus dem bürgerlichen Leben," *Lutherisches Volksblatt*, 7 June 1894, 91.

18 *Gedenkbuechlein, 1837–1912* (Waterloo, ON: Sentinel Print, 1912), 23.

19 Ibid., 23.

20 Ibid., 21.

21 *100th Anniversary. St. John's Evangelical Lutheran Church*, 39.

22 *Annual Report 1930, St. John's Evangelical Lutheran Church, Waterloo, Ontario* (No bibliographic information), 4.

23 Ibid., 30.

24 *St Matthews Evangelical Lutheran Church, Kitchener, Ontario, Annual Report, 1922* (No bibliographic information), 5.

25 Ibid., 3.

26 Ibid., 2, 5.

27 *St. Matthews Lutheran Church, Kitchener, Ontario, Annual Report and Directory, 1925* (No bibliographic information), 4.

28 *St Matthews Evangelical Lutheran Church, Kitchener, Ontario, Annual Report, 1922* (No bibliographic information), 4.

29 *St Matthews Evangelical Lutheran, Kitchener, Ontario, Annual Report 1927* (No bibliographic information), 10.

30 Ibid., 10–11.

31 *100th Anniversary, St. Paul's Evangelical Lutheran Church, Kitchener, Ontario, 1835–1935* (No bibliographic information), 41.

32 *Annual Statement of the Ev. Luth. St. Paul's Church Kitchener, Ontario, 1929* (No bibliographic information), 15.

33 *St Matthews Evangelical Lutheran Church, Kitchener, Ontario, Annual Report, 1922* (No bibliographic information), 4.

34 *St. Matthews Lutheran Church, Kitchener, Ontario, Annual Report and Directory, 1925* (No bibliographic information), 4.

35 *St Matthews Evangelical Lutheran, Kitchener, Ontario, Annual Report 1927* (No bibliographic information), 10.

36 *St Matthews Lutheran Church, Annual Report 1930* (No bibliographic information), 12.

37 *St Matthews Evangelical Lutheran Church, Kitchener, Ontario, Annual Report, 1922* (No bibliographic information), 6.

38 *Verhandlungen der 55sten Jahres-Versammlung der Evangelisch-Lutherischen Synode von Canada, 1917* (No bibliographic information), 56.

39 E.M. Genzmer, "Spezial-Correspondenzen aus Torontos deutschen Kreisen," *Deutsche Zeitung*, 22 December 1891, 5.

40 See, for example, "Special-Correspondenzen. Aus Torontos deutschen Kreisen," *Deutsche Zeitung*, 19 April 1892, 5; "Special-Correspondenzen aus Torontos deutschen Kreisen," *Deutsche Zeitung*, 4 May 1892, 5.

41 E.M. Genzmer, "Spezial-Correspondenzen aus Torontos deutschen Kreisen," *Deutsche Zeitung*, 22 December 1891, 5.

42 Ibid.

43 Ibid.

44 Ibid.

45 Heinrich Rembe, "Bundeslied für unseren Jugendbund" *Kirchenblatt*, 11 November 1909, 7.

46 *Verhandlungen der 63sten Jahresversammlungen der Evangelisch-Lutherischen Synode von Canada, 1925* (No bibliographic information), 44.

47 *Verhandlungen der 64sten Jahresversammlung der Evangelisch-Lutherischen Synode von Canada, 1926* (No bibliographic information), 76.

48 *Verhandlungen der einundzwanzigsten Jahres-Versammlung der Evangelisch-Lutherischen Synode von Canada, 1881* (Neu-Hamburg: Gedruckt von Preßprich and Ritz, Volkblatt Office, 1881), 16.

49 *Verhandlungen der 49sten Jahres-Versammlung der Evangelisch-Lutherischen Synode von Canada, 1910* (Pembroke, ON: Deutsche Post, 1910), 15.

50 *Verhandlungen der 55sten Jahres-Versammlung der Evangelisch-Lutherischen Synode von Canada, 1917* (No bibliographic information), 28.

51 *Verhandlungen der 53sten Jahres-Versammlung der Evangelisch-Lutherischen Synode von Canada, 1914* (No bibliographic information), 33.

52 Schindler, *Im Dienst des Volkes 1929–1969*, 18.

53 Kaelble, *Das erste Jahrzehnt*, 28–9.

54 I first discussed this in Bryce, *To Belong in Buenos Aires*, 125–7. See also Conzen, *Germans in Minnesota*, 44–50.

55 Savard, *Jules-Paul Tardivel*, 238; Perin, *Rome in Canada*, 162; Cahensly, *Der St. Raphaelsverein zum Schutze katholischer deutscher Auswanderer*, 35–40; "Stimmen aus Amerika für die Denkschrift der europäischen Raphaels-Vereine an den hl. Vater," *St. Raphaels-Blatt. Organ des St. Raphaels-Vereins zum Schutze katholischer deutscher Auswanderer*, no. 1, January 1893, 2; "Die Sprachenfrage und die Verluste der katholischen Kirche in den Vereinigten Staaten von Nordamerika," *St. Raphaels-Blatt. Organ des St. Raphaels-Vereins zum Schutze katholischer deutscher Auswanderer*, no. 3, July 1900, 39, 48.

56 Cahensly, *Der St. Raphaelsverein zum Schutze katholischer deutscher Auswanderer*, 29–30.

57 Ibid.

58 Kaelble, *Das erste Jahrzehnt*, 27.

59 Ibid., 10.

60 Ibid., 12.

61 Ibid., 18.
62 Ibid., 32.
63 Ibid., 35.
64 *Centennial, 1857–1957. St. Mary's Church, Kitchener, Ontario* (No bibliographic information), 10.
65 Grams, *German Emigration to Canada*, 235–6; Wagner, *A History of Migration from Germany to Canada*, 11.

Chapter Six

1 Grosjean, *Bilingual*, 4.
2 Kratz and Milnes, "Kitchener German," 184–98, 274–83; Moelleken, "Die russlanddeutschen Mennoniten."
3 *Gedenkbuechlein, 1837–1912*, 2.
4 The congregation was founded in 1904 as the result of a schism in the St Paul's Church, a congregation belonging to the Canada District of the Missouri Synod. The St Matthäus congregation joined the Canada Synod.
5 *Einweihung der Evangelisch-Lutherischen St. Matthäuskirche, Berlin* (No bibliographic information, 1915), 17–19.
6 *St. Matthews Annual Report 1924* (No bibliographic information), insert; *St. Matthews Lutheran Church, Kitchener, Ontario, Annual Report and Directory, 1925* (No bibliographic information), insert.
7 In 1923, Schmieder boasted that the congregation had 2,300 souls and that "every tenth person in the City of Kitchener is a member of St. Matthew's Church" (*St. Matthews Evangelical Lutheran Church, Kitchener, Ontario, Annual Report 1923* [No bibliographic information], 7).
8 *St. Matthews Evangelical Lutheran Church, Kitchener, Ontario, Annual Report 1923* (No bibliographic information), 4–5.
9 Ibid.
10 Ibid.
11 *Gedenkbuechlein*, 21.
12 Kaelble, *Das erste Jahrzehnt*, 27.
13 "Amalgamation Committee, 1927," Box B4, Archive of the Erste Evangelisch-Lutherische Kirche/First Evangelical Lutheran Church, Toronto; H. Grunwald, *History of First Lutheran Church, Toronto, Ontario* (No bibliographic information, 1951), 11.
14 This was the case, for example, at two of the largest congregations in the Canada Synod, the St Matthäus congregation in Kitchener and the St Johannis congregation in Waterloo. *St. Matthews Evangelical Lutheran Church, Kitchener, Ontario, Annual Report 1923* (No bibliographic information), 6; *St. Matthews Annual Report 1924* (No bibliographic information), 34; *St. Matthews Evangelical Lutheran Church, Kitchener, Ontario, Annual Report, 1926* (No bibliographic information), 34; *St Matthews Lutheran Church, Annual*

Report 1930 (No bibliographic information), 33; *Annual Report 1930, St. John's Evangelical Lutheran Church, Waterloo, Ontario* (No bibliographic information), 30.

15 See annual reports of the St Matthew's and St Paul's congregations in Berlin/ Kitchener, of St John's in Waterloo, and the Trinitatis congregation in Toronto.

16 This report provided information about the congregation's finances, the names of the elected church board, membership statistics, and the amount that members contributed to the congregation. This congregation belonged to the Canada District of the Missouri Synod.

17 *100th Anniversary, St. Paul's Evangelical Lutheran Church, Kitchener, Ontario, 1835–1935* (No bibliographic information), 41, 53.

18 "Book of Minutes of St. Paul's Lutheran Ladies Aid. Protokoll-Buch des Frauen-Vereins der St. Paul's Kirche, Kitchener, Ontario," 1 January 1927, Archive of St. Paul's Church, Kitchener, Ontario.

19 "St. Paul's Ladies' Aid, 1 January 1927–7 December 1932," Archive of St Paul's Church, Kitchener, Ontario.

20 "St. Paul's Ladies Society and Young Ladies Society, 1890–1926," Archive of St Paul's Church, Kitchener, Ontario; *90th Anniversary of St. Paul's Lutheran Ladies Aid, Kitchener, Ont. 1865-1955* (No bibliographic information), 3–4.

21 *100th Anniversary. St. John's Evangelical Lutheran Church. 1837–1937. Waterloo, Ontario* (No bibliographic information), 42; *Common Service Book of the Lutheran Church* (Philadelphia: The Board of Publication of the United Lutheran Church in America, 1918).

22 "Es lebe der Kaiser: Feier des Geburtstages seiner Majestät in Berlin," *Berliner Journal,* 1 February 1905, 2.

23 Editors, "An die Leser des ,Journal' und der ,Glocke'," *Berliner Journal,* 13 July 1904, 4.

24 "Fremde Sprachen," *Berliner Journal,* 29 January 1913, 2.

25 Bryce, *To Belong in Buenos Aires,* 58–60.

26 Lesser and Rein, "Motherlands of Choice," 258.

27 *Jubiläums-Büchlein,* 9–15.

28 Ibid.

29 *Verhandlungen der 55sten Jahres-Versammlung der Evangelisch-Lutherischen Synode von Canada, 1917* (No bibliographic inforamtion), 71; *Verhandlungen der 56sten Jahres-Versammlung der Evangelisch-Lutherischen Synode von Canada, 1918* (No bibliographic inforamtion), 38; *Verhandlungen der 63sten Jahresversammlungen der Evangelisch-Lutherischen Synode von Canada, 1925* (No bibliographic information), 46.

30 *Verhandlungen der 63sten Jahresversammlungen der Evangelisch-Lutherischen Synode von Canada, 1925* (No bibliographic information), 86.

31 *St. Matthews Annual Report 1924* (No bibliographic information), 5.

32 "Kirchliche Nachrichten," *Kirchen-Blatt,* 14 January 1909, 7.

33 Bryce, *To Belong in Buenos Aires,* 2.

34 Engerman, "Introduction," 1402.

35 Koselleck, *Futures Past*, 268.

36 Ibid., 270.

37 Bryce, *To Belong in Buenos Aires*, 2.

38 Perin, "French-Speaking Canada from 1840," 215–16, 220.

39 Cecillon, *Prayers, Petitions, and Protests*, 3.

40 There was a German Catholic parish in Toronto between 1881 and 1886. A new one opened in 1929 (Kaelble, *Das erste Jahrzehnt*, 7).

41 *Centennial, 1857–1957. St. Mary's Church, Kitchener, Ontario* (No bibliographic information), 25.

42 "St. Mary's Church Building Fund 1892–1904, Minute Book," Archive of the Congregation of the Resurrection, St Jerome's University.

43 "St Mary's Announcements. 1910-1912," CR 1-1-2 A20, Archive of the Congregation of the Resurrection, St Jerome's University.

44 Theobald Spetz, *The Catholic Church in Waterloo County* (Toronto: The Catholic Register and Extension, 1916), 39.

45 New Germany became Maryhill in 1941 ("The History of Maryhill," Maryhill Historical Society, accessed 10 July 2020, http://maryhillroots.com/history/)

46 "Weiler Papers," Archive of the Congregation of the Resurrection, St Jerome's University.

47 "Obituary: Theobald Spetz," *Daily Record*, 2 December 1921.

48 "Zinger Papers," Archive of the Congregation of the Resurrection, St Jerome's University; *Centennial, 1857–1957. St. Mary's Church, Kitchener, Ontario* (No bibliographic information), 25.

Conclusion

1 Lundberg, "Paying the Price of Citizenship," 217.

2 Ibid.

3 I first discussed the ideas in this paragraph in Benjamin Bryce and David M.K. Sheinin, "Introduction: Citizenship in Twentieth-Century Argentina," in *Making Citizens in Argentina*, edited by Benjamin Bryce and David M.K. Sheinin, 2–3.

4 Sonya Rose, "Fit to Fight but Not to Vote? Masculinity and Citizenship in Britain, 1832–1918," in *Representing Masculinity*, edited by Stefan Dudink, Karen Hagemann, and Anna Clark, 133.

5 Anna Clark, "The Rhetoric of Masculine Citizenship: Concepts and Representations in Modern Western Political Culture," in *Representing Masculinity*, edited by Stefan Dudink, Karen Hagemann, and Anna Clark, 15.

6 Bryce and Sheinin, "Introduction: Citizenship in Twentieth-Century Argentina," 6.

7 Brubaker, *Citizenship and Nationhood*, ix–x.

8 Canning and Rose, "Gender, Citizenship and Subjectivity," 431.

9   Between 1867 and 1914, 4,537,600 immigrated to Canada. While there was important out-migration to the United States in this period, many of those departures were of people born in Canada and not solely foreign nationals passing through Canadian ports. Statistics Canada, "150 Years of Immigration in Canada," https://www150.statcan.gc.ca/n1/pub/11-630-x/11-630-x2016006-eng.htm, accessed 5 March 2021. See also Ramirez, *Crossing the 49th Parallel*; Widdis, *With Scarcely a Ripple*.

10 Hayday, *So They Want Us to Learn French*, 4–5.

Bibliography

Primary Sources, Canada

PUBLISHED DOCUMENTS

Association canadienne-française d'éducation d'Ontario. *Bi-lingualism in Ontario: Common Sense and Prejudice*. Ottawa: Association canadienne-française d'éducation d'Ontario, 1912.

Belcourt, Napoléon-Antoine. *Regulation 17 ultra vires: Argument of Hon. N.A. Belcourt before the Supreme Court of Ontario, November 2, 1914*. Toronto: Imprimerie du 'Droit', 1914.

Berlin Business College 1907. No bibliographic information.

Berlin Collegiate – Calendar of Pupils, 1855–1904. No bibliographic information.

Burpee, Lawrence, et al. *Canada in the Great World War: An Authentic Account of the Military History of Canada from the Earliest Days to the Close of the War of the Nations, vol. II, Days of Preparation*. Toronto: United Publishers of Canada, Ltd, 1921.

The Canadian Newspaper Directory. Montreal: A. McKim and Co., Publishers, 1892.

Catalogue of Books. Berlin Free Library. Berlin, ON: Rittinger and Motz Printers and Publishers, 1900.

Catalogue of Books in the Berlin Free Library, 1894. Berlin, ON: Daily Record, Printers and Publishers, 1894.

Catalogue of Books of the Waterloo Free Public Library. Waterloo, ON: Chronicle Office, 1888.

Der Deutsche in Canada: Ein Organ für deutsches Leben und Streben in Canada. Hamilton, ON: Marxhausen'schen Buchhandlung, 1872.

Die Dominion Canada: Ein Wegweiser für Deutsche Einwanderer nach Canada. Ottawa: n.p., 1876.

Einführungs-Gottesdienst des Herrn Pastor Orzen in der Ev. Luth. St. Paul's Kirche, 1922. No bibliographic information.

Einweihung der Evangelisch-Lutherischen St. Matthäuskirche, Berlin. N.p., 1915.

Figuier, Louis. *Les grandes inventions modernes dans les sciences, l'industrie et les arts*. Nouvelle édition complètement refondue. Paris: Hachette, 1912.

Funcken, Eugen. *Bernhard von Methon, oder Die Entstehung des Hospizes auf dem St. Bernhard*. Cincinnati: Wahrheitsfreund, 1863.

— *Gedichten von Vater Eugen Funcken, Apostol. Missionär in Ober-Canada. Zum besten eines deutschen Waisen-Hauses in Ober-Canada*. New York and Cincinnati: Gebrüder Karl und Nikolaus Benzinger, 1868.

Gesangs-Gottesdienst in der Ev. Luth. St. Pauls Kirche. Berlin, ON: No publisher information, 1904.

Grunwald, A. *History of First Lutheran Church, Toronto, Ontario*. No bibliographic information.

Heintz, Gladys. "German Immigration into Upper Canada and Ontario from 1783 to the Present Day." MA thesis, Queen's University, 1938.

Hopkins, J. Castell. *The Canadian Annual Review War Series, 1916*. Toronto: The Canadian Annual Review Ltd, 1918.

Kitchener, the Industrial City: The Birthplace of the Great Niagara Power Movement. No bibliographic information.

Kitchener and Waterloo Collegiate Institute. *Evening Industrial Classes, 1922–23*. No bibliographic information.

Krafft, A. *In der Filiale: Eine Erzählung für das "Luth. Volksblatt."* Elmira, ON: Verlag des Luth. Volksblatt, 1890.

Library Hand-Book, Berlin, 1904. No bibliographic information.

Liebbrandt, Gottlieb. *100 Jahre Concordia Club, 1873–1973*. No bibliographic information.

Liste der beitragenden Mitglieder der Ev.luth. St. Matthäus Gemeinde, Kitchener, Ontario, 1917. No bibliographic information.

Malinsky, Frank. *Grace and Blessing. A History of the Ontario District of the Lutheran Church-Missouri Synod*. N.p., 1954.

Monaghan, P.J., *Congregation of the Sisters of St. Joseph*. Hamilton, ON: Epsicopus Hamiltonensis, 1943.

Neu-Ontario. Berlin, ON: Gedruckt von Rittinger and Motz, n.d.

Oppel, Alwin. *Kanada und die Deutschen*. Dresden: Heimat und Welt-Verlag, 1916.

Rededication: St. John's Evangelical Lutheran Church. Waterloo, ON. N.p., 1953.

Robertson, John Ross. *Robertson's Landmarks of Toronto*. Vol. 4. N.p., 1904.

Schott, Carl. *Landnahme und Kolonisation in Canada am Beispiel Südontarios*. Kiel, Germany: Geographisches Institut der Universität Kiel, 1936.

Sherk, A.B. "The Pennsylvania Germans of Waterloo County, Ontario." *Ontario Historical Society. Papers and Records* 7 (1906): 98–108.

Spetz, Theobald. *The Catholic Church in Waterloo County*. Catholic Register and Extension, 1916.

Timperlake, J. *Illustrated Toronto: Past and Present*. Toronto: Peter A. Gross, 1877.

Toronto Turnverein 1889. CIHM no 47951.

Tremblay, Jules. *Le français en Ontario: Son usage et son enseignement sont définis par le droit provenant de l'occupation première, par le droit des gens, par la coutume, par le droit constitutionnel et même par les statuts provinciaux.* Montreal: Arthur Nault, éditeur, 1913.

Uttley, W.V. *A History of Kitchener, Ontario.* Kitchener, ON: n.p., 1937.

Worman, James. *Elementary Grammar of the German Language.* New York: A.S. Barnes and Company, 1873.

PUBLICATIONS OF THE EDUCATION DEPARTMENT OF ONTARIO

Acts of the Department of Education, Province of Ontario 1909. Toronto: Warwick Bros and Rutter Ltd, 1909.

Acts Relating to the Education Department. Public and High Schools and Truancy. Ontario 1891. Toronto: Warwick and Sons, 1891.

Acts Relating to the Education Department. Public and High Schools and Truancy. Ontario 1896. Toronto: Warwick Bros and Rutter, 1896.

Acts Relating to the Education Department. Public and High Schools and Truancy. Ontario 1901. Toronto: Warwick Bros and Rutter, 1901.

Ahn, F. *A New Practical and Easy Method of Learning the German Language. First course.* Toronto: Copp, Clark and Co., 1877.

– *A New Practical and Easy Method of Learning the German Language. Second course.* Toronto: Copp, Clark and Co., 1877.

Bernhardt, Wilhelm, ed. *Aus goldenen Tagen: Studien und Abenteuer* von Heinrich Seidel. Toronto: The Copp, Clark Company, Ltd, 1906.

Blake, Crooks, and Harcourt Ross. *Pamphlets on Education.* N.p., 1871–1913.

Catalogue of Books Recommended by the Ontario Department of Education for Libraries of Collegiate Institutes, High Schools, and Continuation Schools. Toronto: A.T. Wilgress, Printer to the King's Most Excellent Majesty, 1918.

Compendium of Acts and Regulations Respecting the Public, Separate and High Schools. Toronto: Hunter, Rose and Col, Printers, 1878.

Educational System of the Province of Ontario. Dominion of Canada. Toronto: Printed for the Department, 1886.

Henn, P. *Ahn's First German Book.* New York: E. Steiger and Co., 1873.

– *Ahn's Fourth German Book.* New York: E. Steiger and Co., 1876.

– *Ahn's Second German Book.* New York: E. Steiger and Co., 1873.

– *Ahn's Third German Book.* New York: E. Steiger and Co. 1875.

Hodgins, George. *The Legislation and History of Separate Schools in Upper Canada: From 1841, until the Close of the Reverend Doctor Ryerson's Administration of the Education Department of Ontario in 1876: Including Various Private Papers and Documents on the Subject.* Toronto: William Briggs, 1897.

Hohlfeld, A.R. ed. *Die Freiherren von Gemperlein* von Marie von Ebner-Eschenbach. Toronto: The Copp, Clark Company Ltd, 1901.

– *Krambamuli* by Marie von Ebner-Eschenbach. Toronto: The Copp, Clark Company Ltd, 1901.

Klotz, Otto. *Leitfaden zur deutschen Sprache oder kurz gefasstes Lehrbuch der deutschen Sprache in Fragen und Antworten.* Preston, ON: Im Selbstverlage des Verfassers, 1867.

Lang, A.E., and G.H. Needler. *Ontario High School German Grammar.* Toronto: The Ryerson Press, 1925.

Macpherson, W.E. *The Ontario Grammar Schools.* Kingston, ON: The Jackson Press, 1916.

Millar, John. *The Educational System of the Province of Ontario, Canada.* Toronto: Warwick and Sons, 1893.

Müller, A. *Selections for Sight Translation and Supplementary Reading in German.* Toronto: The Copp, Clark Co. Ltd, 1896.

Müller, Margarete, and Carla Wenckebach, eds. *Legenden von Gottfried Keller.* Toronto: The Copp, Clark Company, Ltd, 1902.

Nichols, A.B. *Two German Tales: Goethe: Die neue Melusine, Zschokke: Der tote Gast.* Toronto: The Copp, Clark Company Ltd, 1905.

Regulations and Correspondence Relating to French and German Schools in the Province of Ontario. Toronto: Warwick and Sons, 1889.

Remarks upon Text-Books Authorized by the Education Department. Toronto: Warwick and Sons, 1889.

Report of Commissioners on Public Schools in Ontario in Which the French Language Is Taught. Toronto: Warwick and Sons, 1889.

Ross, George. *The Progress of Our Schools, Text Books, and Religious Instruction.* N.p., 1886.

– "The French Language in our Public Schools." Speech, 8 March 1889 (Toronto: Hunter, Rose and Co., Printers, 1889).

– *The Separate School Question and the French Language.* Toronto: Hunter, Rose and Co., Printers, 1889.

– *Report of Compulsory Education in Canada, Great Britain, Germany and the United States.* Toronto: Warwick and Sons, 1891.

– *The Schools of England and Germany.* Toronto: Warwick Bros and Rutter, 1894.

Sissons, C.B. *Bilingual Schools in Canada.* London, Paris, Toronto: J.M. Dent and Sons, Ltd, 1917.

– "The Language Issue in the Schools of Canada." Lecture delivered at the FORUM in Ottawa, January 1920.

Teuscher, Jakob. ABC *Buchstabir- u. Lesebüchlein für die Elementar-Schulen in Canada.* Berlin, ON: Boedecker und Stuebing, 1868.

Text Books Authorized for Use in Public Schools, High Schools and Training Schools/ Departmental Text-Book Regulations and Text-books Authorized for Use in Public, High and Continuation Schools and Collegiate Institutes. Toronto: Education Department, 1889–1930.

Van der Smissen, W.H and W.H. Fraser. *High School German Grammar.* Toronto: The Copp, Clark Company Ltd, 1888.

– *High School German Grammar and Exercises.* Toronto: The Copp Clark Company Ltd, 1909.

– *The High School German Grammar and Reader with Elementary Exercises in Composition and Vocabularies.* Toronto: The Copp, Clark Company Ltd, 1900.

Wells, B.W. ed. *Der Bibliothekar* by Gustav von Moser. Toronto: The Copp, Clark Company Ltd, 1897.

COMMEMORATIVE PUBLICATIONS

Berlin, Ontario. Issued in Commemoration of Its Celebration of Cityhood. Berlin, ON: German Printing and Publishing Company, 1912.

Berlin To-Day, 1806–1906. Berlin, ON: New Record, 1906.

Busy Berlin, Jubilee Souvenir. Berlin, ON: Berlin News Record, 1897.

Centennial, 1857–1957: St. Mary's Church, Kitchener, Ontario. No bibliographic information.

Gedenkbuechlein, 1837–1912. Waterloo: Sentinel Print, 1912.

Germania 100 Jahre, 1864–1964. No bibliographic information.

Jubiläums-Büchlein: Festschrift zur Feier des 50-jährigen Jubiläums der evang.-luther. Synode von Canada. No bibliographic information, 1911.

100 Years of Progress in Waterloo County, Canada. Semi-Centennial Souvenir, 1856–1906. Waterloo, ON: Chronicle-Telegraph, 1906.

100th Anniversary, St. Paul's Evangelical Lutheran Church, Kitchener, Ontario, 1835–1935. No bibliographic information.

90th Anniversary of St. Paul's Lutheran Ladies Aid, Kitchener, Ont. 1865–1955. No bibliographic information.

Roberts, C.S. *100th Anniversary. St. John's Evangelical Lutheran Church.* 1837–1937. Waterloo, ON: N.p., 1937.

Schindler, Karl. *Im Dienst des Volkes 1929–1969. Jahrbuch zum 40-Jährigen Jubiläum der deutschsprachigen katholischen Gemeinde in Toronto.* Toronto: St Joseph Press, 1969.

St. Matthews 70 Years of Service. No bibliographic information.

St. Mary's Church, Kitchener, Ontario, 1900–1950. No bibliographic information.

NEWSPAPERS AND PERIODICALS

Berlin Daily Record, 1924

Berliner Journal, 1890–1916

Deutsch-Canadischer Herold. Illustrierte Kultur-Zeitschrift über Landwirst, Handel, Industrie u. Jagd in Canada, 1928–29

Deutsche Zeitung, 1891–99

Kirchen-Blatt, 1880–1910
Lutherisches Volksblatt, 1871–1918
The New Era: A Monthly Missionary Review, 1910–14
Ontario Journal, 1917–18
Pädagogische Monatshefte: Zeitschrift für das deutschamerikanische Schulwesen, 1899–1901
Toronto Evening Telegram, 1910

CALENDARS

Canada Kalendar, 1882–1920
The Canadian Almanac and Repository of Useful Knowledge/The Canadian Almanac and Miscellaneous Directory, 1880–1930

FEDERAL GOVERNMENT OF CANADA

Acts of the Parliament of Canada. 12th Parliament, 3rd Session. Ottawa: Brown Chamberlin, Law Printer to the Queen's Most Excellent Majesty, 1914.
Acts of the Parliament of the Dominion of Canada. Passed in the session held in the seventh and eighth years of the reign of His Majesty King George V. Vol. 1. Public general acts. Ottawa: J. de Labroquerie Taché, 1917.
Auskunft über die Dominion Canada für deutsche Ansiedler. Ottawa: Ministerium für Landwirtschaft der canadischen Regierung, 1882.
Census of Canada, 1881–1931.
Illiteracy and School Attendance in Canada. Ottawa: F.A. Acland, Printer to the King's Most Excellent Majesty, 1926.
Official Report of the Debates of the House of Commons of the Dominion of Canada, Seventh Session, Twelfth Parliament. 7–8 George V, 1917. Ottawa: J. de Labroquerie Taché, 1918.
Origin, Birthplace, Nationality and Language of the Canadian People. Ottawa: F.A. Acland, Printer to the King's Most Excellent Majesty, 1929.
Otter, William. *Internment Operations, 1914–1920.* Ottawa: Thomas Mulvey, Printer to the King's Most Excellent Majesty, 1921.

ORDERS-IN-COUNCIL

Order-in-Council 1914-2085. "German officers and reservists in Canada – Message Secretary of State of Colonies." Approved 7 August 1914, Series A-1-d. Volume 2811, RG2, Privy Council Office.
Order-in-Council 1914-2150. "War with Germany and with Austria Hungary – Authority to Police and Militia to arrest and intern all German and Austrian subjects suspecting of joining armed forces of the enemy or intending to give aid to release

under certain conditions those who sign engagement not to serve." Approved 15 August 1914, Series A-1-a. RG2, Privy Council Office.

Order-in-Council 1914-2283. "Ammunition etc not to be in the possession of any persons of Austro-Hungarian and German nationality." Approved 3 September 1914, Series A-1-d , Volume 2810, RG2, Privy Council Office.

Order-in-Council 1915-0858. "German and Austrian labourers in Vancouver permitted to go to the United States to obtain employment if they promise not to take part in the war." Approved 24 April 1915. Series A-1-d, Volume 2811, RG2, Privy Council Office.

Order-in-Council 1915-1501, "Aliens of Enemy Nationality who are found competing for employment with aliens of our allies or whose presence in company with friendly aliens on public works." Approved 26 June 1915, Series A-1-a, Volume 2811, RG2, Privy Council Office.

Order-in-Council 1915-2039. "German Civilian Prisoners in Canada – Note Verbal of German Govt [Government] that prisoners Kapuskasing, Ont. [Ontario] and forced to work answered that only those willing work and are paid – S. S. External Affairs [Secretary of State External Affairs] 1915/08." Approved 28 August 1915. Series A-1-d. Volume 2811. RG2, Privy Council Office.

Order-in-Council 1915-2699. "Exeats for Aliens of Enemy Nationality to leave the Country to be issued by officers in Victoria, B.C. and Toronto." Approved 20 November 1915. Series A-1-d, Volume 2811, RG2, Privy Council Office.

Order-in-Council 1918-2381. "Order Respecting Enemy Publications." *The Canada Gazette*, 52:14 (5 October 1918), 1277.

ANNUAL REPORTS

Annual Report of the German and English College at Berlin, 1866–68

Annual Report of the Inspector of Prisons and Public Charities on the Asylums for the Insane and Asylum for Idiots of the Province of Ontario, 1882–1922

Annual Report of the Waterloo Historical Society, Berlin Canada, 1913–30

Annual Statement of the Ev. Luth. St. Paul's Church. Kitchener, Ontario, 1917–30

Catalogue of St Jerome's College, 1887–1930

Commencement exercises, Berlin-Waterloo Collegiate, 1901–27

Jahresbericht der evangelisch-lutherischen Trinitatis-Gemeinde in Toronto, Ont., 1906

Kassenbericht der Evang. Lutherischen St. Pauls Gemeinde zu Berlin, Ontario, 1904–16

Lutheran Theological Seminary/ Catalogue of the Evangelical Lutheran Seminary/ Announcement, Waterloo College School, 1909–30

Report of the Minister of Education, Ontario, 1880–1930

St. John's Evangelical Lutheran Church. Waterloo, Ontario, 1930

St. Matthew's Evangelical Lutheran Church, Kitchener, Ontario, 1920–29

Synodal-Bericht. Verhandlungen der deutschen evang.-luth. Synode von Missouri, Ohio und anderen Staaten. Canada-Districts, 1903

Trustees' Report. Annual Meeting of the Berlin and Waterloo Hospital Trust, 1896–1922

Verhandlungen der Jahres-Versammlung der Evangelisch-Lutherischen Synode von Canada, 1880–1930

MINUTES

Book of Minutes of St. Paul's Lutheran Ladies Aid/Protokoll-Buch des Frauen-Vereins der St. Paul's Kirche. Kitchener, Ontario, 1927–32

High School Register of Daily Attendance. Berlin High School, 1900

Minute Book of the Berlin High School Board, 1902–04

Minutes of the Ladies Hospital Auxiliary, Berlin/Kitchener, 1909–19, 1926–31

Protokollbuch No 2. St. Pauls Kirche, Berlin, 1896–1934

Protokoll- und Rechnungsbuch des Frauen-Vereins der ev.-luth. St. Pauls Gemeinde zu Berlin, Ontario, 1876–1926

Report of the School Work of Wilfrid Bitzer. Berlin Collegiate and Technical Institute, 1909

CONSTITUTIONS AND STATUTES

Constitution of the Evangelical Lutheran Synod of Canada. N.p., 1925.

Constitution des Evangelisch-Lutherischen Sonntagschul-Lehrer-Vereins der St. Petri Kirche zu Berlin, Ont. N.p., 1884.

Nebengesetze der Berliner Loge. Berlin: Rittinger und Motz, 1895.

Statuten und Nebengesetze des Deutschen Unterstützungs-Vereins in Toronto, Ontario. Berlin: Rittinger and Motz, 1871.

ARCHIVE OF SUDDABY SCHOOL, KITCHENER, ONTARIO

County of Waterloo Promotion Examination. 14–16 March 1900

Education Department High School Entrance Examination, 1900

Patriotic Programmes, 1908–09

Regulations of the School Attendance Act and the Adolescent School Attendance Act, 1930

Suddaby School. Entrance Examination Papers, 1895–1899. Toronto: Educational Publishing Co.

FISHER LIBRARY, UNIVERSITY OF TORONTO

Van der Smissen Family Papers. MS. Coll. 68. Box 2

ARCHIVES OF ONTARIO, TORONTO

MU 9478-9487
RG 2-42-0-3518
MHSO Reels – German
MHSO Reels – St Jerome's College

ARCHIVES OF THE CONGREGATION OF THE RESURRECTION AT ST JEROME'S UNIVERSITY, WATERLOO, ONTARIO

Affiliation Papers, CR 1-2-3 B51
Beninger Papers
Dantzer Papers
Funcken Papers. Box CR 1-1-4 C13
Girodat, Edmund. *A Biography of Rev. Theobald Spetz, C.R., D.D., Patron of Waterloo Knights of Columbus*. Unpublished, 1972.
Kloepfer Papers
List of Donations on account of improvements of St. Mary's Church, 1913
Schweitzer Papers
Spetz Papers. Box CR 1-1-3. B37
St Mary's Church. CR 1-1-2 A20
Weiler Papers
Zinger Papers

ARCHIVE OF WIFRID LAURIER UNIVERSITY, WATERLOO, ONTARIO

"Hoffmann, Emil." 5.0.6 Lutheran Synod.

DORA LEWIS RARE BOOKS COLLECTION, UNIVERSITY OF WATERLOO, WATERLOO, ONTARIO

BHC Breithaupt, Albert Liborius: Correspondence. Files 59, 62.
Breithaupt, Albert Liborius. BHC 2005. Files 123-125, 152-153.

WATERLOO CATHOLIC DISTRICT SCHOOL BOARD, KITCHENER, ONTARIO

Account Book 1918–45. SB/F/Budget: 1b
Account Book of the Roman C.S. School of Berlin, 1860–68
Cash Book and Minutes #5 Wellesley 1902–37 SB/F/Budget: 9
Cash Book and Minutes R.C.S.S. #11 Wellesley, December 1883–December 1937
Cassabuch der RC Separatschule zu Berlin, 1870–80
Contobuch der Berliner Separatschule. Berlin. 1870
Minutes. Berlin Catholic School Board, 1911–21
Minutes. Waterloo Catholic School Board 1890–97. SB/A/ Minutes: 2
Minutes. Berlin Catholic School Board. 1902–10. SB/A/Minutes: 3

School Conto Corrente – 1884–94. SB/F/Budget: 4
St Agatha Mintues, 1928–33, 1962. SB/A/Minutes: 12

WATERLOO REGION DISTRICT SCHOOL BOARD, KITCHENER, ONTARIO

Berlin Teachers' Association, 1891–1913
County Model Schools: Amended Regulations, 1882
General Circular. Education Department, Ontario, 1882
Inspector's Reports, 1874–1928
Inspector's Reports. Public School Board. Thomas Pearce, 1899–1907
Kitchener Public School Board Minutes, 1915–20
Preston, Barry. *Berlin Public School Board, 1905.* Self-published, 1980.

ARCHIVE OF FIRST LUTHERAN CHURCH, TORONTO

Amalgamation Committee, 1927. Box B4
Pastors. Box C5
Protokolle des Jugendvereins. Februar 1892–Mai 1908. Box B3.1
Protokolle des Kirchenrathes, 1908–29
Van der Smissen Family History. Box C5
Youth Group Minutes. 1913–17. Box B3.1

RARE BOOKS AND SPECIAL COLLECTIONS, UNIVERSITY OF BRITISH COLUMBIA

Box 123-3, "Reference Files Maps and Other Documents 1922–1931," Chung Collection

Primary Sources, Germany

PUBLISHED DOCUMENTS

Cahensly, Peter Paul. *Der St. Raphaelsverein zum Schutze katholischer deutscher Auswanderer. Sein Werden, Wirken und Kämpfen während des 30jährigen Bestehens.* Freiburg in Breisgau: Verlag des Charitasverbandes für das kathol, 1900.
Dedekind, M. *75 Jahre deutsch-evangelischer Diasporaarbeit in Nord- und Südamerika: Festschrift zum 75jährigen Jubiläum der Evangelischen Gesellschaft für die protestantischen Deutschen in Amerika (Barmen).* Barmen: D.B. Wiemann, 1912.
"German Imperial and State Citizenship Law. July 22, 1913." *The American Journal of International Law* 8, no. 3 (1914): 217–27.
Hamilton, Louis. *Deutschland und Canada.* Berlin: Verlag Ernst Wasmuth A.-G., 1928.

Hassel, Georg. *Die Auslandsdeutschen. Ihr Schaffen und ihre Verbreitung über die Erde. Historisch-wirtschaftliche Studie von den Kreuzzügen bis zur Gegenwart.* Berlin: Verlag von Otto Salle, 1926.

Kleinschmidt, Beda. *Auslanddeutschtum und Kirche: Ein Hand- und Nachschlagbuch auf geschichtlich-statistischer Grundlage. Zweiter Band. Die Auslanddeutschen in Übersee.* Münster: Aschendorffsche Verlagsbuchhandlung, 1930.

Lehmann, Heinz. *Zur Geschichte des Deutschtums in Ostkanada. Band I: Das Deutschtum in Ostkanada.* Stuttgart: Ausland und Heimat Verlags-Aktiengesellschaft, 1931.

Möllmann, Albert. *Das Deutschtum in Montreal.* Jena: Verlag von Gustav Fischer, 1937.

Müller, J.P. *Deutsche Schulen und deutscher Unterricht im Auslande.* Leipzig: Th. Thomas, 1901.

Schmidt, Franz, and Otto Boelitz, eds. *Aus deutscher Bildungsarbeit im Ausland: Erlebnisse und Erfahrungen in Selbzeugenissen aus aller Welt.* Zweiter Band: Außereuropa. Langensalza: Verlag von Julius Beltz, 1928.

Weiser, Christian Friedrich. *Der nationale Wiederaufbau und der Verein für das Deutschtum im Ausland.* Berlin: Verein für das Deutschtum im Ausland, 1919.

NEWSPAPERS AND PERIODICALS

St. Raphaels-Blatt. Organ des St. Raphaels-Vereins zum Schutze katholischer deutscher Auswanderer, 1890–1900

POLITISCHES ARCHIV DES AUSWÄRTIGEN AMTS (POLITICAL ARCHIVE OF THE FOREIGN OFFICE), BERLIN

R 60032. Deutschtum in Canada, 1922–32

R 62549. Schulen. Allgemein

R 63634. Schulen. Allgemein, 1919–20

R 67793. Canada. Evangelische Angelegenheiten, 1907–40

R 67794. Religion in Canada

R 77347. Deutschtum in Canada, 1922–33

BUNDESARCHIV (FEDERAL ARCHIVE) BERLIN

R 901 30575. Die Überwachung der Auswanderer aus Deutschland nach britisch-amerikanischen Kolonien, 1880–86

R 901 30590. Die Überwachung der Auswanderer aus Deutschland nach britisch-amerikanischen Kolonien, 1906–07

R 901 63543. Geistliche, Schul- u. Stift-S, 1896–1902

EVANGELISCHES ZENTRALARCHIV (EVANGELICAL CENTRAL ARCHIVE), BERLIN

EZA 5.2811. Kanada, 1907–28
EZA. 5.2852. Montreal, 1902
EZA 5.2866. Allgemeine kirchliche Verhältnisse in Canada, 1907–29
EZA 5.51448. Kirchliches Außenamt. 1904–11
EZA 5.51428. Auslandsdiaspora Generalia, No. 7. 1884–1928
200.1.4775. Gustav-Adolf-Werk. Montreal, 1897

Secondary Sources

Alexander, Kristine. "Agency and Emotion Work." *Jeunesse: Young People, Texts, Cultures* 7, no. 2 (2015): 120–8.

Anderson, Benedict. *Imagined Communities: Reflections on the Origin and Spread of Nationalism.* 2nd ed. New York: Verso, 1991.

Arndt, Karl, and May Olson. *The German Language Press of the Americas, 1732–1968.* Pullach, Germany: Verlag Dokumentation Saur, 1973.

Avery, Donald. *"Dangerous Foreigners": European Immigrant Workers and Labour Radicalism in Canada, 1896–1932.* Toronto: McClelland and Stewart, 1979.

– *Reluctant Host: Canada's Response to Immigrant Workers, 1896–1994.* Toronto: McClelland and Stewart, 1995.

Axelrod, Paul. *Scholars and Dollars: Politics, Economics, and the Universities of Ontario, 1945–1980.* Toronto: University of Toronto Press, 1982.

Axelrod, Paul, and John Reid, eds. *Youth, University and Canadian Society: Essays on the Social History of Higher Education.* Kingston and Montreal: McGill-Queen's University Press, 1989.

Azuma, Eiichiro. *Between Two Empires: Race, History, and Transnationalism in Japanese America.* New York: Oxford University Press, 2005.

– *In Search of Our Frontier: Japanese America and Settler Colonialism in the Construction of Japan's Borderless Empire.* Oakland: University of California Press, 2019.

Barth, Frederik, ed. *Ethnic Groups and Boundaries: The Social Organization of Culture Difference.* Boston: Little, Brown and Co., 1969.

Bausenhart, Werner. *German Immigration and Assimilation in Ontario, 1783–1918.* Toronto: Legas, 1989.

– "The Ontario German Language Press and Its Suppression by Order-in-Council in 1918." *Canadian Ethnic Studies/Études Ethniques au Canada* 4, no. 1 (1972): 35–48.

Beglo, Barton, ed. *A Time for Building: Essays on Lutherans in Canada.* Kitchener, ON: St. Mark's Press, 1988.

Bender, Thomas. *A Nation among Nations: America's Place in World History*. New York: Hill and Wang, 2006.

Benes, Tuska. *In Babel's Shadow: Language, Philology, and the Nation in Nineteenth-Century Germany*. Detroit, MI: Wayne State University Press, 2008.

Bertram, Laurie K. "'Eskimo' Immigrants and Colonial Soldiers: Icelandic Immigrants and the North-West Resistance, 1885." *Canadian Historical Review* 99, no. 1 (2018): 63–97.

– *The Viking Immigrants: Icelandic North Americans*. Toronto: University of Toronto Press, 2020.

Blanton, Carlos Kevin. *The Strange Career of Bilingual Education in Texas, 1836–1981*. College Station: Texas A & M University Press, 2004.

Boas, Hans. *The Life and Death of Texas German*. Durham, NC: Duke University Press, 2009.

Bock, Michel. *A Nation beyond Borders: Lionel Groulx on French-Canadian Minorities*. Ottawa: University of Ottawa Press, 2014.

Bredbenner, Candice Lewis. *A Nationality of Her Own: Women, Marriage, and the Law of Citizenship*. Berkeley: University of California Press, 1998.

Breton, Raymond. "Institutional Completeness of Ethnic Communities and the Personal Relations of Immigrants." *American Journal of Sociology* 70 (1964): 193–205.

Brinkmann, Tobias. *Von der Gemeinde zur ‚Community': Jüdische Einwanderer in Chicago, 1840–1900*. Osnabrück, Germany: Universitätsverlag Rasch, 2002.

Brouwer, Ruth Compton. *Modern Women Modernizing Men: The Changing Missions of Three Professional Women in Asia and Africa, 1902–1969*. Vancouver: UBC Press, 2002.

– *New Women for God: Canadian Presbyterian Women and India Missions, 1876–1914*. Toronto: University of Toronto Press, 1990.

Brown, Kate. *A Biography of No Place: From Ethnic Borderland to Soviet Heartland*. Cambridge, MA: Harvard University Press, 2004.

Brown, Robert Craig, and Ramsay Cook. *Canada 1896–1921: A Nation Transformed*. Toronto: McClelland and Stewart, 1974.

Brubaker, Rogers. *Citizenship and Nationhood in France and Germany*. Cambridge, MA: Harvard University Press, 1992.

– "Migration, Membership, and the Modern Nation-State: Internal and External Dimensions of the Politics of Belonging Migration and Membership." *Journal of Interdisciplinary History* 41, no. 1 (2010): 61–78.

Brubaker, Rogers, and Frederick Cooper. "Beyond 'Identity.'" *Theory and Society* 29, no. 1 (2000): 1–47.

Bryce, Benjamin. "Germans in Ontario and Buenos Aires, 1905–1918: *Das Berliner Journal* and *Das Argentinische Tageblatt*'s Discourse about Ethnicity and Its Changes during World War I." Major Research Paper, MA, York University, 2008.

– "Seeing Japan: A Canadian Missionary's Photography and Transpacific Audiences, 1888–1925." *Pacific Historical Review* 91, no. 2 (2022): 190–219.

– *To Belong in Buenos Aires: Germans, Argentines, and the Rise of a Pluralist Society.*
Stanford: Stanford University Press, 2018.

Bryce, Benjamin, and David M.K. Sheinin, eds. *Making Citizens in Argentina.* Pittsburgh, PA: University of Pittsburgh Press, 2017.

Buckner, Phillip, and R. Douglas Francis, eds. *Canada and the British World: Culture, Migration, and Identity.* Vancouver: UBC Press, 2006.

Canning, Kathleen, and Sonya Rose. "Gender, Citizenship and Subjectivity: Some Historical and Theoretical Considerations." *Gender and History* 13, no. 3 (2001): 427–43.

Cecillon, Jack. *Prayers, Petitions, and Protests: The Catholic Church and the Ontario Schools Crisis in the Windsor Border Region, 1910–1928.* Montreal and Kingston: McGill-Queen's University Press, 2013.

Chilton, Lisa. *Agents of Empire: British Female Migration to Canada and Australia, 1860–1930.* Toronto: University of Toronto Press, 2007.

Choquette, Robert. *Language and Religion: History of English-French Conflict in Ontario.* Ottawa: University of Ottawa Press, 1975.

– *L'Ontario francais, historique.* Saint-Laurent, Québec: Éditions Études Vivantes, 1980.

Christie, Nancy. *Transatlantic Subjects: Ideas, Institutions, and Social Experience in Post-Revolutionary British North America.* Montreal and Kingston: McGill-Queen's University Press, 2008.

Christie, Nancy, ed. *Households of Faith: Family, Gender, and Community in Canada, 1760–1969.* Montreal and Kingston: McGill-Queen's University Press, 2002.

Christie, Nancy, and Michael Gauvreau. *Christian Churches and Their Peoples, 1840–1965: A Social History of Religion in Canada.* Toronto: University of Toronto Press, 2010.

Clarke, Brian. "English-Speaking Canada from 1854." In *A Concise History of Christianity in Canada*, edited by Terrence Murphy and Roberto Perin, 261–360. Toronto: Oxford University Press, 1996.

– *Piety and Nationalism: Lay Voluntary Associations and the Creation of an Irish-Catholic Community in Toronto, 1850–1895.* Montreal: McGill-Queen's University Press, 1993.

Comacchio, Cynthia. *Dominion of Youth: Adolescence and the Making of a Modern Canada, 1920–1950.* Waterloo, ON: Wilfrid Laurier University Press, 2006.

Conolly-Smith, Peter. *Translating America: An Immigrant Press Visualizes American Popular Culture, 1895–1918.* Washington, DC: Smithsonian Books, 2004.

Conrad, Sebastian. *Globalisation and the Nation in Imperial Germany.* Cambridge: Cambridge University Press, 2010.

Constant, Jean-François, and Michel Ducharme. *Liberalism and Hegemony: Debating the Canadian Liberal Revolution.* Toronto: University of Toronto Press, 2009.

Conzen, Kathleen Neils. *Germans in Minnesota.* St Paul, MN: Minnesota Historical Society, 2003.

– *Immigrant Milwaukee, 1836–1860: Accommodation and Community in a Frontier City*. Cambridge, MA: Harvard University Press, 1976.

– "Immigrant Religion and the Public Sphere: The German Catholic Milieu in America." In *German-American Immigration and Ethnicity in Comparative Perspective*, edited by Wolfgang Helbich and Walter Kamphoefner, 69–114. Madison, WI: Max Kade Institute for German-American Studies, 2004.

Conzen, Kathleen Neils, David Gerber, Ewa Morawska, George Pozzetta, and Rudolph Vecoli. "The Invention of Ethnicity: A Perspective from the U.S.A." *Journal of American Ethnic History* 12, no. 1 (1992): 3–41.

Coschi, Mario Nathan. "'Be British or Be D—d': Primary Education in Berlin-Kitchener, Ontario, during the First World War." *Histoire sociale/Social History* 47, no. 94 (2014): 311–32.

– "From Wilhelm to Hans: Ethnicity, Citizenship, and the German Community of Berlin/Kitchener, Ontario, 1871–1970s." PhD thesis, McMaster University, 2018.

Crunican, Paul. *Priests and Politicians: Manitoba Schools and the Election of 1896*. Toronto: University of Toronto Press, 1974.

Curtis, Bruce. *Building the Educational State: Canada West, 1836–1871*. London, ON: Falmer Press, 1988.

– *The Politics of Population: State Formation, Statistics, and the Census of Canada, 1840–1875*. Toronto: University of Toronto Press, 2001.

– *Ruling by Schooling Quebec: Conquest to Liberal Governmentality – A Historical Sociology*. Toronto: University of Toronto Press, 2012.

– *True Government by Choice Men? Inspection, Education, and State Formation in Canada West*. Toronto: University of Toronto Press, 1992.

Danylewycz, Marta, and Alison Prentice. "Teachers, Gender, and Bureaucratizing School Systems in Nineteenth Century Montreal and Toronto." *History of Education Quarterly* 24, no. 1 (1984): 75–100.

Dart, Douglas. "George William Ross, Minister of Education for Ontario, 1883–1899." MA thesis, University of Guelph, 1971.

Doerries, Reinhard. "German Transatlantic Migration from the Early Nineteenth Century to the Outbreak of World War II." In *Population, Labour and Migration in 19th- and 20th-Century Germany*, edited by Klaus Bade, 115–34. Leamington Spa, UK: Berg Publishers, 1987.

Ducharme, Michel. *Le concept de liberté au Canada à l'époque des Révolutions atlantiques (1776–1838)*. Montreal and Kingston: McGill-Queen's University Press, 2010.

Dudink, Stefan, Karen Hagemann, and Anna Clark, eds. *Representing Masculinity: Male Citizenship in Modern Western Culture*. New York: Palgrave Macmillan, 2007.

Emery, George. *The Methodist Church on the Prairies, 1896–1914*. Montreal and Kingston: McGill-Queen's University Press, 2001.

Engerman, David. "Introduction: Histories of the Future and the Futures of History." *American Historical Review* 117, no. 5 (2012): 1402–10.

English, John R. "Wartime Elections Act." *The Canadian Encyclopedia*. Historica Canada. Article published 7 February 2006; last edited 18 September 2015. https://www.thecanadianencyclopedia.ca/en/article/wartime-elections-act.

English, John, and Kenneth McLaughlin. *Kitchener: An Illustrated History*. Waterloo, ON: Wilfrid Laurier University Press, 1983.

Epp, Marlene. *Women without Men: Mennonite Refugees of the Second World War*. Toronto: University of Toronto Press, 2000.

Fair, Ross. "'Theirs Was a Deeper Purpose': The Pennsylvania Germans of Ontario and the Craft of the Homemaking Myth." *Canadian Historical Reveiw* 87, no. 4 (2006): 653–84.

Frisse, Ulrich. *Berlin Ontario (1800–1916): Historische Identitäten von „Kanadas deutscher Hauptstadt": Ein Beitrag zur deutsch-kanadischen Migrations-, Akkulturations- und Perzeptionsgeschichte des 19. und frühen 20. Jahrhunderts*. New Dundee, ON: TransAtlantic Publishing, 2003.

Gabaccia, Donna, and Dirk Hoerder, eds. *Connecting Seas and Connected Ocean Rims: Indian, Atlantic, and Pacific Oceans and China Seas Migrations from the 1830s to the 1930s*. Leiden and Boston: Brill, 2011.

Gabaccia, Donna, and Franca Iacovetta, eds. *Women, Gender and Transnational Lives: Italian Workers of the World*. Toronto: University of Toronto Press, 2002.

Gaffield, Chad. *Language, Schooling, and Cultural Conflict: The Origins of the French-Language Controversy in Ontario*. Montreal: McGill-Queen's University Press, 1987.

Gal, Susan. *Language Shift: Social Determinants of Linguistic Change in Bilingual Austria*. New York: Academic Press, Inc., 1979.

Gauvreau, Michael. *The Evangelical Century: College and Creed in English Canada from the Great Revival to the Great Depression*. Montreal and Kingston: McGill-Queen's University Press, 1991.

Geyer, Michael, and Hartmut Lehmann, eds. *Religion und Nation, Nation und Religion: Beiträge zu einer unbewältigten Geschichte*. Göttingen: Wallstein, 2004.

Gidney, R.D., and D.A. Lawr. "Bureaucracy vs. Community? The Origins of Bureaucratic Procedure in the Upper Canadian School System." *Journal of Social History* 13, no. 3 (1980): 438–57.

Gidney, R.D., and W.P.J. Millar. *How Schools Worked: Public Education in English Canada, 1900–1940*. Montreal and Kingston: McGill-Queen's University Press, 2012.

– *Inventing Secondary Education: The Rise of the High School in Nineteenth-Century Ontario*. Montreal and Kingston: McGill-Queen's University Press, 1990.

Gleason, Mona. "Avoiding the Agency Trap: Caveats for Historians of Children, Youth, and Education." *History of Education* 45, no. 4 (2016): 446–59.

– *Small Matters: Canadian Children in Sickness and Health*. Montreal and Kingston: McGill-Queen's University Press, 2013.

Goldberg, Jennifer. "'I Thought the People Wanted to Get Rid of the Teacher:' Educational Authority in Late-Nineteenth Century Ontario." *Historical Studies in Education/Revue d'histoire de l'éducation* 23 (2011): 41–60.

Goldstein, David, and Audrey Thacker, eds. *Complicating Constructions: Race, Ethnicity, and Hybridity in American Texts.* Seattle: University of Washington Press, 2007.

Grams, Grant. "Der Verein für das Deutschtum im Ausland and Its Observations of Canada Prior to World War One." *Canadian Ethnic Studies* (2002): 117–25.

– *German Emigration to Canada and the Supports of Its Deutschtum during the Weimar Republic.* Frankfurt am Main: Peter Lang, 2001.

– "Sankt Raphaels Verein and German-Catholic Emigration to Canada from 1919 to 1939." *The Catholic Historical Review* 91, no. 1 (2005): 84–103.

Grenke, Arthur. *The German Community of Winnipeg 1872 to 1919.* New York: AMS Press, 1991.

Grosjean, François. *Bilingual: Life and Reality.* Cambridge, MA: Harvard University Press, 2011.

– *Life with Two Languages: An Introduction to Bilingualism.* Cambridge, MA: Harvard University Press, 1982.

Harris, Robin. *A History of Higher Education in Canada, 1663–1960.* Toronto: University of Toronto Press, 1976.

Haupt, Heinz-Gerhard, and Jürgen Kocka, eds. *Comparative and Transnational History: Central European Approaches and New Perspectives.* New York: Berghahn Books, 2009.

Hayday, Matthew. *So They Want Us to Learn French: Promoting and Opposing Bilingualism in English-Speaking Canada.* Vancouver: UBC Press, 2015.

Hébert, Raymond. *Manitoba's French-Language Crisis: A Cautionary Tale.* Montreal and Kingston: McGill-Queen's University Press, 2004.

Helbich, Wolfgang, and Walter Kamphoefner, eds. *German-American Immigration and Ethnicity in Comparative Perspective.* Madison, WI: Max Kade Institute for German-American Studies, University of Wisconsin-Madison, 2004.

Herrmann, Wilhelm. "The Kropp Lutheran Seminary 'Eben-Ezer' Germany, and Its Relation to the United Lutheran Church in America." Master of Sacred Theology thesis, Lutheran Theological Seminary at Philadelphia, 1938.

Hinther, Rhonda, and Jim Mochoruk, eds. *Civilian Internment in Canada: Histories and Legacies.* Winnipeg: University of Manitoba Press, 2020.

Hobsbawm, Eric. *Nations and Nationalism since 1780: Programme, Myth, Reality.* Cambridge: Cambridge University Press, 1990.

Hollinger, David. *Protestants Abroad: How Missionaries Tried to Change the World but Changed America.* Princeton, NJ: Princeton University Press, 2017.

Houston, Susan, and Alison Prentice. *Schooling in Nineteenth-Century Ontario.* Toronto: University of Toronto Press, 1988.

Iacovetta, Franca. *Gatekeepers: Reshaping Immigrant Lives in Cold War Canada.* Toronto: Between the Lines, 2006.

- "'In the Case of a Woman' or 'The Headache': Married Women's Nationality and Canada's Citizenship Act at Home and Europe, 1946–50. *Women's History Review* 28, no. 3 (2019): 396–420.

Ion, Hamish. *The Cross and the Rising Sun: The Canadian Protestant Missionary Movement in the Japanese Empire, 1872–1931*. Waterloo, ON: Wilfrid Laurier University Press, 1990.

Iwicki, John. *Resurrectionist Charism: A History of the Congregation of the Resurrection*. Vol. 2, 1887–1932. Rome: Tip. Poliglotta della Pontificia Università Gregoriana, 1992.

Iwicki, John, and James Wahl. *Resurrectionist Charism: A History of the Congregation of the Resurrection, 150 Years*. Vol. 1, 1836–1886. Rome: Tip. Poliglotta della Pontificia Università Gregoriana, 1986.

Jacobson, Matthew Frye. *Whiteness of a Different Color: European Immigrants and the Alchemy of Race*. Cambridge, MA: Harvard University Press, 1998.

Jaenen, Cornelius, ed. *Les Franco-Ontariens*. Ottawa: Presses de l'Université d'Ottawa, 1993.

Kalbfleisch, Herbert Karl. *The History of the Pioneer German Language Press of Ontario, Canada, 1835–1918*. Toronto: University of Toronto Press, 1968.

Katz, Michael. "The Emergence of Bureaucracy in Urban Education: The Boston Case, 1850–1884: Part I." *History of Education Quarterly* 8, no. 2 (1968): 155–88.

- "The Emergence of Bureaucracy in Urban Education: The Boston Case, 1850–1884: Part II." *History of Education Quarterly* 8, no. 3 (1968): 319–57.

Katz, Michael, and Paul H. Mattingly. *Education and Social Change: Themes from Ontario's Past*. New York: New York University Press, 1975.

Kazal, Russell. *Becoming Old Stock: The Paradox of German-American Identity*. Princeton, NJ: Princeton University Press, 2004.

- "Revisiting Assimilation: The Rise, Fall, and Reappraisal of a Concept in American Ethnic History." *The American Historical Review* 100, no. 2 (1995): 437–71.

Kealey, Gregory S. "State Repression of Labour and the Left in Canada, 1914–20: The Impact of the First World War." *Canadian Historical Review* 73, no. 3 (1992): 281–314.

Kelley, Ninette, and Michael Trebilcock. *The Making of the Mosaic: A History of Canadian Immigration Policy*. 2nd ed. Toronto: University of Toronto Press, 2010.

Keshen, Jeff. "All the News That Was Fit to Print: Ernest Chambers and Information Control in Canada, 1914–19." *Canadian Historical Review* 73, no. 3 (1992): 315–43.

Kinbacher, Kurt. "Life in the Russian Bottoms: Community Building and Identity Transformation among Germans from Russia in Lincoln, Nebraska, 1876 to 1926." *Journal of American Ethnic History* (2007): 22–57.

Kleiner, John W. Henry *Melchoir Muhlenberg: The Roots of 250 Years of Organized Lutheranism in North America. Essays in Memory of Helmut T. Lehmann*. Lewiston, NY: Edwin Mellen Press, 1998.

Kloosterhuis, Jürgen. *Friedliche Imperialisten: Deutsche Auslandsvereine und Auswärtige Kulturpolitik, 1906–1918*. Frankfurt: Lang, 1994.

Kmiec, Patricia. "'Take This Normal Class Idea and Carry It Throughout the Land':
Sunday School Teacher Training in Ontario, 1870–1890." *Historical Studies in
Education/Revue d'histoire de l'éducation* 24 (2012): 195–211.

Kordan, Bohdan. *Enemy Aliens, Prisoners of War: Internment in Canada during the
Great War.* Montreal: McGill-Queen's University Press, 2002.

– "First World War Internment in Canada: Enemy Aliens and the Blurring of the
Military/Civilian Distinction." *Canadian Military History* 29, no. 2 (2020): 1–28.

Koselleck, Reinhart. *Futures Past: On the Semantics of Historical Time.* Cambridge,
MA: The MIT Press, 1985.

Kratz, Henry, and Humphrey Milnes. "Kitchener German: A Pennsylvania German
Dialect." *Modern Language Quarterly* 14 (1953): 184–98, 274–83.

Lears, Jackson. "The Concept of Cultural Hegemony: Problems and Possibilities." *The
American Historical Review* 90, no. 3 (1985): 567–593.

– *No Place of Grace: Antimodernism and the Transformation of American Culture,
1880–1920.* New York: Pantheon Books, 1981.

Lesser, Jeffrey. *Immigration, Ethnicity, and National Identity in Brazil, 1808 to the
Present.* New York: Cambridge University Press, 2013.

– *Negotiating National Identity: Immigrants, Minorities, and the Struggle for Ethnicity
in Brazil.* Durham, NC: Duke University Press, 1999.

Lesser, Jeffrey, and Raanan Rein. "Challenging Particularity: Jews as a Lens on Latin
American Ethnicity." *Latin American and Caribbean Ethnic Studies* 1 (2006): 249–63.

– "Motherlands of Choice: Ethnicity, Belonging, and Identities among Jewish-Latin
Americans." In *Immigration and National Identities in Latin America*, edited by
Nicola Foote and Michael Goebel, 141–59. Gainesville, FL: University Press of
Florida, 2014.

Löchte, Anne. *Das Berliner Journal (1859–1918): Eine deutschsprachige Zeitung in
Kanada.* Göttingen: VandR unipress, 2007.

Loewen, Royden. *Diaspora in the Countryside: Two Mennonite Communities and
Mid-Twentieth-Century Rural Disjuncture.* Urbana: University of Illinois Press,
2006.

– *Family, Church, and Market: A Mennonite Community in the Old and New Worlds,
1850–1930.* Urbana and Chicago: University of Illinois Press, 1993.

Lorenzkowski, Barabara. "Languages of Ethnicity: Teaching German in Waterloo
County's Schools, 1850–1915." *Histoire Sociale/Social History* 41 (2008): 1–40.

– *Sounds of Ethnicity: Listening to German North America, 1850–1914.* Winnipeg:
University of Manitoba Press, 2010.

Luebke, Frederick. *Bonds of Loyalty: German-Americans and World War I.* DeKalb:
Northern Illinois University Press, 1974.

– *Germans in Brazil: A Comparative History of Cultural Conflict during World War
I.* Baton Rouge: Louisiana State University, 1987.

– "Legal Restrictions on Foreign Languages in the Great Plains States, 1917–1923."
In *Languages in Conflict: Linguistic Acculturation on the Great Plains*, edited by
Paul Schach, 1–19. Lincoln: University of Nebraska Press, 1980.

Lundberg, Anna. "Paying the Price of Citizenship: Gender and Social Policy on Venereal Disease in Stockholm, 1919–1944." *Social Science History* 32 (2008): 215–34.

Lyon, Barry. *The First 60 Years: A History of Waterloo Lutheran University from the Opening of Waterloo Lutheran Seminary in 1911, to the Present Day*. Waterloo, ON: Waterloo Lutheran University Press, 1971.

Manz, Stefan. "'Wir Stehen fest zusammen/Zu Kaiser und zu Reich!': Nationalism among Germans in Britain, 1871–1918." *German Life and Letters* 55, no. 4 (2002): 398–415.

Manz, Stefan, Panikos Panayi, and Matthew Stibbe, eds. *Internment during the First World War: A Mass Global Phenomenon*. New York: Routledge, 2019.

Marks, Lynne. *Revivals and Roller Rinks: Religion, Leisure, and Identity in Late-Nineteenth-Century Small-Town Ontario*. Toronto: University of Toronto Press, 1996.

Martel, Marcel. *French Canada: An Account of Its Creation and Break-up, 1850–1967*. Ottawa: Canadian Historical Association, 1998.

Martel, Marcel, and Martin Pâquet. *Langue et politique au Canada et au Québec: Une synthèse historique*. Montreal: Boréal, 2010.

Maza, Sarah. "The Kids Aren't All Right: Historians and the Problem of Childhood." *American Historical Review* 125, no. 4 (2020): 1261–85.

McCalla, Douglas. *Planting the Province: The Economic History of Upper Canada, 1784–1870*. Toronto: University of Toronto Press, 1993.

McGowan, Mark. *The Waning of the Green: Catholics, the Irish, and Identity in Toronto, 1887–1922*. Montreal: McGill-Queen's University Press, 1999.

McKay, Ian. "The Liberal Order Framework: A Prospectus for a Reconnaissance of Canadian History." *Canadian Historical Review* 81 (2000): 617–45.

McKegney, Patricia. *The Kaiser's Bust: A Study of War-Time Propaganda in Berlin, Ontario, 1914–1918*. Kitchener, ON: Bamberg Heritage Series, 1991.

McLaughlin, Kenneth. *The Germans in Canada*. Ottawa: Canadian Historical Association, 1985.

Milewski, Patrice. "'I Paid No Attention To It': An Oral History of Curricular Change in the 1930s." *Historical Studies in Education/Revue d'histoire de l'éducation* 24 (2012): 112–129.

Miller, J.R. *Compact, Contract, Covenant: Aboriginal Treaty-Making in Canada*. Toronto: University of Toronto Press, 2009.

– *Shingwauk's Vision: A History of Native Residential Schools*. Toronto: University of Toronto Press, 2006.

Mintz, Steven. "Children's History Matters." *American Historical Review* 125, no. 4 (2020): 1286–92.

– "Why the History of Childhood Matters." *The Journal of the History of Childhood and Youth* 5, no. 1 (2012): 15–28.

Mitchell, Nancy, *The Danger of Dreams: German and American Imperialism in Latin America*. Chapel Hill: University of North Carolina Press, 1999.

Moelleken, Wolfgang Wilfried. "Die russlanddeutschen Mennoniten in Kanada und Mexiko: Sprachliche Entwicklung und diglossische Situation." *Zeitschrift für Dialektologie und Linguistik* 54, no. 2 (1987): 145–83.

Mosse, George. *The Crisis of German Ideology: Intellectual Origins of the Third Reich.* London: Lowe and Brydone, 1966.

Moya, José. "A Continent of Immigrants: Postcolonial Shifts in the Western Hemisphere." *Hispanic American Historical Review* 86 (2006): 1–28.

– "Immigrants and Associations: A Global and Historical Perspective." *Journal of Ethnic and Migration Studies* 31 (2005): 833–64.

Noël, Françoise. "The Impact of Regulation 17 on the Study of District Schools: Some Methodological Considerations." *Historical Studies in Education/Revue d'histoire de l'éducation* 24 (2012): 72–92.

Nugent, Walter. *Crossings: The Great Transatlantic Migrations, 1870–1914.* Bloomington: Indiana University Press, 1992.

O'Donnell, Krista, Renate Bridenthal, and Nancy Reagin, eds. *The Heimat Abroad: The Boundaries of Germanness.* Ann Arbor: University of Michigan Press, 2005.

Oliver, Peter. "The Resolution of the Ontario Bilingual School Crisis, 1919–1929." *Journal of Canadian Studies* 7 (1972): 22–45.

Orsi, Robert. *The Madonna of 115th Street: Faith and Community in Italian Harlem, 1880–1950.* New Haven, CT: Yale University Press, 1985.

Ostrower, Francie. *Why The Wealthy Give: The Culture of Elite Philanthropy.* Princeton, NJ: Princeton University Press, 1995.

Otero, Hernán. *Historia de los franceses en la Argentina.* Buenos Aires: Editorial Biblos, 2012.

Otte, T.G. "A 'German Paperchase': The 'Scrap of Paper' Controversy and the Problem of Myth and Memory in International History." *Diplomacy and Statecraft* 18, no. 1 (2007): 53–87.

Paddison, Joshua. *American Heathens: Religion, Race, and Reconstruction in California.* Berkeley: University of California Press, 2012.

Parr, Joy. *The Gender of Breadwinners: Women, Men, and Change in Two Industrial Towns, 1880–1950.* Toronto: University of Toronto Press, 1990.

Pavlenko, Aneta. *Emotions and Multilingualism.* Cambridge: Cambridge University Press, 2005.

Perin, Roberto. "Churches and Immigrant Integration in Toronto, 1947–65." In *The Churches and Social Order in Nineteenth- and Twentieth-Century Canada*, edited by Michael Gauvreau and Ollivier Hubert, 274–91. Montreal: McGill-Queen's University Press, 2006.

– "French-Speaking Canada from 1840." In *A Concise History of Christianity in Canada*, edited by Terrence Murphy and Roberto Perin, 190–260. Toronto: Oxford University Press, 1996.

– *The Immigrants' Church: The Third Force in Canadian Catholicism, 1880–1920.* Ottawa: Canadian Historical Association, 1998.

– *The Many Rooms of This House: Diversity and Toronto's Places of Worship since 1840.* Toronto: University of Toronto Press, 2017.

– *Rome in Canada: The Vatican and Canadian Affairs in the Late Victorian Age.* Toronto: University of Toronto Press, 1990.

Peterson, Brent. *Popular Narratives and Ethnic Identity: Literature and Community in* Die Abendschule. Ithaca, NY: Cornell University Press, 1991.

Pickles, Katie. *Female Imperialism and National Identity: Imperial Order Daughters of the Empire.* Manchester: Manchester University Press, 2002.

Prang, Margaret. "Clerics, Politicians, and the Bilingual Schools Issue in Ontario, 1910–1917." *Canadian Historical Review* 41 (1960): 281–307.

– *A Heart at Leisure from Itself: Caroline Macdonald of Japan.* Vancouver: UBC Press, 1995.

Prentice, Alison. *The School Promoters: Education and Social Class in Mid-Nineteenth Century Upper Canada.* Toronto: McClelland and Stewart, 1977.

Price, Peter. "Naturalising Subjects, Creating Citizens: Naturalisation Law and the Conditioning of 'Citizenship' in Canada, 1881–1914." *The Journal of Imperial and Commonwealth History* 45, no. 1 (2017): 1–21.

Ramirez, Bruno. *Crossing the 49th Parallel: Migration from Canada to the United States, 1900–1930.* Ithaca, NY: Cornell University Press, 2001.

Ramsey, Paul. "In the Region of Babel: Public Bilingual Schooling in the Midwest, 1840s–1880s." *History of Education Quarterly* 49 (2009): 267–90.

Raptis, Helen. "Exploring the Factors Prompting British Columbia's First Integration Initiative: The Case of Port Essington Indian Day School." *History of Education Quarterly* 51 (2011): 520–43.

Raska, Jan. *Czech Refugees in Cold War Canada.* Winnipeg: University of Manitoba Press, 2018.

Roediger, David. *How Race Survived U.S. History: From Settlement and Slavery to the Obama Phenomenon.* New York: Verso, 2008.

Rose, Nikolas, Pat O'Malley, and Mariana Valverde. "Governmentality." *Annual Review of Law and Social Science* 2 (2006): 83–104.

Roy, Patricia E. "Internment in Canada." *The Canadian Encyclopedia.* Historica Canada. Article published 27 August 2013; last edited 10 August 2018. https://www.thecanadianencyclopedia.ca/en/article/internment.

Savard, Pierre. *Jules-Paul Tardivel, la France et les États-Unis 1851–1905.* Québec: Les Presses de l'Université Laval, 1967.

Sauer, Angelika, and Matthias Zimmer, eds. *A Chorus of Different Voices.* New York: Peter Lang, 1998.

Schober, Michaela. "Austrian Immigration to Canada in the Imperial Period." In *A History of the Austrian Migration to Canada,* edited by Frederick Engelmann, Manfred Prokop, and Franz Szabo, 45–58. Ottawa: Carleton University Press, 1996.

Scott, James C. *Seeing Like a State: How Certain Schemes to Improve the Human Condition Have Failed.* New Haven, CT: Yale University Press, 1998.

Simon, Victor. *Le Règlement XVII: Sa mise en vigueur à travers l'Ontario 1912–1927.* Sudbury, ON: Université de Sudbury, 1983.

Solberg, Carl. *The Prairies and the Pampas: Agrarian Policy in Canada and Argentina, 1880–1930.* Stanford: Stanford University Press, 1987.

Sollors, Werner, ed. *The Invention of Ethnicity*. New York: Oxford University Press, 1989.

Smith, Helmut Walser. *Protestants, Catholics, and Jews in Germany, 1800–1914*. New York: Berghahn, 2001.

Stamp, Robert. *The Schools of Ontario, 1876–1976*. Toronto: University of Toronto Press, 1982.

Stern, Fritz. *The Politics of Cultural Despair: A Study in the Rise of the Germanic Ideology*. Berkeley: University of California Press, 1961.

Suárez-Orozco, Carola, and Marcelo Suárez-Orozco. *Children of Immigration*. Cambridge, MA: Harvard University Press, 2001.

Sutherland, Neil. *Growing Up: Childhood in English Canada from the Great War to the Age of Television*. Toronto: University of Toronto Press, 1997.

Swyripa, Frances, and John Herd Thompson, ed. *Loyalties in Conflict: Ukrainians in Canada during the Great War*. Edmonton: Canadian Institute of Ukrainian Studies, University of Alberta, 1983.

Taylor, Joseph E., III. "Boundary Terminology." *Environmental History* 13, no. 3 (2008): 454–81.

The Reverend Ernest Hahn: His Life, Work and Place among Us. No publisher information, 1951.

Thompson, John Herd. *Ethnic Minorities during Two World Wars*. Ottawa: Canadian Historical Association, 1991.

Tomkins, George. *A Common Countenance: Stability and Change in the Canadian Curriculum*. Scarborough, ON: Prentice-Hall Canada, 1986.

Toth, Carolyn. *German-English Bilingual Schools in America: The Cincinnati Tradition in Historical Context*. New York: Peter Lang, 1990.

Tuennerman-Kaplan, Laura. *Helping Others, Helping Ourselves: Power, Giving, and Community Identity in Cleveland, Ohio, 1880–1930*. Kent, OH: Kent State University Press, 2001.

Tyack, David. *The One Best System: A History of American Urban Education*. Cambridge, MA: Harvard University Press, 1974.

Valverde, Mariana. *The Age of Light, Soap, and Water: Moral Reform in English Canada, 1885–1925*. Toronto: McClelland and Stewart, 1991.

Vaudry, Richard. *Anglicans and the Atlantic World: High Churchmen, Evangelicals, and the Quebec Connection*. Montreal and Kingston: McGill-Queen's University Press, 2003.

Wagner, Jonathan. *A History of Migration from Germany to Canada 1850–1939*. Vancouver: UBC Press, 2006.

Wahl, James. "Father Louis Funcken's Contribution to German Catholicism in Waterloo County, Ontario." *CCHA Study Sessions*, no. 50 (1983): 513–31.

Weaver, John. *The Great Land Rush and the Making of the Modern World, 1650–1900*. Montreal: McGill-Queen's University Press, 2003.

Weber, Eugen. *Peasants into Frenchmen: The Modernization of Rural France*. Stanford: Stanford University Press, 1976.

Welch David. "Early Franco-Ontarian Schooling as a Reflection and Creator of Community Identity." *Ontario History* 85 (1993): 312–47.

Westfall, William. *Two Worlds: The Protestant Culture of Nineteenth-Century Ontario.* Kingston, ON: McGill-Queen's University Press, 1989.

Widdis, Randy. *With Scarcely a Ripple: Anglo-Canadian Migration into the United States and Western Canada, 1880–1920.* Montreal and Kingston: McGill-Queen's University Press, 1998.

Wilson, Donald, Robert Stamp, and Louis-Pilippe Audet, eds. *Canadian Education: A History.* Scarborough, ON: Prentice Hall, 1970.

Winks, Robin. *The Blacks in Canada: A History.* Montreal: McGill-Queen's University Press, 1971.

Worsfold, Elliot. "Welcoming Strangers: Race, Religion, and Ethnicity in German Lutheran Ontario and Missouri, 1939–1970." PhD thesis, University of Western Ontario, 2018.

Wright, Barry, Eric Tucker, and Susan Binnie, eds. *Canadian State Trials, Volume IV: Security, Dissent, and the Limits of Toleration in War and Peace, 1914–1939.* Toronto: University of Toronto Press, 2015.

Yildiz, Yasemin. *Beyond the Mother Tongue: The Postmonolingual Condition.* New York: Fordham University Press, 2012.

Zahra, Tara. *The Great Departure: Mass Migration from Eastern Europe and the Making of the Free World.* New York: W.W. Norton and Company, 2016.

– *Kidnapped Souls: National Indifference and the Battle for Children in the Bohemian Lands, 1900–1948.* Ithaca, NY: Cornell University Press, 2008.

Index